2500 COINS
OF THE WORLD

2500 COINS
OF THE WORLD

A stunning global history covering 180 countries, from the first coins ever struck to present-day innovations, fully illustrated with over 2500 images

Captures the beauty and diversity of coins, including classical Greek owls, Chinese copper cash, gold trade coins, silver dollar prototypes, and more

Dr James Mackay

southwater

This edition is published by Southwater, an imprint of Anness Publishing Ltd
Hermes House, 88–89 Blackfriars Road, London SE1 8HA;
tel. 020 7401 2077; fax 020 7633 9499;
www.southwaterbooks.com;
www.annesspublishing.com

© Anness Publishing Ltd 2008

Anness Publishing has a new picture agency outlet for publishing, promotions and advertising. Please visit our website www.practicalpictures.com for more information.

UK agent: The Manning Partnership Ltd;
tel. 01225 478444; fax 01225 478440;
sales@manning-partnership.co.uk

UK distributor: Grantham Book Services Ltd;
tel. 01476 541080; fax 01476 541061;
orders@gbs.tbs-ltd.co.uk

North American agent/distributor:
National Book Network; tel. 301 459 3366;
fax 301 429 5746; www.nbnbooks.com

Australian agent/distributor:
Pan Macmillan Australia;
tel. 1300 135 113; fax 1300 135 103;
customer.service@macmillan.com.au

New Zealand agent/distributor: David Bateman Ltd;
tel. (09) 415 7664; fax (09) 415 8892

A CIP catalogue record for this book is available from the British Library.

Publisher: Joanna Lorenz
Editorial Director: Helen Sudell
Project Editor: Catherine Stuart
Production Controller: Helen Wang
Designer: Nigel Partridge
Photographer: Mark Wood

ETHICAL TRADING POLICY

Because of our ongoing ecological investment programme, you, as our customer, can have the pleasure and reassurance of knowing that a tree is being cultivated on your behalf to naturally replace the materials used to make the book you are holding. For further information about this scheme, go to www.annesspublishing.com/trees

Previously published as part of a larger volume, *The World Encyclopedia of Coins and Coin Collecting*.

NOTE

Every effort has been made to reproduce coins at their actual size. Some coins have been enlarged or reduced slightly to make features more legible, but such modifications have been kept to a minimum.

CONTENTS

INTRODUCTION

Coins, as we think of them today, came into existence some 2,700 years ago, an arrival that was roughly concurrent in Asia Minor and the Far East. Of course, the history of trade predates that of coins by thousands of years. There is evidence that the earliest civilizations of the Mediterranean and Middle East exchanged goods of value such as cattle, cow hide and salt – indeed, the Latin word *sal* (salt) gives us the modern term salary. We now refer to payment in goods as "barter", and it is not entirely obsolete in the modern world. Many African countries have long traditions of trading salt, while tins of rice were used as currency in Pol Pot's Cambodia following the establishment of his "moneyless society". Today, hard-to-find goods still form the basis of everyday transactions in times of economic upheaval or war.

THE ORIGINS OF COINS

Gradually, civilizations in Persia, India and China began to develop what might be thought of as the first true "currencies" – items given a notional value and used chiefly for the purpose of monetary exchange. Sometimes these currencies were modelled on

Below: This 1st-century relief shows the kind of money bag a travelling moneyer would have taken to a Roman treasury.

utilitarian items, such as the bronze currencies shaped as spades, knives and keys exchanged in ancient China. Sea shells, in particular the cowrie shell, were used as money in the Far East, the Pacific and Africa, where they were often threaded on to strings or fashioned into armlets. Cowries were even mimicked by some of the early metal currencies: bronze casts of the shells were traded in China until about 200BC, and the name "cowrie" has inspired coins in India (the Kutch kori) and Africa (the cauri of Guinea).

Despite some impressive examples of metallurgy, such as the Chinese knife and key money mentioned above, many metal currencies began life in fairly simple form – often as lumps or strips. Roman coins originated with the *aes rude*, which was, as its Latin name suggests, little more than an unadorned lump of bronze. Modern Russian coins take their name from the Old Russian *rubl,* which basically translates as a "cut strip", possibly from a silver metal bar. The Indo-European root of the Indian *rupee* is thought to have similar origins.

The kind of metal used varied from place to place. The Lydian kings – an exceptionally affluent Persian dynasty

Below: Coining is entwined with metal craft. The Gold Weigher, *by Dutch artist Gerard Dou, appeared in 1664.*

Above: This convex shield of Macedon with the head of Pan is a fine example of early allegorical portraiture.

– mined electrum, a natural alloy of gold and silver, from the river beds of their empire. These coins, at first crudely marked with a nail, are now generally recognized as the first true European coins, and have been traced to the late 7th century BC. Silver coins were also traded in ancient Persia, and poured into neighbouring Middle Eastern fiefdoms. Copper was mined in Cyprus from about 3000BC, and, when alloyed with tin to form bronze, was exchanged as bullion bars, or "talents", in the ancient Greek world. At the peak of Hellenic power, the Athenian silver was traded far and wide as drachmae and obolo.

The Romans generally preferred silver to gold for its abundance and hard-wearing nature, although their gold imperial coins, such as the aureus, circulated as far as India. The eastern empire of Byzantium, formed in AD 364, produced some of the most exquisite gold coins ever to have existed. Gold was not favoured as a trading metal by China until reforms sought by the Han ruler Wang Mang just before the first millennium. Rather, copper, bronze, brass and even iron were used to produce the earliest Chinese coins, and formed the basis of their enduring cash currency. Ancient conical copper items have also been recovered by archaeologists in India.

DENOMINATION AND DESIGN

The face value – or denomination – of a coin was traditionally determined by the weight and purity of the metal used. Subdivisions calculated in the ancient world formed the basis of long-standing denominations that ultimately stood the test of time. The Roman system of dividing the libra (or pound) into 20 solidi or 240 denarii was retained by the Carolingian dynasty long after the fall of Rome, and under-pinned the French franc and Italian lira until the arrival of the euro.

The earliest coins were often unmarked, as their value was invested solely in their weight. However, forward-thinking principalities and mercenary strongholds began to mark metals as a guarantee of value, to save time. At first these basic signatures were little more than the strike of a nail or a blow of a hammer, but gradually a more advanced form of inscription developed. Ancient Greek designs such as the turtles of Aegina and owls of Athens were superbly influential in their day, and crude copies, as well as superior adaptations, were made from Celtic Europe to Pharaonic Africa.

Below: A page from an American coin album designed to house Lincoln cents of each date and mint-mark.

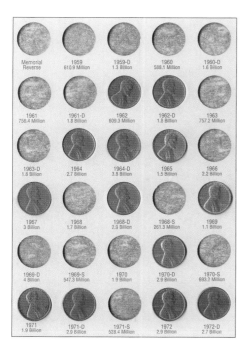

Above: Bronze bu (knife and key) currency was revived in China during 1st century AD.

Portraiture and allegory, which gathered momentum under the Romans and achieved near-perfection in the hands of Byzantine rulers, were revived in the intaglio-produced coins of medieval Europe. Among the most notable were the thalers (or dollars) and ducatos produced by the Habsburg and Medici dynasties respectively. Historic Middle Eastern and Islamic coins, although non-figurative, also bore very creative designs, with lengthy inscriptions that proclaimed victories and allegiances, many mirroring the concentric patterns of the Fatimids.

After centuries of craftsmanship, the first milled coins were developed in northern Europe during the 16th century, and, in duplicating elaborate designs with lightning speed, turned the mints of the world into power-houses of production. Colonial mints from Mexico to Bengal produced coins that married imperial symbols with local imagery.

COINS TODAY

Today the role of coins in everyday life is being supplanted by plastic in the form of credit cards and cash cards. Yet, despite this gradual narrowing in the usage of metal money, coins as collectables have developed dramatically. Not only are the mints and treasuries of the world producing more and more deluxe items for collectors, but the coins in general circulation are more varied than at any time since the fall of the Roman Empire.

One of the more challenging aspects of collecting coins is the actual identification process. Inscription and denomination can be helpful in this regard, but ancient coins are more of a problem; the time-worn obliteration of any lettering, effigy or emblem may obstruct obvious clues to their origin. Where inscriptions do exist and are legible, you can look for dates or mint-marks identifying the place where the coins were struck. The coins in this book have been selected to chronicle the key developments in design and production that have defined each country's coinage, so that enduring motifs and other distinguishing features become familiar to the reader. Should you wish to learn more, there are a wealth of excellent numismatic organizations on-line devoted to the research and identification of coins, while coin clubs, and collectors' fairs, are good opportunities to discuss your coins with fellow numismatists.

There can be little doubt that the true value of coins lies in their reflection of social and economic shifts; of poverty and power. In the pages that follow, you will see civilizations rise and fall, civil wars and invaders make their mark, empires extend their influence, independent republics come into being, and national heritage rediscovered. You will also witness seminal designs, revived currencies and misjudged innovations, such as the supremely heavy copper plate coins of Catherine the Great. Coins also commemorate world-changing events, from the assassination of Julius Caesar to the voyage of Captain Cook. Whether unique or common, cryptic or ostentatious, these tactile, portable, and often ornate metal objects have not only powered economies old and new for nearly three thousand years, but, in doing so, have also chronicled the power struggles of the modern world.

Left: President George Washington of the United States originally felt the inclusion of his portrait on coins to be an affront to democracy, favouring the figural representation of Liberty. Today, the word remains inscribed on US coins – as does Washington's portrait.

1   2

3   4

5   6

7   8

9   10

11   12

13

14   15

AMERICA

The earliest coinage consisted of crude pesos struck in the Spanish colonies from locally mined silver. The *peso a ocho reales* (8 real piece) later became the standard currency medium throughout the French and British colonies in North America and laid the foundation for the dollar system.

CANADA

One of the world's largest countries, Canada was colonized by the French after 1534. Although John Cabot discovered Newfoundland in 1497, it was not annexed by England until 1583, and no attempt was made to colonize it until 1610. Britain formally acquired Hudson's Bay, Newfoundland and Nova Scotia in 1713 and gained control of New France in 1763 after a decisive victory at Quebec in 1759. The early colonists used French, English, Spanish or Dutch coins, but suffered frequent shortages of money from France and resorted to using playing cards, stamped locally. In 1670 silver coins denominated in sols were struck at the Paris Mint, specifically for use in New France, but were unpopular as they could not be used to buy supplies from France. A second attempt to provide a purely local coinage was made in 1721, when the mint at La Rochelle struck copper deniers, but they were no more successful. The British colonies were supplied with gold and silver coins from England, but subsidiary coinage was in the form of tokens struck by the major banks. Federal coinage was adopted in 1870, following the Confederation of Canada in 1867. New Brunswick, Nova Scotia and Prince Edward Island issued copper or bronze coins before joining the Confederation in 1873, while Newfoundland had its own coins until 1949, when it joined Canada.

Left: The dollar of 1982, celebrating the 125th anniversary of Confederation, reproduces the painting entitled The Fathers of Confederation *by Robert Harris, showing delegates at the Quebec Conference of 1864, which led to the unification of the colonies in British North America.*

BANK TOKENS

From 1800 the chronic shortage of coins from Europe led tradesmen to issue copper tokens, but these were gradually suppressed from 1835 and replaced by copper or bronze tokens issued by the major banks. The first of these were the Bouquet Sous of the Bank of Montreal [1–2], followed by issues in Quebec showing the bank emblem with a farmer or bank building on the reverse [3], though the last issue had the farmer on the obverse and an allegorical scene on the reverse [4]. The Bank of Upper Canada (now Ontario) struck pennies and halfpence in 1850–7, with St George and the Dragon on one side and the bank's arms on the other [5–6]. The tokens were withdrawn in 1858, when bronze cents were introduced for the whole province of Canada.

PROVINCIAL COINAGE

Copper or bronze halfpence and pennies were issued by the Maritime Provinces before they joined the Confederation. New Brunswick had coins showing Queen Victoria on the obverse [7] and a shipping scene on the reverse, while Nova Scotia had coins featuring a Scottish thistle on one side and busts of George IV or Victoria on the other [8]. Both colonies also struck cents in the 1860s. Prince Edward Island produced only a single coin, a cent of 1871 [9–10], before joining the Confederation in 1873, but Newfoundland [11–12] had its own coins until 1949.

DEFINITIVES

The coins of the Confederation bear the effigy of the reigning monarch to this day. Prior to 1935 the reverses showed the value in words, set within a wreath and surmounted by a crown, but in 1920 a small cent was adopted with maple leaves flanking the value; two years later the nickel 5 cents replaced the tiny silver coin [13]. In 1937 a pictorial series was adopted: the reverses showing maple leaves (1 cent), beaver (5 cents), the schooner *Bluenose* (10 cents), caribou (25 cents) and national arms (50 cents) continue to this day [14–18]. The silver dollar first appeared in 1935, celebrating the silver jubilee of George V, and its motif of a Voyageur canoe was retained until 1987, when it was replaced by a circulating coin in aureate-bronze plated nickel depicting a loon [19]. A bimetallic $2 coin showing a polar bear was added in 1996 [20]. Gold coins began with a Canadian version of the British sovereign (1908–19) alongside $5 and $10 coins (1912–14). Gold bullion coins in the Maple Leaf series have appeared since 1983.

BULLION COINS

Canada is one of the world's leading producers of precious metals, and this inspired the development of the Maple Leaf in 1979, a coin containing a troy ounce of pure gold, originally struck to a fineness of .999. The reverse featured the national emblem, hence its name. The legal tender value of $50 appeared on the obverse. Since 1983 this coin has been struck in .9999 fine – "four nines gold" – which appears alongside the maple leaf. In addition to smaller gold coins, Canada has also produced platinum bullion coins since 1988.

From Barter to Beaver

Relics of the days when Canada's chief industry was fur trapping are the coins struck by the Hudson's Bay Company. These brass pieces, with the arms of the company on the obverse, had a cryptic reverse showing ligated H B over E M, then 1 or a fraction, with N B at the foot. The last initials were actually an error for M B ("made beaver") and denoted a value in terms of prime beaver pelts, which were highly prized for men's hats.

COMMEMORATIVE COINS

From 1935 the silver dollar was the preferred medium for commemorative coins, but since 1943 Canada has also produced many as base-metal circulating coins, beginning with the 5 cent coins in tombac brass or chromium-plated steel instead of nickel (which was required for the war effort). These substitutes featured the V-sign and had a victory slogan in Morse code around the rim [21–22]. The bicentennial of the nickel industry (1951) resulted in a special 5 cent coin, and this set the precedent for the entire series from 1 cent to $1, with motifs and double dates to celebrate the centennial of Confederation (1967).

More recently, 5 and 25 cent coins [23] have often been used as commemoratives, notably the 1992 series of provincial quarters [24] to mark the 125th anniversary. Special issues have proliferated since the 1970s, notably the series for the Montreal Olympics (1973–6) and the Calgary Winter Games (1985–7) [25–26], and the 150th anniversary of Toronto [27]. Gold and platinum have also been used in recent years for coins in thematic sets featuring Canadian wildlife.

1
2
3
4
5
6
7
8
9
10
11
12
13

UNITED STATES DEFINITIVES

Although the Continental Congress of 1777 resolved to establish a national mint, it was not until 1792 that the first mint was opened in Philadelphia. Up to that time the currency was chaotic, with base-metal subsidiary coins valued in pence or halfpence and silver based on the Spanish dollar. In common parlance the Spanish real was known as a "bit", and a quarter dollar was known as a "two-bit coin", a term still used to signify 25 cents. From the outset however, the infant United States adopted a decimal system (following the examples of Russia and France), although the original 10 cent piece soon changed its name from "disme" to "dime". An interesting feature of United States coins is the inclusion of initials denoting the various branch mints, which were set up to refine and coin gold and silver mined locally. This practice survives to this day, although most US coins are now confined to base alloys.

Left: Among the prototypes for a distinctive American coinage were the coins that have acquired the nickname of Fugio Cents, from the Latin word meaning "I fly" inscribed over a sundial. This reminder that time flies and the more trenchant legend "Mind Your Business" are believed to have been suggested by Benjamin Franklin. The reverse shows 13 rings, symbolizing the original states.

STATES OF THE CONFEDERATION

From the Declaration of Independence in 1776 until the introduction of a federal coinage in 1792, it was left to individual states to produce subsidiary coins. Massachusetts struck cents and half cents depicting a Native American and the eagle [1–2], but others, notably Connecticut, New Hampshire, New York and Vermont, imitated British and Irish coins, often with busts of George Washington laureated in the Roman manner and looking suspiciously like George III [3]. Even the seated Britannia was only slightly modified for many of the reverses.

EARLY COINS

The first coins consisted of cents and half cents, followed by silver dollars [5–6], half dollars [7–8] and half dimes (5 cents) in 1794, and the dime [11–12] and quarter dollar [13] in 1795. The half cent vanished in 1857 when the size of the cent was considerably reduced [4]. The remaining six denominations have continued ever since, although now for all practical purposes only the coins from 1–25 cents generally circulate. Some odd values have been struck from time to time, including the bronze 2 cents (1864–73) [14–15], the silver 3 cents with a shield in a star (1851–73) [16] and a larger piece in nickel with a head of Liberty and the value in Roman numerals (1865–89) [17–18]. Between 1875 and 1878, 20 cent coins appeared briefly, showing a seated figure of Liberty on the obverse and an eagle on the reverse.

The silver half dime, with the seated Liberty on one side [9] and the value in words on the other [10], continued until 1873 but was challenged in 1866 by a larger coin minted in nickel with a shield obverse and the value in numerals on the reverse. Both coins circulated side by side for several years and the latter acquired the nickname – nickel – by which it is still commonly known today, even though the circulating "silver" coins (dimes, quarters and half dollars) have been produced in a similar alloy since 1964.

The mid-19th century gold rush had a massive impact on US coinage, reflected by the dominance of gold in the eagle ($10), the double eagle ($20) [21–22] and its subdivisions of half ($5) and quarter ($2.50), deriving its name from the reverse motifs, which showed an American eagle in various guises, either heraldic or flying [19–20] or even walking. As if this were not sufficient, the 19th century saw tiny gold dollars as well as $2, $3, $4 and $50 denominations, though some of these were intended for commemorative purposes. Following the California gold rush of 1849, gold coins of 50 cents or $1 were struck locally in addition to the federal gold dollars. Many of these tiny coins were octagonal in shape and fairly basic in design [23].

MODERN COINS

Although the figure or profile of Liberty dominated American coins for many years, there were some attempts to replace her with other motifs. When the size of the cent was reduced in 1857 Liberty was replaced by a flying eagle, followed two years later by the head of a Native American wearing a war bonnet [30]. This motif continued until 1909, when it was replaced by a bust of Abraham Lincoln, marking the centenary of his birth [24]. Almost a century later it is still in use, second only to the world's longest-running coin design – Pistrucci's St George and the Dragon on the British gold coins. In 1943 cents were struck in zinc-coated steel [24–25]. In 1959, on Lincoln's 150th anniversary, the ears of wheat [25–26] were replaced by a Lincoln Memorial reverse [27–28].

The Indian Head Penny, as it is commonly known, inspired the changes made to the nickel in 1913,

Above: The profile of Dwight D. Eisenhower on the dollar of 1971.

When Precious Metal Replaced Base Alloy

Between 1942 and 1945 the nickel was actually struck in silver. It may not be a precious metal but nickel was vital to the war effort, hence its replacement by coins containing 35 per cent silver alloyed with copper and manganese. To distinguish the silver from the nickel coins a mintmark was placed above the dome on the reverse; these marks included a P – the first (and for many years the only) time the coins from the main mint at Philadelphia had been thus distinguished.

when pictorial motifs were used for both sides. James Earle Fraser produced the head of a Native American chief based on profiles of John Tree, Iron Tail and Two Moon, but the "buffalo" on the reverse (which gives this coin its nickname) was actually Black Diamond, the American bison in the New York Zoo. In 1938 it was replaced by designs portraying Thomas Jefferson (obverse) and his home, Monticello (reverse). Nostalgia being what it is, the Buffalo reverse was revived in 2005.

George Washington [29] replaced Liberty on the quarter in 1932, the bicentenary of his birth, while Franklin D. Roosevelt was the first president to receive this honour barely months after his death [31]. Similarly, Kennedy (1964) and Eisenhower (1971) appeared on the half dollar and dollar, the former replacing Benjamin Franklin and the Liberty Bell, which had graced the half dollar since 1948.

1

2

3

4

5

6

7

8

9

10

11

12

13

14

15

AMERICAN COMMEMORATIVE AND SPECIAL ISSUES

Although the United States was one of the first countries to produce commemorative coins (1893), this practice was overdone in the 1920s and 1930s to such an extent that it was virtually abandoned in 1938. No fewer than 48 different half dollars were produced in this first period, but with variants in date and mint-mark the total rose to 142, which collectors eventually protested at as being excessive. In the same period there was one quarter and one silver dollar, plus a pair of quarter eagles and two massive $50 gold coins. Apart from three circulating, double-dated coins celebrating the bicentenary of the Declaration of Independence (1976), commemoratives were not generally revived until 1982. Output since then has far exceeded that of the first period.

Left: The United States struck a number of gold commemoratives for the Pan-Pacific Exposition in 1915, marking the opening of the Panama Canal. Many, like these half-dollar coins, had typically ornate designs. Among the most collectable, however, are the gold $50 coins struck at San Francisco in 1915, which circulated in circular and octagonal versions [1–4].

EARLIEST COMMEMORATIVES

The first half dollars appeared in 1892 to celebrate the 400th anniversary of Columbus's voyage to America, as well as to publicize (and help finance) the Columbian Exposition in Chicago. This opened in 1893, hence coins of both dates were issued [7–8]. The half dollar bears the bust of Columbus on one side and on the other his flagship *Santa Maria* above the twin globes representing the hemispheres. The Ladies Committee of the Exposition pressed for a coin of their own, resulting in the silver quarter portraying Queen Isabella. Tiny gold dollars were struck between 1903 and 1922 to mark the centenaries of the Louisiana Purchase and the birth of Ulysses Grant [5–6]. William McKinley, assassinated in 1901, had the unusual distinction of appearing on one of the Louisiana coins of 1903 as well as coins of 1916–17 with his memorial on the reverse. The last of these tiny pieces marked the inauguration of Grant's memorial. Gold quarter eagles appeared in 1915 for the Pan-Pacific Exposition celebrating the completion

of the Panama Canal, and in 1926 for the 150th anniversary of Philadelphia as the cradle of the Revolution. A silver dollar bearing the conjoined profiles of Washington and Lafayette appeared in 1900.

SILVER HALF DOLLARS

A silver half dollar was included in the set of 1915 marking the Pan-Pacific Exposition, but no further commemoratives of this denomination appeared until 1918, when the centennial of the state of Illinois was marked by a coin portraying Lincoln and an eagle [12–13]. Two years later the tercentenary of the Pilgrim Fathers was marked by coins showing a Pilgrim (obverse) and the *Mayflower* (reverse). In the same year a coin celebrated the state of Maine, with its arms on the obverse and the value on the reverse, establishing the precedent for several others commemorating statehood anniversaries [14–17]. Native Americans featured on the reverse of the Missouri Centennial half dollar in 1921 (with frontiersman) [18–19], and on the obverse of the Oregon Trail memorial in 1926 (with covered wagon on reverse)

The Spirit of '76

Although the definitive obverses were retained in 1976, the quarter, half and dollar bore the double date 1776–1996, with entirely new motifs on the reverse. A drummer boy of the Continental Army and Independence Hall, Philadelphia, graced the quarter and half respectively, while the dollar featured the Liberty Bell with a full Moon in the background, alluding to the recent Apollo missions.

[20–21]. Ulysses Grant was again commemorated on a half dollar of 1922 [10–11]. In the early years the events honoured were relatively important and included the Huguenot-Walloon tercentenary (1924) and the 150th anniversary of Cook's landing in Hawaii (1928), but by 1930 the pace of issues was escalating as the importance of the events diminished: even individual towns petitioned Congress for coins to mark their anniversaries. This reached its nadir in 1936, when no fewer than 16 coins appeared, celebrating the centenary of Bridgeport, Connecticut, the opening of the Bay Bridge linking San Francisco and Oakland, and even the opening of the Cincinnati Music Center [22–23]. More portentously, a silver half dollar was struck in preparation for the 75th anniversary of the Battle of Gettysburg in 1938. It featured conjoined busts on the obverse, plus two shields flanking a fasces (the ancient Roman symbol for authority and power over life and death) on the reverse.

Not only were these issues too frequent, but rumours of manipulation and speculation brought the programme into disrepute. Nevertheless, they are handsome examples of the numismatic art, and most are now quite expensive because the average mintage was very small. The post-World War II exceptions, honouring Booker T. Washington and George Washington Carver, were produced in plentiful quantities on a nationwide basis, and were even reissued in subsequent years to satisfy public demand.

MODERN COMMEMORATIVES

After a gap of almost three decades commemorative half dollars resumed in 1982, to mark the 250th anniversary of the birth of George Washington. Since then, they have been used sparingly, for the centenary of the Statue of Liberty, the bicentenary of Congress, Mount Rushmore's golden jubilee, the 450th anniversary of Columbus, the Bill of Rights and World War II.

The shape of things to come was manifest in the coins launched in 1983 for the forthcoming Olympic Games in Los Angeles, followed by coins for the 1994 World Cup soccer championship, hosted by the USA and, more recently, the Centennial Olympic Games in Atlanta. The last were celebrated by no fewer than six gold $5, ten silver dollars and six cupro-nickel half dollars [24–27]. Apart from these Olympic coins, half dollars have not been issued since 1996. The preferred denomination is the silver dollar, retaining its traditional size and weight.

Modern commemorative issues are much more prolific than the pre-war half dollars but tend to be restricted to events and personalities of national or international importance. Particularly poignant are the 1994 coins honouring US prisoners of war and Vietnam veterans. By contrast, the USA is now following Canada's example, with low-value circulating commemoratives [9].

THE STATE QUARTERS OF 1999–2008

Certain American coins, notably the commemorative half dollars of the early 20th century, alluded to particular states, but this was haphazard and piecemeal. Conversely, even individual towns and cities have been honoured solely because they petitioned Congress for a coin marking their jubilee or centenary. Every state of the Union is honoured equally for the first time in the ten-year celebration that began in 1999 and continues at the rate of five coins a year.

HOW IT ALL BEGAN

Although the 13 colonies declared their independence in 1776 and fought a long and bitter war to secure their freedom in 1783, a federal constitution was not finally drawn up until 1787 and then had to be ratified by each state. The first to do so was Delaware, on December 7, 1787. Pennsylvania followed five days later, and then New Jersey on December 18. Georgia ratified the Constitution on January 2, 1788, and Connecticut a week later. These five states were therefore selected for depiction on the quarter dollars released in 1999.

On December 1, 1997, President Clinton signed Public Law 105–124 (the 60 States Commemorative Coin Program Act), authorizing the United States Mint to celebrate each state with a special coin. The general circulating

Below (clockwise from top-left): state and keystone (PA), Charter Oak (CT), statutory George Washington obverse used for all quarters, Delaware River crossing (NJ), Caesar Rodney (DE).

versions of the five coins issued each year have a copper core and a cupronickel cladding. They are struck at Philadelphia and Denver, identified by the P or D mint-marks below the motto on the obverse. Proof versions of each coin are struck at the mint in San Francisco and bear the S mint-mark.

The quarter was chosen for this ambitious series because it is the most widely circulated coin, as well as the largest of the four coins in everyday use. The US Mint invited the governors of each state to submit suggestions for the designs on the reverse of each coin. These were considered by the Mint, the Citizens' Commemorative Coin Advisory Committee and the Commission of Fine Arts. They were then sent to the Secretary of the Treasury for final review and approval.

No other quarters are being struck during this ten-year period. Five quarters are being released each year, in the order in which the states ratified the Constitution or attained statehood.

DIVERSITY OF SUBJECTS

Obviously, when there is only a fairly limited amount of space for a motif, the choice of subject is very important. What is intriguing is the wide range of subject matter depicted on these coins, reflecting different outlooks and attitudes across the United States.

The designs for the first coins, issued on behalf of the states that were quick to ratify the new Constitution, have adopted a historical approach. Delaware chose a figure on horseback, Caesar Rodney, who, like the much more famous Paul Revere, made a midnight ride of 130km/80 miles in a thunderstorm on July 1, 1776, to break

Above (clockwise from top-left): Jamestown (VA), young Abraham Lincoln (IL), Helen Keller (AL), Kitty Hawk (NC), Gateway to Discovery (FL), pelican (LA), space odyssey (OH).

the deadlock in the Delaware vote for independence. A major-general in the Delaware militia, he held more public offices than anyone else in a career spanning 40 years. Connecticut chose its Charter Oak, but the most dramatic motif is to be found on the New Jersey quarter, with the caption "Crossroads of the Revolution" below the image of Washington crossing the Delaware to defeat the British at Trenton, the turning point in the war. A Minuteman – a member of the colonial militia, who fought the British from the outset, appears on the Massachusetts coin.

Above: Many states have chosen famous landmarks. Mount Rushmore appears on the South Dakota quarter.

HISTORIC EVENTS AND PERSONALITIES

Some of the states formerly ranked among the earliest colonies allude to events of another era. Virginia shows ships at Jamestown, which celebrates its 400th anniversary in 2007. By contrast, others have selected events and celebrities of much more recent vintage, ranging from a young Abraham Lincoln (Illinois) to Helen Keller (Alabama), who overcame both deafness and blindness to teach others. Appropriately the coin also bears her name in Braille. Ohio alludes to its role as the birthplace of aviation pioneers with an astronaut, John Glenn, in a spacesuit and the *Wright Flyer*. The latter is also featured on the coin from North Carolina, where the first flight actually took place near Kitty Hawk in December 1903.

Guitars and a trumpet celebrate the musical heritage of Tennessee, an oblique reference to jazz pioneer W.C. Handy and, of course, Elvis Presley. Florida has the slogan "Gateway to Discovery", contrasting a Spanish galleon with the Columbia Shuttle.

LANDMARKS

Some state quarters have picked an outstanding landmark. The strange geological feature aptly named the Old Man of the Mountain is shown on the coin from New Hampshire, while the Statue of Liberty was an obvious choice for New York. Other manmade features that appear include the most easterly lighthouse (Maine) and the dome of the state capitol (Maryland). Missouri has chosen the great arch at St Louis in the background to a scene showing the Corps of Discovery, led by Lewis and Clark, setting off on their expedition in 1804.

MAPS AND SPECIALITIES

Many of the designs incorporate a map of the state, often with the state bird such as the pelican (Louisiana), the great Carolina wren (South Carolina) or a loon on one of the 10,000 lakes of Minnesota. Arkansas features the mockingbird, an ear of corn and a diamond, alluding to the fact that it is the only state where diamonds are mined. Pennsylvania includes an allegorical statue with the caption "Virtue Liberty Independence", while Texas has the

Above (clockwise from top-left): Old Man of the Mountain (NH), Statue of Liberty (NY), Pemaquid Point (ME), Lewis and Clarke (MO), Statehouse Dome (MD).

lone star and Georgia has a peach. Other states omit the map and concentrate on what they are best known for: cattle, corn and cheese (Wisconsin), sailing (Rhode Island), magnolias (Mississippi), breeding horses (Kentucky) and car racing (Indiana).

By the time the series is completed in 2008, with coins representing New Mexico and Arizona, which gained statehood in 1912, and Alaska and Hawaii, which attained that status in 1959, collectors worldwide will have a better picture of the various maps, birds, landmarks and achievements that characterize each State of the Union.

Below (clockwise from top-left): Camel's Hump (VT), musical heritage (TN), Great Lakes (MI), Minuteman (MA).

Below (clockwise from top-left): Palmetto tree and Carolina wren (SC), Lone Star (TX), cattle and cheese (WI), peach (GA).

Below (clockwise from top-left): Ocean State (RI), magnolia (MS), Indy Car Races (IN), thoroughbred (KY).

1

2

3

4

5

6

7

8

9

10

11

12

13

14

15

16

17

BAHAMAS, BERMUDA AND WEST INDIES

Contrary to popular belief, the Bahamas and Bermuda are not in the West Indies but lie in the North Atlantic rather than the Caribbean. Barbados was regarded as one of the Windward Islands but lies well to the east of the archipelago, while Trinidad and Tobago are at the southern end of the islands, off the coast of South America. In the 17th and 18th centuries, throughout the Caribbean, extensive use was made of Spanish, French and British coins, cut into pieces and countermarked for local circulation.

Left: The earliest coinage in this area consisted of the Hogge Money of Bermuda, produced in 1616 and so called on account of the image of a pig on the reverse, alluding to the wild hogs that succoured shipwrecked mariners. The image has been used on the reverse of 1 cent coins since their inception in 1970.

BAHAMAS

The Commonwealth of the Bahamas is an archipelago of about 3000 islands, cays, rocks and reefs east of Florida. The Bahamas have the distinction of being the first land sighted by Columbus in 1492, but they were colonized by the English in 1626 and, although they attained full independence in 1973, the British monarch remains the head of state.

A penny with the effigy of George III and the colony's badge was struck at Birmingham in 1806–7. British coins were legal tender until 1966, when distinctive coins from 1 cent to $5 were adopted with the bust of Elizabeth II on the obverse and images of island fauna and flora on the reverse [1–2]. The Bahamian sloop (25 cents) and blue marlin (50 cents) allude to the main tourist attractions. The same reverses were retained for a new series in 1974, with the arms of the Bahamas replacing the Queen's effigy [3–4]. The original series was struck at the Royal Mint; from 1974 to 1985 they were produced by the Franklin Mint and are now produced by the Royal Canadian Mint. Small gold coins marked the adoption of the new constitution (1967) while cupro-nickel or silver commemoratives have appeared since 1974, notably celebrating anniversaries of the arrival of Columbus.

BARBADOS

Although the island was discovered and named by the Portuguese in 1563, it was not settled until 1627. It remained in British hands from then until it achieved independence in 1966, Elizabeth II continuing as head of state.

Countermarked Spanish silver (1791–9) and copper tokens with a Negro head obverse and Neptune reverse (1788–92) [5–6] were followed by mainly British coins. Coins of the British Caribbean Territories (Eastern Group) were in use from 1955 to 1973, when a distinctive series from 1 cent to $5 was introduced [7–9], with the arms of the island (obverse) and landmarks, birds and fishes (reverse). Double-dated versions appeared in 1976 to mark the tenth anniversary of independence. Gold coins since 1975 and $10, $20 and $50 silver coins since 1981 have been struck as commemoratives, and they include the world's first cricket coin (1991).

BERMUDA

The "still-vex'd Bermoothes" of Shakespeare's *The Tempest*, the island was settled involuntarily when a shipload of British colonists bound for Virginia was wrecked there in 1609. The settlement became permanent in 1612. Apart from the crude Hogge Money (in denominations of 2, 3, 6 and 12 pence), Bermuda had a token coinage from 1793 [10–11] until 1842, when British coins became legal tender.

Bermuda abandoned sterling [12–13] in 1970 and adopted the dollar of 100 cents. Birds, fish and flowers form the subjects of the reverses, while various effigies of Elizabeth II have appeared on the obverse [14–18]. A brass $5 coin was added in 1983 for general circulation. A series of 25 cent coins appeared in 1984, with the arms of Bermuda or its ten parishes on the reverse, to celebrate the 375th anniversary of the colony. Large silver (and latterly cupro-nickel) dollars have served as a commemorative medium since 1970 while higher values ($2, $5 and $25) have been produced for the same purpose since 1975. Gold coins from $10 to $250 have also been issued for special events and anniversaries.

TRINIDAD AND TOBAGO

Discovered by Columbus in 1498, these islands were colonized by the French and Dutch but captured by the British in 1797 and formally annexed in 1814. Originally administered as separate colonies, they merged in 1888. They formed part of the British West Indies Federation until 1962, when they became an independent state, adopting a republican constitution in 1976.

Spanish, French or British countermarked or cut coins circulated in Tobago (1798) and Trinidad (1804 and 1811 respectively), followed in 1825 by British coins, which were replaced in 1955 by those of the East Caribbean. Distinctive coinage (1–50 cents) was adopted in 1966, with numerals of value on one side and the republic's arms on the other [19–20]. Higher denominations consist of $1 (1969), $5 (1971) and $10 (1976) in base metals, with silver and gold coins in higher values for commemoratives. Pictorial motifs were substituted from 1974 onwards, many featuring Caribbean landmarks, fauna and flora [21–24] but also giving prominence to cultural heritage, such as the steel bands for which Trinidad is world famous.

The Bermuda Triangle

Since 1996 Bermuda has produced coins to publicize the great mystery of navigation known as the Bermuda Triangle. The coins have, appropriately, three sides and are denominated as $3 or a multiple. The first coins ($3, $6 and $30) showed a map, a compass and a sinking ship; later issues have featured specific ships, such as the *Sea Venture*, wrecked in 1609, and the *Deliverance*, built by the survivors.

NETHERLANDS ANTILLES

These islands, forming part of the Kingdom of the Netherlands, comprised two groups: Aruba, Bonaire and Curaçao near the coast of Venezuela, and St Eustatius, Saba and part of St Martin south-east of Puerto Rico. Aruba became a separate state in 1986.

A general issue of coins for the Dutch West Indies appeared in 1794. Copper cents and silver stuivers were issued at Curaçao in the name of the Batavian Republic (1799–1803) and later, stuivers and reaals, often cut into segments under the Dutch kingdom. Cut or countermarked Spanish coins were used during the British occupation (1807–16) and after the restoration of Dutch rule, until 1821, when coins specifically minted for Curaçao were resumed.

Modern coins date from World War II, when the islands were cut off from Holland while it was under German occupation. These coins were similar to their Dutch counterparts, but with "Curaçao" inscribed on the reverse [25–27]. Distinctive coins inscribed "Nederlandse Antillen" have been in use since 1952, with a separate series for Aruba since 1986 [28–31].

1
2
3
4
5
6
7
8
9
10
11
12
13
14
15
16
17
18

CUBA, HISPANIOLA AND JAMAICA

The three largest islands of the Caribbean lie in its northernmost part, south of Florida and the Bahamas. Spanish-speaking Cuba is the largest and most westerly of the group. To the east lies the island of Hispaniola, the western third constituting the French-speaking Republic of Haiti and the remaining two-thirds the Spanish-speaking Dominican Republic. South of Cuba lies Jamaica, which is English-speaking and now a republic within the British Commonwealth. Associated with Jamaica are the Cayman Islands and the Turks and Caicos Islands, which were formerly its dependencies.

Left: Jamaica remained within the sterling area until 1969, and in this period produced its first commemorative coin, a crown-sized 5 shillings to celebrate its hosting of the 1966 Commonwealth Games.

CUBA

Reached by Columbus in 1492 and settled by the Spaniards in the early 1500s, Cuba remained a Spanish colony until 1898. The island was captured by the United States during the Spanish-American War and granted independence in 1902. The dictatorship of Fulgencio Batista was overthrown in 1959 by Fidel Castro, who instituted a communist regime. Although trade sanctions are still imposed by the USA, Cuba has become a popular tourist resort in recent years.

Distinctive coins based on the peso of 100 centavos were introduced in 1915, with an armorial obverse and a five-pointed star inscribed "Patria y Libertad" ("Fatherland and Liberty") on the reverse [1–2]. The Castro regime retained these motifs but changed the motto to "Patria o Muerte" ("Fatherland or Death") on some of the coins. In 1915 dollar-sized silver pesos were accompanied by a tiny gold coin portraying the martyr José Marti. Silver pesos ceased in 1939 but since 1977 smaller cupro-nickel coins have been extensively used as a vehicle for commemoration: by 2004 there had been well over 400 different issues [3–8]. Since 1975, 5 and 10 pesos have been almost as prolific, with even larger denominations in silver or gold.

HAITI

Hispaniola ("Little Spain") was, like Cuba, claimed by Columbus on his first voyage and colonized by Spain, but in the early 17th century the western district was taken over by French pirates, who ceded it to France in 1697. The coffee and sugar plantations worked by slaves imported from Africa made Saint-Domingue one of France's richest colonies, but a slave rebellion led by Henri Christophe led to the creation of the Republic of Haiti in 1804, the oldest Negro republic in the world and (second only to the USA) the oldest republic in the western hemisphere.

Countermarked French, Spanish and Portuguese coins circulated in the 18th century, followed by a local coinage denominated in escalins. Coins in deniers and sols, introduced in 1807, were rapidly superseded by a decimal system based on the gourde of 100 centimes, a currency that continues to this day. Circulating coins have the arms on one side and Liberty (1881–94), followed by profiles of historic figures (since 1904) on the other. Apart from the circulating coins from 1 centime to 1 gourde in nickel- or brass-plated steel [9], Haiti has issued many gold and silver commemoratives since 1971.

DOMINICAN REPUBLIC

The larger part of Hispaniola, which the Spaniards called Santo Domingo, remained under their control until 1822, when the Haitians invaded it. They occupied the entire island until 1844. In that year Juan Pablo Duarte raised a revolt and drove out the invaders, establishing the independent Dominican Republic. It voluntarily submitted to Spain from 1861 to 1866 but has been independent ever since.

A Spanish mint was established at Santo Domingo in 1542 and struck silver and copper coins. Distinctive coins appeared in 1814–21 under the name of Fernando VII. Copper or brass quarter reales of 1844–8 were struck, but no other distinctive coinage emerged until 1877, when the peso of 100 centavos was adopted. The earliest coins were non-figural, with the date on one side and the value on the other, but an armorial design was introduced in 1937 [10–16], with a palm tree or

native American head on the other side. Numerous commemoratives, in gold, silver or platinum, have appeared in more recent years.

JAMAICA

Columbus reached Jamaica in 1494 and it was colonized by Spain in 1509 but captured by Britain in 1655. It joined the West Indies Federation in 1958 but seceded in 1961, gaining full independence a year later. Cut or countermarked coins were in circulation in the 18th century, followed by the coins of the British West Indies in 1822. Sterling was introduced in 1834, represented by silver coins of small denominations. Cupro-nickel coins were introduced in 1869 with the effigy of the monarch (obverse) and colonial arms (reverse); these continued until 1969 [17–22]. The dollar was adopted in 1969; the arms moved to the obverse [23, 29] and pictorial motifs (fauna and flora) occupied the reverse of the cents [24], while Sir Alexander Bustamente, the first prime minister, was portrayed on the dollar [25]. Subsequently, other political figures were depicted [26–28, 30]. Since the 1990s inflation has led to a great reduction in the size of coins and the introduction of higher denominations for general circulation. Silver and gold commemoratives, up to $500, have also been produced.

FORMER JAMAICAN DEPENDENCIES

The Cayman Islands west of Jamaica and the Turks and Caicos group to the north-east were formerly Spanish but ceded to Britain in 1670 and 1799 respectively. The latter group was long a dependency of the Bahamas, then briefly a separate colony, before becoming a dependency of Jamaica in 1873. Jamaican coinage was used in both groups until 1959, when they joined the West Indies Federation. Distinctive coins have been issued by the Cayman Islands since 1972 [31–32, 34–35] and the Turks and Caicos Islands since 1969 [33], but both groups prefer US coinage in general circulation.

Colourful Coins

In 1994 Cuba became one of the first countries in the world to issue coins with a multicoloured surface. While the arms of the republic appeared in plain silver on the obverse, the reverse featured Caribbean fauna in full colour. The following year a similar series portrayed pirates of the Caribbean.

1

2

3

4

5

6

7

8

9

10

11

12

13

14

15

16

EAST CARIBBEAN

Columbus laid claim to the smaller islands of the east Caribbean during his second and subsequent voyages, and they were originally colonized by Spain but were frequently fought over by France and Britain in the 17th and 18th centuries, before finally coming under permanent British control. These crown colonies joined together in 1958 to form the West Indies Federation, but when that broke up they were granted associate statehood, with self-government, as a prelude to full independence within the British Commonwealth. They used British currency until 1955, when the coinage of the British East Caribbean Territories was introduced, followed by that of the East Caribbean Territories in 1980.

Left: The first coins inscribed for each territory of the British East Caribbean were the $4 coins of 1970, which formed part of the Food for All programme instituted by the United Nations Food and Agriculture Organization. These coins had standard obverse and reverse, depicting the East Caribbean arms [11] and bananas respectively, but individual names were inscribed below the arms.

The standard issues of the British East Caribbean Territories had a crowned bust of Elizabeth II on the obverse, and numerals (low values), Columbus's flagship the *Santa Maria* (5, 10 and 25 cents) or Neptune driving a sea chariot (50 cents) on the reverse [1–6]. The coins of the East Caribbean Territories bear the Machin bust of Queen Elizabeth and laureated numerals (1, 2 and 5 cents) and the *Santa Maria* (10 and 25 cents and $1) [7–10].

ANTIGUA AND BARBUDA
At the eastern end of the Leeward Islands, Antigua and its dependency of Barbuda achieved self-government in 1967 and became a wholly independent member of the Commonwealth in 1981, with the British monarch as head of state. Although copper token farthings, some struck in the Bahamas, were issued in the mid-19th century, the first distinctive coins appeared in 1982 to mark the 250th anniversary of George Washington's birth; they comprised three $30 silver proofs showing scenes of the American Revolutionary War. A $10 coin appeared in 1985 to celebrate Queen Elizabeth's visit, while more recent coins have focused on Caribbean wildlife.

DOMINICA
Lying in the Windward Islands, Dominica was confirmed as a British possession in 1805 and at that time had a curious currency consisting of rings, dumps or fragments of Spanish coins denominated in bits. Spanish dollars had a crenellated piece cut out of the centre to form the moco (1½ bits) [12] while the rest was tariffed at 11 or 16 bits according to size and weight.

Dominica was granted associated statehood in 1967 and became wholly independent in 1978. Coins were issued in 1970 to mark the signing of an agreement among 18 Caribbean states, to promote economic development in the region [11], and $10 coin, released that year to celebrate independence, featured carnival dancers. The relatively few commemoratives include those for royal and papal visits and the Middle East peace brokered by Bill Clinton (1979).

ST KITTS AND NEVIS
Though colonized by Sir Thomas Warner in 1623, St Christopher (usually known as St Kitts) became a permanent British possession in 1783. Billon French deniers were countermarked SK and issued in 1801. Known

Coins on Coins

In 2004 the British Virgin Islands issued a pair of coins, denominated $1 (cupro-nickel) or $10 (sterling silver), to mark the Athens Olympic Games, featuring athletes from the ancient Games on the reverse. As well as scenes of runners and a chariot race alongside striking bronze busts, they bore facsimiles of ancient Greek coins, an Athenian owl and a coin showing a head of Zeus with Nike, goddess of victory.

18

19

colloquially as Black Dogs, and used as small change, they were withdrawn from St Kitts in 1849 and Nevis in 1858 [13]. Spanish silver dollars cut into eighths were countermarked S for circulation in St Kitts. More recently, it has issued a few coins marking a royal visit, bicentenaries of battles and anniversaries of independence [14–15].

Its former dependency of Anguilla seceded in 1967, countermarking various dollar-sized coins of Mexico, Peru and the Yemen to assert its independence. It was taken under direct British control in 1971 and accorded autonomy in 1976. In recent years, a few coins, including tiny $5 gold pieces, have featured local landmarks.

VIRGIN ISLANDS

Cut and countermarked Mexican coins were used in Tortola in the British Virgin Islands [16–17] in the late 18th century, although the circulation of countermarked Spanish and French coins was not authorized until 1801. More recently, the islands have preferred US coinage, which continues to circulate freely, although distinctive coins from 1 cent to $1 were issued in 1973 with Elizabeth II's profile (obverse) and fauna and flora (reverse). Gold $100 coins were added in 1975, mostly encapsulated in philanumismatic covers. Since 1977 the islands

have produced many commemoratives in denominations from $5 upwards [18–21]. Loyalty to the British crown is reflected in numerous coins marking the Queen's coronation, birthdays, jubilees, and anniversaries; others have honoured the Queen Mother, Princess Diana and, most recently, the marriage of Prince Charles and Camilla Parker-Bowles. Dollar-sized silver coins are also now produced in thematic sets.

OTHER ISLANDS

Fragments of Spanish coins countermarked G were current in the much fought-over island of Grenada, finally ceded to Britain in 1783. Since 1985 the very few commemoratives that have appeared have marked the Queen's visit and featured wildlife.

St Lucia, reached by Columbus in 1502, was subject to similar territorial ambition until Britain gained permanent possession in 1814. It had an assortment of escalins, sous and livres, countermarked on Spanish silver [22]. The handful of commemoratives since 1986 include coins for papal and royal visits, the bicentenary of the Battle of the Saints and the Commonwealth Finance Ministers' Meeting (1986). St Vincent has followed the same pattern, using bits and holey dollars in the early 19th century but issuing even fewer commemoratives since 1985.

20

21

22

MEXICO

The United States of Mexico, to give it its full name, is one of the largest and most populous countries in the western hemisphere, third after the USA and Brazil. Boasting a civilization stretching back to pre-Christian times, it was the centre of the mighty Aztec empire, which survived until 1521 when it was subjugated by Hernando Cortez at the head of a small band of Spanish conquistadors. For three centuries Mexico was at the heart of the Spanish Empire and was known as New Spain. It became a republic in 1823 and has experienced frequent periods of economic instability since that time, reflected in attempts to reform and revalue its currency.

Below: Coins from the colonial period of Mexico's history are relatively easy to come by. This gold 8 escudo piece of 1802 is engraved with a bust of Charles IV of Spain on the obverse and, on the reverse, the regal arms surmounted by a crown and surrounded by the collar and badge of the Order of the Golden Fleece. It was struck at the height of Spanish colonial power, before Spain was hard hit by the Napoleonic Wars.

INDEPENDENCE

A mint was established at Mexico City as early as 1536 and coined Spanish currency until 1811. Coins were often roughly cut from bars and crudely stamped [1–2]. Numerous other mints were opened in the ensuing centuries, producing a vast range of silver and gold coins. Latterly, large coins such as the silver 8 reales [3–4] and gold 8 escudos [5–6] were well struck.

On September 18, 1810, Father Miguel Hidalgo raised the cry of independence, though more than a decade elapsed before it was accomplished by General Agustín de Itúrbide. He proclaimed himself emperor in 1822 but was deposed a year later and a republic instituted [7]. During this turbulent time temporary mints functioned at San Felipe de Chihuahua and Durango, and royalist coins were frequently countermarked by the rebels. The chronic instability of Mexico from then until 1867 saw frequent changes of dictators as well as the rise and subsequent decline of a second emperor, the luckless Austrian Maximilian. It was one year prior to Maximilian's rule that the first decimal coinage, based on the peso of 100 centavos, was introduced (in 1863), paving the way for a republican series of 1869. Under Benito Juárez (president until 1872) liberal democracy was briefly established, but by the end of the century Mexico was under the iron grip of Porfirio Díaz. In this period, the old silver 8 reales coinage was revived (1873–98) [11], yet Díaz's government also introduced the sweeping reforms of 1905, which corrected the balance between gold and silver. Díaz was overthrown in 1911, but this precipitated a wave of revolutions that lasted until 1917. During its first century of independence Mexico was kept afloat by its extraordinary mineral wealth, reflected in the abundance of coinage and a bewildering array of mint-marks as coin production devolved on individual states. No fewer than 14 mints functioned, from Alamos to Zacatecas.

CIVIL WARS

The overthrow of Díaz brought Francisco Madero to power, but he was murdered in 1913. His death triggered civil war. The Constitutionalists were led by Pancho Villa and Emiliano Zapata in opposition to Victoriano Huerta. Other guerrilla leaders, such as Venustiano Carranza and Alvaro Obregón, jostled for the presidency and the country was in turmoil until Carranza emerged as president in 1916 and eventually forced through a constitution acceptable to most factions.

During this period of turbulence separate issues of coins were made in the Mexican states of Aguascalientes, Chihuahua, Durango, Guerrero, Jalisco, Estado de Mexico, Morelos, Oaxaca, Puebla and Sinaloa, and in many cases separate issues appeared in towns and cities within these states. The coins ranged from the crudely cast pieces of Buelna and Carrasco and the rectangular pieces of Oaxaca to coins of Duranga inscribed "Muera Huerta" ("Death to Huerta").

UNITED STATES OF MEXICO

Up to 1905 coins bore the legend "Republica Mexicana" but since then "Estados Unidos Mexicanos" has been

---

Decline and Fall

The silver peso serves as a barometer for the decline of the Mexican economy in the course of the 20th century. The Cabalitos of 1903–14 were minted in .903 silver, while the Sunray pesos were struck in .800 silver (1918–19), then in .720 silver (1920–45). Thereafter the fineness of the silver was reduced to .500 (1947–9), .300 (1950) and finally .100 (1957–67). It was not until 1970 that Mexico at last admitted defeat and substituted cupro-nickel (1970–83) and stainless steel (1984–87).

---

preferred [8]. Considering the number of mints functioning in the country, it seems ironic that Mexico has sometimes relied on the Birmingham Mint (1909–14) and the Royal Canadian Mint in more recent years.

Not only has a wide range of different metals and alloys been used, especially in the subsidiary coinage (bronze, brass, stainless steel, nickel and cupro-nickel of varying composition) [9–10], but Mexico also holds the record of striking pesos in the greatest range of finenesses, from almost pure silver to a mere .100 fine [12–15].

PICTORIAL MOTIFS

Most coins in the period up to the 1940s had an obverse showing an eagle and serpent and a reverse showing a radiate Cap of Liberty, with wreathed numerals on the lower denominations. The exceptions were the pesos of 1910–14, nicknamed Cabalitos for their depiction of a horseman. A pictorial approach was generally inaugurated in 1943, when a large bronze 20 centavos was introduced with a view of Chichen Itza on the reverse [14]. Portrait reverses were produced from 1950 and, for the next three decades, bore historical figures ranging from Cuauhtémoc (the last Aztec emperor) [15] to José Morelos, leader of the war of independence [16], Hidalgo [17] and Madero. In the same period, the smallest coins featured a corn cob, symbolic of the agrarian economy. The 5 peso coins became a popular medium for commemoratives marking the anniversaries of major celebrities.

CONTEMPORARY COINAGE

Mexico's periods of inflation in the 1980s were reflected in frequent changes of coinage as major denominations shrunk in size and fineness, while ever-higher values were required for everyday use. In an attempt to maintain some kind of ratio of weight to value, it ended up with some very large coins, notably the massive brass 1000 pesos of 1988–92 and the cupro-nickel 5000 pesos of 1988 [18–21].

1
2
3
4
5
6
7
8
9
10
11
12
13
14

CENTRAL AMERICA

The Caribbean coast of Central America was sighted by Columbus during his last voyage (1502). Panama was explored by Vasco de Balboa in 1513 and settled in 1519, but the territories to the north were not conquered until 1522–3. Of the seven Central American countries, six were under Spanish rule while the seventh was a British colony. In the colonial period silver coins, mainly from Mexico, were in use, with numerous provisional issues of countermarked pesos and the very crude pieces known as "cobs".

Left: Vasco Nuñez de Balboa (1475–1519) arrived in Central America in 1511 as a stowaway but within two years had established himself as leader of the Spanish settlement at Darien. He explored the surrounding region and was the first European to sight the Pacific Ocean. Balboa lost his head (literally) after a disagreement with the new Spanish governor, but he gives his name to the unit of currency in Panama and appears on many of its coins.

CENTRAL AMERICAN REPUBLIC
The region threw off the Spanish yoke in 1821 and formed the Republic of Central America, with coins featuring the Tree of Liberty [1] and five mountain peaks [2], but by the mid-19th century Costa Rica, El Salvador, Guatemala, Honduras and Nicaragua were separate republics. Coins in a common design showing five peaks but inscribed with the name of each state were issued in this period.

COSTA RICA
Decimal currency based on the peso of 100 centavos was adopted in 1865 [3–4]. The peso was replaced in 1896 by the colon (named after Columbus) of 100 centimos, the coins of this series having an armorial obverse [6–8] but the value on the reverse. Costa Rica lives up to its name ("rich coast") by being the most prosperous and stable in Central America. A nickel 10 colon piece celebrated the 25th anniversary of the Central Bank (1975) [5], presaging some large, handsome commemoratives in silver or gold.

GUATEMALA
A mint was established at Antigua Guatemala in 1731 and moved to Nueva Guatemala in 1776, striking coins in the Spanish colonial style

[9–10]. Guatemala, the most northerly of the Central American group, was briefly absorbed by the Mexican Empire of Itúrbide (1822–3) before joining the Central American federation. Its secession in 1839 hastened the break-up of the union.

It was only in 1859 that a distinctive coinage was adopted, based on the real, with an obverse of three peaks and the value on the reverse for the low values; the higher values featured an allegorical figure or a profile of Rafael Carrera, founder of the republic. A new style of arms (1892) incorporated a quetzal, the national bird, and when the currency was reformed by the dictator Trujillo in 1924 the quetzal of 100 centavos was introduced. An armorial obverse and a reverse bust of Fray Bartolome de las Casas (who introduced Christianity and defended the rights of the indigenous people against the ruling regime) appeared on the centavo [11–12], but the higher value reverses bore a quetzal or a Mayan monolith [13–14].

HONDURAS
The earliest coin was an 8-reales minted at Tegucigalpa in 1813, while the entire region was under Mexican control. As the union disintegrated there were some local issues, superseded by the series of 1869–70. The first decimal

coins (1879) had a pyramid emblem on the obverse and the value on the reverse [26]. Like the others, Honduras abandoned the peso (with its connotations of colonial rule) in 1931 and adopted a distinctive unit, the lempira, named after an Indian chief whose exploits against the Spanish were legendary. Lempira himself was portrayed on the obverse of the higher values [16, 19], with the arms on the reverse [15, 20]. On the smaller coins the arms occupied the obverse and the value appeared on the reverse [17–18].

NICARAGUA

This republic got by with Spanish pesos and the coins of its neighbours until 1878, when it acquired its own coinage, struck by the Heaton Mint of Birmingham, although the full range, from the half centavo to the cordoba [21–24], was not completed until 1912. The unit was named in honour of Francisco Fernandez de Cordoba who explored the area (1515–24). After the earthquake disaster of 1975 Nicaragua produced a silver 20 cordoba coin to raise funds for the victims, a very early example of a charity coin.

EL SALVADOR

Apart from an interesting issue of 1828–35, when the federation was collapsing, inscribed "For the freedom of Salvador", Central American federation

Below: Panama's silver 20 balboas was the largest coin in the world when it was issued in 1971, with a diameter of 61mm/2½in.

Country Named After a Town

British Honduras was settled by sailors shipwrecked in 1638 and later became the haunt of buccaneers who founded Belize, a town allegedly named after a pirate called Wallace. The country took the name of Belize in 1973 when it became independent. Coins portraying the reigning monarch were introduced in 1885, and since 1973 have had pictorial reverses.

reales and countermarked Spanish coins served El Salvador until 1889, when the peso of 100 centavos was adopted. While silver pesos and half pesos showing the flag or a bust of Columbus, and a gold series with the head of Liberty, were struck in San Salvador, some centavo denominations, in cupro-nickel, were produced by Heaton. In 1920 the colon replaced the peso as the unit of currency. Armorial obverses have alternated with a profile of Francisco Morazan, hero of the struggle for liberation and president of the Central American Republic from 1829 to 1840 [25]. Gold coins were revived in 1971, the prelude to many special issues of recent years [29–32].

PANAMA

After seceding from Colombia in 1903, Panama adopted the balboa of 100 centesimos [26–27], although an actual 1 balboa coin did not appear until 1947 [28]. Balboa himself has dominated the obverse of the coins since their inception; other historical figures have appeared since 1975. Panama has the distinction of producing both the region's smallest and (until recently) largest coins – the tiny silver 2 centesimos or "Panama pill" and the giant 20 balboas portraying Simon Bolivar.

1

2

3

4

5

6

7

8

9

10

11

12

COLOMBIA, ECUADOR AND VENEZUELA

Columbus reached the Atlantic coasts of Colombia and Venezuela in 1498 but no Spanish settlement took place there until the mid-16th century. These three countries in the north-east of South America originally formed the vice-royalty of New Granada, but revolted against Spanish rule in 1811. Although they achieved their independence in 1821, Spain did not recognize it until 1845. Initially the three countries united to form Greater Colombia or the Granadine Confederation, striking reales or using countermarked Spanish pieces, with numerous local issues during the war of independence. When the confederation disintegrated in 1830 each country went its own way. Panama seceded from Colombia in 1903, having used the coins of that country up to that time.

Below: Simon Bolivar (right), born at Caracas, Venezuela, in 1783, led the 1911 revolt against Spanish rule and is the great national hero of Colombia, Ecuador and Venezuela as well as Peru and Bolivia. The last of these was named in his honour, and from this derived the currency unit, the boliviano, while the Colombian state of Bolivar also perpetuates his memory. In his native land his name was given to the unit of currency, while that of his lieutenant, Antonio Sucre (left), was used for the currency unit in Ecuador.

VENEZUELA

Bolivar's homeland issued reales until the 1860s, although a reformed currency, based on the venezolano of 100 centavos, was in parallel use from1873 to 1879, when it was replaced by the bolivar of 100 centimos. Early coins bore the head of Liberty, but since 1874 Simon Bolivar the Liberator has been portrayed instead [1], with a heraldic shield on the reverse [2–6]. Since 1975 a number of large gold or silver coins have commemorated historic events and personalities or appeared in sets highlighting nature conservation and other worthy causes.

ECUADOR

Francisco Pizarro penetrated the northwest Pacific coast of South America in 1526, and within a decade Ecuador had been pacified by Sebastian de Benalcazar, who founded Quito in 1534. Revolts against Spain were crushed in 1810 and 1812 and it was not until 1822 that Ecuador was liberated by Antonio Sucre.

Distinctive coins date from 1833 and were originally inscribed "Ecuador in Colombia", but "Republica del Ecuador" was substituted in 1837. The head of Liberty [7] and the sunrise over twin peaks were the main features of the early issues [8]. Decimal coinage based on the sucre of 10 decimos or 100 centavos was adopted in 1872, the obverses showing an elaborate coat of arms with the wreathed value in words on the reverse – a design that has endured for decades [9–11]. The effigy of Sucre appeared in 1884 and has dominated the higher values ever since [12], although pictorial designs still featured on the lower values [13–14]. Unusually, some coins of Ecuador include the word "Mexico" at the foot of the reverse to denote the place of minting [15]. Since 1988 nickel-clad

Leper Coins

Special coins were produced by Colombia from 1901 onward for the use of patients in the government-managed leper colonies at Agua de Dios, Cano de Loro and Contratacion. The standard obverse bore the name of the country with "Lazareto" across the middle. The coins, ranging from 1 centavo to 10 pesos, continued in use until the leper colonies were shut down in 1959. Venezuela also issued distinctive coins between 1913 and 1936 for each of its leper colonies at Maracaibo, Providencia and Cabo Blanco, and Panama produced coins for its leper colony at Palo Seco in 1907.

steel coins of Ecuador have matched a new armorial obverse [16] to images of the independence memorial [17] or indigenous sculpture and artefacts. Very few commemoratives have so far appeared, notably the series of 1991 for the Columbus quincentenary.

COLOMBIA

If the coinage of Ecuador and Venezuela has been relatively straightforward, that of Colombia has been exceedingly complex, reflecting turbulent times and periods of rampant inflation. A mint was opened at Bogota in the 1620s, striking silver pesos and also, from 1756, gold coins such as the beautiful 8 escudos portraying Charles III [18] with the crowned royal arms of Spain on the reverse [19], struck at the Bogota Mint in 1785. A subsidiary mint producing silver also functioned at Popayan from 1729. Spanish royalists and republican rebels struck coins in areas under their control during the prolonged wars of independence, the former at Popayan and Santa Marta

and the latter in Cartagena and Cundinamarca. A national coinage of escudos and reales appeared in 1820, richly symbolic with flowers, cornucopiae and doves of peace as well as the obligatory head of Liberty.

The first attempt to decimalize the currency (1847) yielded the peso of 10 reales or decimos. These coins continued the previous symbols but had the value on the reverse. The peso of 100 centavos was adopted in 1872, Liberty heads and arms or symbols providing the motifs, with profiles of Bolivar and other national figures more prominent from 1912 [20–22]. Bronze (and later copper-clad steel) subsidiary coins were introduced in 1962 with a wreathed Cap of Liberty on the obverse and a numeral of value flanked by flowers and a cornucopia on the reverse. Higher denominations with armorial motifs were struck in brass [24] while bimetallic high values were adopted in 1993 [23]. Recently, inflation has necessitated base-metal coins up to 5000 pesos. These have the value on one side and motifs derived from indigenous art on the other [25–26].

Special issues began in 1968, with cupro-nickel 5 pesos and gold 100 pesos to mark the Eucharistic Congress, while a 5 pesos of 1971 celebrated the Pan-American Games. The relatively few commemoratives issued since have mostly been of very high denominations (500, 1000, 1500 or 2000 pesos), struck in gold.

Colombia was rent by civil wars in the early 20th century, and the territory of Panama seceded with the connivance of the USA. In that period uniface coins of 10, 20 and 50 centavos were struck from thin sheets of brass at Santander under the command of General Ramon Gonzales Valencia. In the immediate postwar years the paper currency depreciated to the point at which a paper peso was worth no more than a centavo in silver coinage; 1, 2 and 5 peso cupro-nickel coins of 1907–16 are inscribed "P/M" below the value on the reverse, signifying "*papel moneda*" (paper money).

13

14

15

16

17

18

19

20

21

22

23

24

25

26

1
2
3
4
5
6
7
8
9
10
11
12
13
14
15

BRAZIL AND GUYANA

The largest of the Latin American nations, Brazil was claimed by the Portuguese explorer Cabral in 1500, and settled by the inhabitants of that country, who imported their currency based on the real. By the late 16th century sugar was serving as a medium of currency, with cowries (known as *zombo* or *gimbombo*) as small change. From 1580 to 1640 Portugal was under Spanish rule, and Spanish silver pesos circulated, followed in 1643 by countermarked coins. Mints were opened at Bahia (1694) and Rio (1698), where the 4000 reis coin of João V was minted in 1719 [1–2], and struck in gold and silver. Guyana is the generic name for the region north of Brazil and east of Venezuela, colonized by the French and Dutch, and later the British: these territories are now a French overseas department, Surinam and Guyana respectively.

Left: In 1900 Brazil celebrated the 400th anniversary of Pedro Alvares Cabral's arrival on its shore with a very large 4000 reis silver coin, the obverse showing the Portuguese explorer setting foot on dry land, cap in hand, while the reverse showed the sunrise flanked by the arms of Portugal and Brazil in upright oval cartouches.

THE EMPIRE

Some of the world's most poignant coins are those struck at the Rio Mint portraying the Portuguese royal family in the late 18th century. Queen Maria I suffered from severe melancholia, which descended into madness following the death of her husband, Pedro III. Their conjoined profiles appeared on the gold peca of 1782 [3–4], but the widowed queen appeared alone on later coins [5–6]. Coins were struck in the name of João VI, who served as regent from 1799 to 1816, including a gold peca of 1811 [7–8].

When Napoleon's armies invaded the Iberian Peninsula the Portuguese royals fled to Brazil and set up court in Rio de Janeiro. After Portugal was liberated by Wellington's troops in 1811, the Prince Regent, who would later accede to the throne as João VI, returned to Lisbon, leaving his son Pedro as his viceroy, but in September 1822 Pedro declared Brazil a wholly independent empire and proclaimed himself emperor. His son succeeded in 1831 and, as Dom Pedro II, ruled wisely until 1889. The abolition of

slavery caused great discontent among the landowning classes and led to a military coup, which abolished the empire and deposed the monarchy.

Imperial coinage had a crowned shield on the obverse and the value on the reverse [9–10]. A singular feature of the early period was the plethora of countermarked copper coins [11] as the government strove to impose a standard system, although it was not until the 1860s that the coinage was reformed. Portraits of the emperor, from boyhood to old age, were confined to gold and a few silver coins.

THE REPUBLIC

As in Spain, Portuguese currency was based on the real, but it became so depreciated that it was counted in large multiples known as reis (the plural of *real* in Portuguese). Even in imperial times the lowest denomination was 5 reis, while silver coins ran up to 2000 reis and gold from 5000 to 20,000 reis. Under the republic the lowest coin was the bronze 20 reis, the highest the gold 20,000 reis minted between 1889 and 1922. Latterly money was counted in

Revaluation

Inflation and depreciation are nothing new to Brazil. Between 1667 and 1683, when the value of money fell in relation to the intrinsic worth of coins, Portuguese gold coins of 1000, 2000 and 4000 reis were countermarked in Brazil and stamped with new values of 1100, 2200 and 4400 reais respectively.

milreis (1000 reis) and the banknotes ran up to 1,000,000 reis, known as a conto. Liberty and the numerals of value dominated the coinage [12–14] but during the dictatorship of Getulio Vargas (1938–42) his profile appeared on the obverse [15]. A few special issues of the inter-war period commemorated the 400th anniversary of settlement and honoured celebrated Brazilians.

CURRENCY REFORMS

Despite the greatest natural resources of any South American country, Brazil has been hard hit by economic and political instability from time to time, coupled with periods of high inflation. This led to a reform of the currency in 1942 when the outmoded milreis gave way to the cruzeiro of 100 centavos. A feature of this series was that a different portrait of a famous Brazilian was used for each value from 10 to 50 centavos, while a map of the country or the federal arms graced the higher values. In every case the value, denoted by large numerals, occupied the reverse.

Inflation in the 1950s led to changes from cupro-nickel to brass and latterly aluminium, notably the series of 1965. Two years later the currency was reformed, the cruzeiro novo being worth 1000 old cruzeiros. In this period occurred the avant-garde coins marking the 150th anniversary of independence [16–17]. The currency was again reformed in 1986 when the new cruzeiro was superseded by the cruzado of 100 centavos [18–22]. Like its predecessors, this series was struck in stainless steel but by 1989 had also depreciated: 1000 cruzados were worth one cruzado novo, which was again replaced by the cruzeiro a year later. In 1993, 1000 cruzeiros equalled one cruzeiro real, but in July 1994, 2750 of these equalled 1 real of 100 centavos. So far, the real (plural *reais*) has managed to hold steady [23–24].

GUYANA

To a large extent coins of the mother country were used in the British, Dutch and French parts of Guyana, although during World War II Dutch coins were struck at the US Mint with a P (Philadelphia) mint-mark for use in Surinam. Appropriately countermarked Spanish coins, holey dollars and dumps were used in Essequibo and Demerara following the British occupation of 1796, made permanent in 1814. In the British colonial period stuivers and guilders portrayed the reigning sovereign [25–26]. British silver groats (4 pence) were superseded by distinctive coins of the same value, augmenting ordinary British coins [27–30]. When the territory gained independence in 1967 the dollar of 100 cents was introduced. The coins had armorial and numeral motifs [31–32], which changed to pictorial reverses in 1976.

The coinage of Dutch Guiana began at Recife in 1645, with gold florins inscribed "Brasil" (the first numismatic use of the name), followed by silver in 1654. These coins were rectangular, with the "GWC" monogram of the Dutch West Indies Company. Distinctive coins were introduced in Surinam in 1962, with an armorial obverse and value reverse. The former Dutch Guiana attained independence in 1975, and celebrated its first anniversary with silver and gold coins.

1   2

3   4

5   6

7   8

9

10

11   12

13   14

BOLIVIA, CHILE AND PERU

The former Inca strongholds were absorbed by Spain's colonial empire in the 1530s. In 1543 silver was discovered in Bolivia at Potosi in the Cerro Rico, which contained the largest silver deposit then known. Pesos were crudely struck at Lima, Peru, from 1565 and at Potosi from 1575, exemplified by the 1723 cob 8 reales of Potosi [1–2], intended mainly as a convenient medium for shipping bullion rather than for local circulation. Although independence was declared in 1809–10 and secured by 1824, Spain made many later attempts to regain the territory and did not finally recognize its independence until 1879. Ironically, by that time relations between the states had deteriorated, leading to the Pacific War of 1879–83, which resulted in victory for Chile, and territorial losses for Bolivia and Peru.

Left: The Andean condor, in flight or, as shown here, alighting on a lofty peak, has long been a popular motif for the coins of the countries dominated by this great mountain range.

BOLIVIA

Known as Upper Peru in Spanish colonial times, the country declared its independence in 1809, following a revolt in La Paz. It was the first of the Spanish territories to do so, but 16 years elapsed before it was secured by Bolivar's crushing defeat of the last Spanish army in South America, at Maipu in 1824. The republic, established in August 1825, took its name from its liberator.

Distinctive coinage began in 1827 with the escudo of 2 pesos or 16 soles, portraying Simon Bolivar with a palm tree on the reverse or the sun rising over the Andes (on gold escudos) [3–4]. A tiny quarter sol was added in 1852, featuring a llama (obverse) and an Andean peak (reverse). The coinage was decimalized in 1864, based on the boliviano of 100 centecimos, replaced by centavos in 1878. Arms, eagle or mountain motifs replaced Bolivar's effigies while the reverse bore the value. This series continued until 1919, although by that date only the 5 and 10 centavo coins were still being struck.

Attempts to re-introduce coins in 1935–7 and 1951 were hampered by rampant inflation. A drastic currency reform in 1963 led to the introduction of the peso boliviano and coinage was resumed in 1965. The first commemoratives, in 1952, consisted of small gold coins celebrating the revolution of that year. By 1980 coins had disappeared from circulation, overtaken by inflation, but in 1987 a monetary reform, replacing 1,000,000 pesos with the new boliviano of 100 centavos, resulted in the first full range of coins in 80 years, with the arms (obverse) and value (reverse) [5–8]. A few special issues since then include the Ibero-American series of 10 boliviano coins and a 50 boliviano silver piece of 1998 for the 450th anniversary of La Paz.

CHILE

Coins were struck at Santiago from 1749 in the prevailing Spanish colonial styles; they included silver pesos and gold coins such as the handsome 8 escudo piece of Ferdinand VII minted in 1813 [9–10]. Following the revolution, distinctive coinage dated from 1817 and consisted of the peso inscribed "Chile Independent" with Santiago at the foot of a motif showing an erupting volcano. Other values from the tiny silver quart (quarter real) to the gold 6 escudos followed, but the peso of 100 centavos was adopted in 1835, with a star, condor or Liberty head (obverse) and value (reverse). Variations on these themes continued until 1942, when peso coins were introduced portraying Bernardo O'Higgins, dictator of Chile (1817–23). The peso was hard hit by inflation and by 1958 the condor or 10 pesos, originally a gold coin, was reduced to aluminium [11–12]. In 1960 the currency was reformed, introducing the escudo of 100 centesimos, with the centesimo worth 10 old pesos.

This series retained the flying condor obverse and value reverse, but since 1971 O'Higgins and other national heroes have been portrayed. In 1975 the coinage was again reformed, making the peso equal to 1000 old escudos. In this series the condor appeared in repose on the lower denominations [13–14], while O'Higgins graced the obverse [17] with a laureated value on the reverse [18]. Gold and silver coins showing a winged Victory appeared in 1976, originally celebrating the revolution of 1973, but the motif was subsequently extended to the base-metal coinage [15–16].

PERU

Low-denomination copper coins appeared in 1822–3 as a prelude to a regular series in silver. The tiny silver quarter real of 1826–56 featured a llama, but the higher values had the standing figure of Liberty (obverse) and arms (reverse). Coins inscribed "Nor-Peruana" or "Repub. Sud-Peruana Confederacion" appeared in 1836–9 and reflected a short-lived confederation with Bolivia.

A decimal system based on the libra (pound) of 100 soles, 100 dineros or 1000 centavos was adopted in 1863. The 1 and 2 centavos were struck in bronze, with a sunburst obverse [21] and a wreathed value reverse [22], but higher denominations were minted in silver with the seated figure of Liberty on the obverse [19] and the national arms on the reverse [20]. The dinero was phased out in 1916, but the gold libra and fifth libra survived until 1969. The brass coins of 1935–65, from the half sol upwards, bore the name of the Central Reserve Bank and a promise to

Tiny Gold

The peso was normally minted in silver, but from 1860 to 1873 Chile struck this denomination in 22 carat (.917 fine) gold, with the standing figure of Liberty on the obverse and a wreathed value on the reverse (see enlarged view, bottom). The tiny coin (14mm/⅝in diameter, top) proved unpopular and very few were struck after the production of silver pesos resumed in 1867.

pay the bearer in gold soles [23]. The promise gave way to an image of a llama on coins of 1966–75 [24–25].

Like other Latin American countries, Peru was hard hit by inflation, resulting in base-metal coins up to 500 soles by 1985. The currency was reformed in that year and adopted the inti (the Inca word for "sun") of 1000 soles de oro, with the value or arms on one side and a bust of the national hero Admiral Grau on the other [26]. Brass coins from 1 to 50 centimos and cupronickel 1 and 5 intis were struck until 1988. Yet another reform in 1991 produced the nuevo sol, worth 1,000,000 intis, and a range of brass coins from 1 centimo to 5 nuevos soles [27–28]. The arms and value were enlivened by the inclusion of tiny birds on the reverse of the highest denominations, while the lower coins incorporated the value in Braille. Among the relatively few commemorative coins should be noted the series of 1965 celebrating the quatercentenary of the Lima Mint, the reverse reproducing a coin of 1565 [29].

1
2
3
4
5
6
7
8
9
10
11
12
13
14
15
16
17

ARGENTINA, PARAGUAY AND URUGUAY

Spanish penetration of the countries bordering the River Plate and its tributaries began in 1515, but settlement was very slow and there was little European development, due largely to the preservation of the indigenous people by the Jesuit missions, which were brutally suppressed in 1767–81. In the decades that followed opposition to the tyrannical rule of Spain escalated and fuelled the movement for independence in 1810–11. Argentina won its independence in 1816. Paraguay followed soon afterwards, but Uruguay was conquered by the Portuguese from Brazil and did not gain its independence, with help from Argentina, until 1830.

Left: Veinticinco de Mayo (May 25) is to Argentines what the Fourth of July is to Americans, commemorating the date on which independence was declared in 1810. The 150th anniversary was celebrated by this peso showing the Old Town Hall in Buenos Aires and the national arms.

ARGENTINA

Republica Argentina (literally "silver republic") owes its name and origin to the mineral wealth in the basin of the Rio de la Plate ("river of silver") and the earliest coins (1813–15) were given Spanish inscriptions signifying "Provinces of the River Plate". They consisted of gold escudos and silver soles and reales with a radiate sun obverse and arms reverse. Continual civil war resulted in separate issues of coins in the provinces of Buenos Aires, Cordoba, Entre Rios and La Rioja at various times until 1867, and it was not until 1881 that a national currency emerged, based on the peso of 100 centavos. Arms and the head of Liberty [1–4] provided the dominant motifs until 1962, but as inflation took hold the need for higher denominations in base metal resulted in some coins portraying historic figures or the sailing ship *Presidente Sarmiento* (5 pesos) and a gaucho (10 pesos) [5–6].

The first of many currency reforms took place in 1970, when the old peso became the new centavo. Coins from 1–50 centavos showed Liberty [8] with the value on the reverse [7]. Inflation led to the re-introduction of peso coins in 1974, the radiate sun being revived [9]. José de San Martin, the father of independence, and the naval commander Almirante Brown appeared on the 50 and 100 pesos brass-clad steel coins of 1980–81 [10–11]. In 1983 the peso argentino, worth 10,000 pesos, was introduced, followed by the austral, worth 1000 pesos argentinos (1985), and the peso of 10,000 australes (1992); the currency has been reasonably stable since then [12–13]. The austral coins included fauna on the low values – a respite from the sun and Liberty head. In recent years Argentina has also produced a number of commemoratives, mainly in base metal, for general circulation.

PARAGUAY

Apart from a copper half real showing a lion and the Cap of Liberty (1845) Paraguay had no coinage until 1870, when the peso of 100 centesimos was introduced. A radiate star in a wreath alternated with the lion emblem on the obverse, with the value on the reverse, apart from the large silver peso of 1889, which used both symbols. A new system, based on the guarani of 100 centimos, was adopted in 1944 and struck in aluminium (centimos) or stainless steel (1–50 guaranies), with brass-plated steel 100 guaranies since 1992. The guarani series has a mixture of allegory and portraiture on the obverse, notably the figure of a soldier alluding to the disastrous Chaco War with Bolivia of 1932–5 [14]. Paraguay had lost half its territory to Argentina, Uruguay and Brazil in the War of the Triple Alliance (1864–70) and was not minded to give up any more. The Chaco War, fought in a harsh terrain, claimed more lives through malaria than combat. It was a pyrrhic victory for Paraguay, which decimated the population and almost bankrupted the economy. The soldier appeared on Paraguayan coins and banknotes from 1975 onwards. By contrast, the 5 guarani coin portrayed a typical Paraguayan woman [17].

The higher denominations, in stainless steel or cupro-nickel zinc, featured landmarks on the reverse, such as the Acaray River hydroelectric dam [15], ancient ruins [19] and modern buildings. The obverses bore national figures, such as Generals Estigarribia, Garay [16] and Caballero [18], beginning in 1968 with a 10,000 guarani coin portraying General Alfredo Stroessner.

Paraguay embarked on a prolific programme of special issues struck in gold or silver. These have portrayed not only local heroes but also a staggering range of international celebrities (Goethe,

Beethoven, Lincoln, Bismarck, Einstein, Garibaldi and Kennedy were among the earliest).

URUGUAY

Coinage in Uruguay was produced very sporadically in the 19th century, beginning with the copper 5 and 20 centesimos of 1840, followed in 1844 by the 40 centesimos and the silver peso. The copper 1, 2 and 4 centesimos appeared in 1869 and the silver 10 and 50 centesimos in 1870. The centesimos had a radiate sun obverse [20] and value reverse [21] but the peso had the republican arms. These types continued until 1953, when base-metal coins bore the national leader, José Artigas [22], previously portrayed in 1916–17. A brass 10 centesimo, issued in 1930 to celebrate the centenary of independence, had the head of Liberty (obverse) and a puma (reverse); it was re-issued in 1936 without the centenary inscription. A wide range of base alloys was used (bronze, cupro-nickel, aluminium-bronze or aluminium) for coins dated 1965, struck in very small quantities for the numismatic market.

Since the monetary reform of 1977, which exchanged 100 old pesos for one new one, aluminium or aluminium-bronze have been used for the circulating coins, with pictorial images and values on obverse and reverse respectively. The motifs were a curious mixture of the allegorical, such as the scales of justice on the 50 centesimo [23], and the agricultural, reflecting the importance of the cattle industry [24]. The nuevo peso denominations, however, featured José Artigas on the obverse [25–26]; Artigas was also the subject of a 5 nuevo peso coin issued in 1975 to celebrate the 150th anniversary of the revolutionary movement [27–28]. The currency was again reformed in 1993, when the peso uruguayano, worth 1000 nuevos pesos, was adopted. In recent years Uruguay has produced numerous medallic or bullion pieces in gold or silver [29–30]; they bear the revolutionary slogan "Libertad o Muerte" (Liberty or Death).

Conquering the Desert

The pacification of the interior of Argentina was not completed until 1879, when a military expedition was sent to Central Patagonia to subjugate the native peoples at the point of a lance. The centenary of the "conquest of the desert", as it is euphemistically known, was celebrated by this coin showing a lancer on horseback.

18

19

20

21

22

23

24

25

26

27

28

29

30

SOUTH ATLANTIC ISLANDS

The islands of the South Atlantic were some of the last outposts of the British Empire. Ordinary British coinage was largely used but in quite recent times distinctive sets in base alloys for general circulation have appeared. Since the 1970s they have also produced numerous commemorative or special issues. St Helena and its dependencies of Ascension and Tristan da Cunha were discovered by the Portuguese in 1501–2, while the Falkland Islands (named after Lord Falkland, Treasurer of the Navy) were discovered by John Davies in 1592. While St Helena (a staging post of the East India Company from 1659) was originally colonized by refugees from London after the Great Fire of 1666, Ascension and Tristan da Cunha were garrisoned in 1815 as a security precaution following the exile of Napoleon to St Helena.

Left: The Falklands, settled by Britain in 1833, have long been claimed by Argentina, resulting in the military invasion of April 1982 and the occupation of both the Falklands and its dependency, South Georgia. The South Atlantic War, which followed, led to the liberation of both island groups in mid-June. Crown-sized 50 pence in cupro-nickel, silver or gold celebrated the liberation and showed the arms of the colony superimposed on the Union Jack.

ST HELENA

Apart from a copper halfpenny of 1821 bearing the colonial arms [1–2], St Helena used coins of the East India Company and countermarked foreign coins until 1834, when British coinage was adopted exclusively for general circulation. In 1984, coins in the same weights and specifications as the British series were introduced with the names of both St Helena and Ascension inscribed on the obverse. The reverses feature South Atlantic fauna and flora.

In 1973, St Helena issued a crown-sized 25 pence in cupro-nickel or proof silver to celebrate the tercentenary of its return to British hands after a period of occupation by the Dutch [3–4]. A similar coin celebrated Elizabth II's silver jubilee in 1977 [5] and in 1978 the 25th anniversary of her coronation was likewise celebrated. Since then relatively few silver or gold coins have marked royal anniversaries and occasions. Crowns valued at the traditional 25

pence continued to be issued, both for St Helena alone [6–7] and with Ascension [8], although other crown values have also appeared. In 1984, a crown-sized 50 pence celebrated the 150th anniversary of St Helena as a crown colony.

ASCENSION

This island, which derives its name from its discovery on Ascension Day 1501, was occupied in 1815 to prevent any attempt by Bonapartists to free Napoleon from exile on St Helena. It acquired a strategic value in World War II and more recently has been an important staging post for communications and a NASA tracking station.

Apart from the joint issues with St Helena, a number of which depict flora and fauna [9–11], Ascension has had several crown-sized coins, generally complementing the issues of St Helena. The first distinctive coin marked the 25th anniversary of the coronation and

The Queen's Beasts

In 1978 the 25th anniversary of the coronation was marked by an omnibus issue of stamps in the various crown colonies and dependent territories. Their theme was the set of 12 heraldic animals known as the Queen's Beasts. The stamps showed a facing portrait of the Queen flanked on one side by one of the original beasts and on the other by a creature relevant to the particular country. St Helena and its dependencies of Ascension and Tristan da Cunha went further by issuing coins to mark the event and made philatelic and numismatic history by reproducing the stamp designs on the reverse of the coins.

includes the error in which the Ascension reverse was muled with an Isle of Man obverse. The coin issued for the royal golden wedding in 1997 featured an equestrian event at the Montreal Olympics. Other Ascension issues marked International Year of the Scout (1983) with a portrait of Lord Baden-Powell, and the nature conservation programme of the World Wide Fund for Nature (1998), for which frigate-birds and long-tailed tropic-birds were shown on a pair of coins.

TRISTAN DA CUNHA

One of the world's remotest islands, situated roughly midway between South America and West Africa, Tristan da Cunha was named in honour of the navigator who discovered it, and like Ascension, it was garrisoned in 1815–16, though most of the present population are the descendants of shipwrecked seamen.

Barter currency of cigarettes or potatoes continued in use until the 1950s, when South African coins were adopted, but the island switched to British money after it was resettled in 1963, following the volcanic eruption of 1961. No circulating coins have been produced but a handful of crown-sized 25 pence and later 50 pence have marked royal events [12–13]. The sole exception is the gold £2 of 1983 for the Year of the Scout.

FALKLAND ISLANDS

British coins used on the islands were superseded by a distinctive series in the same weights and specifications in 1974, with the Queen's bust (obverse) and fauna (reverse) [14–15], including a gold sovereign and half sovereign featuring a Romney Marsh ram. Special issues began with the silver jubilee crown (1977) but began to proliferate after the South Atlantic War, including a lengthy series of 1996 entitled Royal Heritage, featuring monarchs from Egbert of Wessex (802–39) to Victoria (1837–1901). Very large silver coins (65mm/2⅝in diameter) tariffed at £25 have also appeared in recent years.

SOUTH GEORGIA AND SOUTH SANDWICH ISLANDS

Until 1985 these sub-Antarctic islands were dependencies of the Falklands, but they were then constituted a separate crown colony. Ordinary British coins are in everyday use, but since 2000 crown-sized £2 coins in cupro-nickel or silver, with occasional higher denominations in gold, have marked historic anniversaries, mainly pertaining to the islands, although also acknowledging royal events [16–19].

1

2

3

4

5

6

7

8

9

10

11

12

13

14

15

16

17

EUROPE

With a coinage that dates back to the 6th century BC, Europe is responsible for the largest number of different coins – far more than the rest of the world put together. This is due primarily to the multiplicity of petty kingdoms and principalities in the Middle Ages, each striking its own coinage. Even after the emergence of nation states with centralized coinage systems, political and economic upheavals, and the growth of commemorative and special issues, resulted in a vast output in the past century alone.

WESTERN SCANDINAVIA

This group includes the most south-westerly of the Scandinavian countries, Denmark, together with its colonies or dependencies in the North Atlantic. Iceland became autonomous in 1918 and a wholly independent republic in 1944. The unit of currency since 1874 has been the krone (crown) of 100 øre, replacing the daler (dollar) and skilling (shilling) of earlier times.

Left: Danish currency was reformed and rationalized with the foundation of the Rigsbank in 1813; the rigsspeciedaler of 96 skilling was replaced by the rigsbankdaler of 96 rigsbank skilling. The rigsbankdaler was worth half a rigspeciedaler, while five of them were worth a speciedaler d'or. Currency changed again in 1854, when the rigsdaler of 96 rigsmont skilling was introduced. Gold coins were known by the ruler's name followed by d'or *("of gold"), such as the Christian d'or.*

DENMARK

The kingdom of Denmark emerged under Gorm the Old in the 10th century, and his descendants have reigned ever since. King Cnut (Canute) united the Norse lands and even ruled over England (1016–35). Harthacnut, son of Cnut, ruled Denmark while his father reigned in England, and struck coins derived from Anglo-Saxon models [1–2]. About 800 the Danes began striking silver deniers and later imitated English pennies. The first distinctive coins appeared about 995 and followed the northern European pattern. Typical cross-type coins were the pennies issued by Eric of Pomerania at Lund in the 14th century [3–4]. In 1522 the first large coins appeared under the name daler. By the 16th century, Danish currency was in total chaos, with more than 150 different coins in circulation in the reign of Christian IV, many of which bore the crowned bust of the monarch on the obverse [5] and a

crown on the reverse [6]. A similar style was continued under his successor Christian V (1670–95), typified by fine portrait ducats [7–8] reflecting the growing importance of Denmark as a trading nation of world rank.

In the 19th century Denmark had a very complex monetary system based on the skilling, rigsbank skilling or rigsmont skilling as subdivisions of the rigspeciedaler, rigsbankdaler or rigsdaler. While the smaller coins featured a crowned monogram or shield, higher values portrayed the reigning monarch [9] with the value on the reverse [10].

DECIMAL COINAGE

On the formation of the Scandinavian Monetary Union the krone of 100 øre was introduced in 1874 and continued the style of the earliest coins, with a crowned monogram on the smallest denominations [11] and a royal effigy on the higher values [18], with the value on the reverse [12, 19]. Iron

Above: The obverses of Iceland show the four mythical guardians as supporters.

replaced bronze in 1918–19, and zinc, adopted as a wartime measure in 1942, continued in use until 1972. Coins with a central hole were first used in 1926 and continue today [13–17]. The silver krone denominations originally featured the monarch's portrait on the obverse with a crowned shield reverse, but when aluminium-bronze was substituted in 1924, a crowned monogram (obverse) and crown (reverse) were adopted. Coins since 1972 have borne two initials, identifying the mintmaster and the moneyer.

The relatively few commemorative coins mostly record royal birthdays, jubilees and weddings; a silver 10 krone (1972) simultaneously mourned the death of Frederik IX and celebrated the accession of Margrethe II.

ICELAND

The coins of Denmark circulated in Iceland, but after the constitutional change of 1918 distinctive coins began to appear from 1922. Many coins issued prior to 1944, when Iceland became an independent republic, bore the crowned monogram in the Danish style or a crowned shield flanked by the royal monogram (obverse) [20–21], while the country's name and value in Icelandic (eyrir, aurar, króna, kronur) distinguished the reverse [22–25]. From 1945 the crown and royal monogram were omitted from the shield [26–27]. A new version of the arms, flanked by the mythical guardians of Iceland, began with the aluminium-bronze krona values (1946). The 50th anniversary of sovereignty was marked in 1968 by a 50 kronur featuring the parliament building and this, minus the commemorative inscriptions, was

retained as a definitive coin until 1980. The currency suffered severe inflation and was reformed in 1961, 10,000 old kronur being worth one new króna. In this series the guardian spirits, individually or together, graced the obverse [28], while the reverse motifs featured different species of fish and marine life [29–30]. The few commemoratives include a gold 500 kronur of 1961 for the 150th birthday of the independence leader Jon Sigurdsson, a set of three silver coins for the millenary of the Norse settlement (1974) and a gold 10,000 kronur for the millenary of Christianity (2000).

GREENLAND

Bronze or cupro-nickel tokens were produced by trading companies from 1875 to 1922, but Danish coins were otherwise used in this colony, politically regarded as part of Europe. Three coins (25 and 50 øre and 1 krone) were introduced in 1926 with crowned arms (obverse) [31] and a polar bear (reverse) [32]; a 5 krone coin was added in 1944. Since 1957 the krone has had the conjoined shields of Denmark and Greenland on the obverse [33] and a wreathed value on the reverse [34].

Wartime Occupation

Danish coins continued during the German occupation of Denmark, but Iceland, Greenland and the Faroes, occupied by the Allies, had coins supplied from Philadelphia or London, distinguished from their Danish contemporaries by the omission of the heart mint-mark of Copenhagen. A pattern coin showing a polar bear was struck in London for use in Iceland but was never generally released.

1

2

3

4

5

6

7

8

9

10

11

12

EASTERN SCANDINAVIA

The Scandinavian peninsula is occupied by Norway and Sweden, which were united under the personal rule of the Swedish kings from 1814 to 1905. The former Grand Duchy of Finland was under Swedish rule until 1809, when it was ceded to Russia. It gained its independence in 1917.

Left: Swedish copper was once mined in such abundance that monarchs such as Queen Christina (1632–54), pictured on these Swedish marks struck towards the end of her reign, sought methods of exporting an important product at a guaranteed price. To this end, plåtmynt *(plate money) – a currency based on copper – was adopted in 1643 and endured until 1768. The 10 daler piece weighed 19.75kg/44lb, and lower denominations of 1–8 daler were of proportionate size and weight. During the 125 years in which these large copper pieces were in circulation, Sweden established a number of mints close to the mines. This resulted in the most northerly mints in the world, at Kengis, Husa and Ljusendal, which functioned from 1644 to 1768. As in China, where cash proved too cumbersome,* plåtmynt *was unpopular and led to Sweden pioneering paper money as a substitute.*

SWEDEN

A wide range of coins, from Frankish deniers to Islamic dinars, has been found in coin hoards in Sweden, testifying to the prolific trade (or booty) of the Vikings in the early Middle Ages. In 995 King Olaf Skottkonung brought Anglo-Saxon moneyers to Sweden to strike coins at Sigtuna modelled on the English penny, and these continued until 1363, occurring in different weights according to where they were minted. The Swedish coinage was then standardized, with the örtug as the principal unit.

During the period of the Union of Kalmar, coins of the Danish type were used. Distinctive coinage reappeared in the 1520s under Gustav Vasa, who founded a dynasty that lasted until 1818 [1]. The daler and its subdivisions were introduced in 1534, followed by the mark and its öre subdivisions in 1536. Diamond-shaped coins called klippe [2–3] were issued by Erik XIV.

Like Denmark, Sweden had a very complex currency system in the 18th and 19th centuries. In 1776 the currency was reformed and the riksdaler of 48 skilling introduced [4–5]. From 1798 to 1830 the gold ducat was worth

two speciedaler or riksdaler of 48 skilling. From 1830, 32 skilling banco equalled a riksdaler riksgalds, four of which equalled a riksdaler specie. From 1855 a riksdaler riksmynt was worth 25 öre, but when the Scandinavian Monetary Union was formed in 1874 the riksdaler was brought in line with the krona (plural *kronor*) of 100 öre. Lower denominations had a crowned monogram or effigy on the obverse, with the value on the reverse, often incorporating the triple crown emblem signifying the kingdom of the Swedes, Wends and Goths [6], whereas the krona values had an effigy (obverse) and arms (reverse).

The decimal coinage since 1874 has followed a similar pattern, the general principles remaining the same, even if the treatment of values, arms and portraits has varied over the years [7–12]. A conservative policy regarding special issues tended to confine them to royal occasions, but a more liberal attitude since 1980 has resulted in silver 50 or 100 kronor being struck for all manner of events, from the 350th anniversary of the Swedish colony in Delaware (1988) to the millenary of the Swedish Mint (1995).

Russian Colony

The Svalbard archipelago in the Arctic Ocean, of which Spitsbergen is the largest island, was annexed by Norway in 1920 on the basis that it was discovered by Norsemen in the 12th century, although it was first charted and named by Willem Barents in 1596. Its coal reserves led to the development of mines by American, Dutch and Scandinavian companies from 1904. Norwegian currency is used, but the Russian mines, established at Barentsburg in 1932, have had their own token coins, struck at the mint in Leningrad (now St Petersburg) and issued by Arktikugol, the state Arctic coal corporation. The series of 1946, of 10–50 kopeks, was non-pictorial, but a 1993 series of 25–100 roubles showed a polar bear atop the North Pole. The current set (1998), from 10 kopeks to 5 roubles, features walruses, a polar bear or a whale above the globe.

NORWAY

Distinctive coins first appeared in Norway in the late 10th century. While the country was under Danish rule, separate coins were struck from the 15th century [13–14]. A separate coinage also appeared in Norway under Swedish rule: it conformed to Swedish weights and specifications, but the obverse featured the crowned lion rampant shield of Norway [15]. The higher values portrayed the king on the obverse and relegated the Norwegian arms to the reverse. The decimal series featured the royal monogram on the reverse of the low values [16–17], and the king's effigy and arms on the higher values. In 1908 new types were intro-duced for the low values, with the crowned monogram of Haakon VII. The series with the monogram of Olaf V or his profile (1958) adopted pictorial reverses [18–20]. Coins of 50, 100, 200 kroner (silver) or 1500 kroner (gold) have been issued recently, mainly for sporting events.

FINLAND

The Finns were converted to Christianity in the 12th century and Finland became a Swedish duchy in 1284. Local issues, from about 1410, were followed by coins in the name of the Swedish king, struck intermittently at Åbo (Turku) from 1558 to 1801. Under Russian rule the markka, worth a quarter rouble, became the unit of currency, divided into 100 penniä, and coins bore the Tsar's monogram (low values) or the imperial double eagle (high values) with the value on the reverse. Following the abolition of the monarchy, coins with the double eagle (minus its crowns) were issued in 1917, but the series adopted by the Republic of Finland (Suomen Tasavalta) [21–26] bore the lion rampant of the Vasa kings until 1969, when an ornamental knot was substituted on the lowest values.

Since 1990 some pictorial elements have crept in. Previously, the 5 markkaa coins featured icebreakers, the ships *Varma* (1972–8) or *Urho* (1979–83). Special issues from 10 to 2000 markkaa have appeared in recent years, cele-brating anniversaries of independence and a few historical figures. Finland produced the first coins marking the modern Olympics (1951–2) and sport-ing events, from the Lahti Games to the World Ski Championship, continue to predominate.

Above: The 5 markkaa of 1986 shows an unusual incuse treatment for numerals and inscriptions.

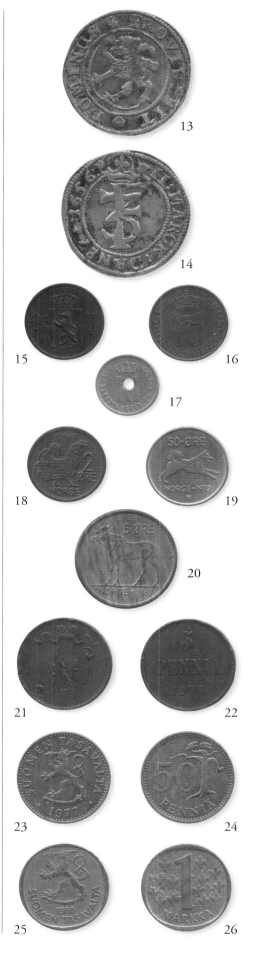

THE OLYMPIC GAMES

The great Panhellenic sporting festival known as the Olympic Games was in existence by 776 BC and continued to be held every four years until AD 393, when it was suppressed. The concept of a great sporting contest of athletes of all nations was revived in 1894 by Baron Pierre de Coubertin and the first modern Olympics were staged at Athens in 1896. The Games have been held every four years since then, except during the World Wars.

Special coins for the classical Games were issued by the tiny Greek state of Elis in the Peloponnese, in whose territory the athletic contest was held, but it was not until 1951–2 that coins were minted to celebrate the Games of the modern era, when Finland produced a silver 500 markkaa to publicize the Helsinki Games. No further Olympic coins were minted until 1964, when Japan produced 100 and 1000 yen coins for the Summer Games at Tokyo that year, and Austria issued a 50 schilling silver coin showing a ski-jumper, in honour of the Innsbruck Winter Games. In 1968, Mexico hosted the Summer Games and issued a 25 peso silver coin. Germany celebrated the Munich Olympics in 1972 by issuing six 10 mark coins, and in the same year Japan released a 100 yen coin for the Winter Games held at Sapporo.

Below: A set of four silver crowns issued by Gibraltar to mark the 1998 Winter Olympic Games in Japan, showing various winter sports.

For the Montreal Olympics in 1976 Canada produced seven sets, each comprising two $5 and $10 silver coins, topped by $100 gold coins in two different sizes and alloys, making a total of 30 coins. By contrast, Austria issued four 100 schilling coins featuring winter events for the Games at Innsbruck in 1976.

Up to that time Olympic coins had been confined to the countries hosting the Summer and Winter Games, but now coins began to appear elsewhere, and in many cases it has to be admitted that these supporting issues were often better designed and more visually attractive than those from the host countries. One example is the handsome crowns, in silver or cupro-nickel, produced by the Isle of Man for the Olympics from 1980 onward, a tradition maintained right down to the present time.

For the 1980 Summer Games in Moscow, the Soviet Union embarked on a lengthy series of coins, spread over the previous three years and struck

Above: A coin from Niue (top) to mark the admission of tennis to the Games in 1987 and an Olympic torchbearer and globe on a $50 coin of 1988 (bottom).

in silver, gold and platinum. Exceptionally, the USA, which hosted the Winter Games at Lake Placid that year, did not issue any commemorative coins. Four years later, however, when the same country hosted the Summer Games at Los Angeles, a 30-year embargo on commemorative coins was broken by the release of a silver dollar and a gold eagle ($10).

The 1984 Winter Olympics were staged in Sarajevo, and, to publicize the Games, Yugoslavia had begun issuing a series of 500 dinar silver coins at six-monthly intervals from 1982 onward, featuring various winter sports on

the reverses. These large coins were accompanied by the annual issue of 5000 dinar gold coins.

South Korea did not wait until the end of the Los Angeles Games but began issuing its advance publicity coins in 1982 – thus lapping the previous Olympiad by two years. A total of eight gold, twelve silver, four nickel and four cupro-nickel coins was released over the ensuing six years, the pictorial motifs often having little or no relevance to the Olympic ideal. When Calgary hosted the Winter Games in 1988 Canada issued ten silver proof $20 coins from September 1985 onward, released in pairs at half-yearly intervals.

For the Albertville Winter Games (1992), France produced eight silver proof 100 franc coins showing various winter sports. In honour of the Barcelona Summer Games, Spain produced a superb collection of four individual issues, each consisting of three gold and four silver coins. Atlanta, Georgia was the venue for the Centennial Games, for which the US Mint produced two gold $5, four silver dollars and two clad cupro-nickel half dollars in 1995, all with attractive motifs showing aspects of Olympic sports as well as the Centennial logo of a torch, rings and the numerals 100. A similar programme appeared in 1996. Gibraltar, Bosnia and the Isle of Man were among the countries that released

Below: San Marino produced a silver 10,000 lire for the 2000 Olympics.

Above: A set of crowns released by the Isle of Man for the Sydney Olympics, 2000, linking Australian maps and landmarks with various sports.

Below: A series of three crowns was issued by the Isle of Man on the occasion of the Los Angeles Summer Games in 1984.

support coins in 1995–6. The most attractive of the support coins of recent years, however, have come from San Marino, often harking back to the timeless quality of the ancient Greek Olympic coins. In the same genre was the series of eight crowns from Gibraltar in 1992, with reverse motifs depicting events from the ancient Games, from boxing to chariot racing.

For the Millennium Games of 2000, Australia struck a prodigious series of coins in various metals. A total of 28 aluminium-bronze coins featured a wide range of Olympic sports: aquatics, archery, athletics, baseball, boxing, equestrian, gymnastics, hockey, pentathlon, rowing, sailing, volleyball, weight lifting, cycling, triathlon, football, canoeing, softball, wrestling, handball, taekwondo, basketball,

shooting, badminton, fencing and table tennis. A set of five coins from the Solomon Islands – two nickel $1, two silver $5 and a gold $50 – featured cartoon characters created by Brian Sage. Kenny the Kangaroo, Kylie the Koala and Eddie the Emu were shown taking part in various Olympic events.

To mark the Athens Games of 2004, Greece produced six sets of coins, each comprising a pair of silver 10 euros and a .9999 fine gold 100 euro piece. The obverses of the silver coins featured ancient and modern images of the same sports, to show the continuity of athletic contests over the millennia, while the gold coins concentrated on historically significant landmarks in Greece. The most recent issue is a set of coins from Italy, which hosted the Winter Games of 2006.

ENGLAND, SCOTLAND AND IRELAND

The three kingdoms of the British Isles maintained separate political identities for hundreds of years, and each struck their own coins before they were united. England and Scotland had distinctive coins until the Act of Union of 1707, while Ireland ceased to mint its own coinage when the United Kingdom was formed by the Act of Union of 1801.

Left: The gold sovereign of Henry VII, showing the monarch enthroned, symbolized the Tudor ascendancy that ended the Wars of the Roses. The reverse shows the Tudor rose crowned and superimposed by the royal arms.

ENGLAND

Gallo-Belgic, Celtic tribal and Roman coins were used in Britain from the 2nd century BC until the withdrawal of the Roman legions in the early fifth century. These included gold Celtic ring money [1–2], Gallo-Belgic staters [3–4] and coins of the major tribes in southern Britain [5–6]. In succeeding generations, southern Britain was invaded by the Angles, Saxons and Jutes, who established petty kingdoms in Northumbria, Kent, Mercia (the Midlands) and East Anglia. The earliest coins were small gold thrymsas and silver sceattas [7] but Offa of Mercia (757–96) introduced the silver penny, which remained the standard coin until the reign of Henry VII (1485–1509), with a stylized full-face portrait (obverse) and a cross (reverse). While its obverse gave the name of the king, the reverse bore the name of the place where the coin was struck.

The Anglo-Saxon style of coinage was retained by the Normans and Plantagenets. Edward I (1277–1307) introduced the halfpenny and farthing [8–9] as well as the groat (4 pence). Edward III struck half groats and the florin, England's first regular gold coin. It was not a success, and was soon replaced by the noble [10], which remained in use for almost a century. Edward IV introduced the gold angel [11] or third of a pound.

During the Hundred Years' War, coins in the English style were struck in those parts of France under English rule. Although the English king's claim to the French throne was effectively crushed by 1450, the French title and fleur de lis emblem survived on coins until the end of the 18th century.

English coinage entered a new era under Henry VII. He introduced the gold sovereign (1489) and the silver testoon or shilling (1500), the latter bearing the first realistic portrait on any English coin, influenced by developments in Renaissance Italy [12]. His grandson, Edward VI [13–14], introduced the large silver crown of 5 shillings, the first English coin to bear a date (1551). His sister Elizabeth (1558–1603) struck more denominations than any other British ruler – 20 different coins from the halfpenny to the sovereign [15–16]. Yet the number of types (about 60 in a 44-year reign) was comparatively small. During her reign the first tentative experiments in mechanization took place.

The Stuart dynasty, imported from Scotland in 1603, ruled England for little more than a century, but it was the most complex in British numismatic history. James I almost rivalled Elizabeth with coins of different names for the same value, such as the unite [17], laurel [18] and sovereign (pound), as well as new denominations like the thistle crown (4 shillings). During the reign of Charles I (1625–49) the Civil War broke out in 1642. While Parliament controlled London and thus the Tower Mint, which continued to strike coins in the king's name [19], the Royalists established mints at Aberystwyth, Shrewsbury, Oxford, York, Bristol [20], Exeter, Truro, Chester, Worcester and strongholds such as Hartlebury Castle. Makeshift coins were also produced in besieged towns, such as the diamond-shaped clipped coins of Pontefract [21–22].

Coins of the Commonwealth (1649–60) had the shield of St George on one side and the conjoined shields of England and Ireland on the other [23]. In 1662, shortly after the Restoration, milled coinage was adopted permanently, and, following the Act of Union of 1707, English coins extended to the whole country.

SCOTLAND
Scotland had no indigenous coinage until the reign of David I (1124–53), and only farthings, halfpennies and pennies were struck until the time of Robert II (1329–71), when gold nobles and silver groats [24] began to appear. Scottish coinage was remarkable for its diversity. Robert III added the lion (gold crown) and demy lion, while James I (1406–37) produced the demy and half demy. James III (1460–88) added the gold rider and its subdivisions, as well as the unicorn, the billon plack and the copper farthing [25–26]. Thereafter the use of base metal escalated, while gold and silver were often heavily debased. Inevitably the value of Scottish money fell in relation to sterling until ultimately the Scottish shilling (12 pence) was worth no more than an English penny [27–28]. After the Union of the Crowns (1603) the Edinburgh Mint continued to strike

---

Gun Money

Emergency coins were minted at Dublin in 1690 in the name of James II and were struck in metal from melted cannons in denominations of a crown, half crown, shilling and sixpence. Apart from the crown, these coins bore both their year and month of issue.

---

distinctive coins, but increasingly they conformed to English weights and fineness, which explains denominations such as 12, 30 and 60 shillings (equivalent to the English shilling, half crown and crown). The last Scottish coins were similar to those in England but bore the E mint-mark below Queen Anne's bust. The Edinburgh Mint closed in 1708.

IRELAND
Silver pennies were struck at Dublin by the Vikings in the 10th century. Following the Anglo-Norman conquest in the 12th century coins were struck showing Prince John as Lord of Ireland. Subsequent coins followed the English pattern but included oddities such as the tiny half farthing of Edward IV and a groat struck by Lambert Simnel, pretender to the throne under the name of Edward V. The harp first appeared on coins in the reign of Henry VIII and survived until 1822, when Irish coins were discontinued.

Below: An Irish groat of Henry VIII with the crowned harp on the reverse.

UNITED KINGDOM

The United Kingdom of Great Britain and Ireland was formed in 1801. In 1922, when the 26 counties of southern Ireland attained independence under the name of the Irish Free State, the United Kingdom of Great Britain and Northern Ireland came into being. Today it comprises the kingdoms of England and Scotland, the principality of Wales and the province of Northern Ireland, all but the first-named now having devolved powers exercised through a parliament in Scotland and assemblies in Wales and Northern Ireland. Scotland and Northern Ireland have their own banknotes, but the United Kingdom has a unified system of coinage.

Left: In 1989, £2 coins were issued to celebrate the tercentenaries of the Bill of Rights (England) and the Claim of Right (Scotland), which provided the basis for the constitutional monarchy under William III and Mary and laid the groundwork for the eventual union of the kingdoms.

HANOVERIAN RULERS

Her many children having pre-deceased her, Queen Anne (half farthing [1–2]) was succeeded by her cousin George Louis, Elector of Hanover, who ascended the throne in 1714 as George I. The quality of the engraving in British coins improved during the 18th century, with portraiture becoming more lifelike, if hardly flattering. Gold coins were struck in denominations of 5, 2, 1 [3–4] and half guinea (the name being derived from the Guinea Coast, whence much of the gold was imported). Although nominally rated at 20 shillings, the value of the guinea rose as high as 30 shillings before settling at 21 shillings, owing to fluctuations in the price of gold.

Silver became increasingly scarce in the Hanoverian period [10–11] and very few of the smaller coins (1–4 pence) were struck. Meanwhile, at the other end of the scale, small gold third and quarter guinea coins circulated, with respective values of 7 shillings, 5 shillings and 3 pence. A feature of British coins in this period was the inclusion of provenance marks, denoting the source of the bullion. In 1745, Admiral George Anson captured a Spanish treasure ship during his voyage round the world. Coins struck from the captured silver bore the word "Lima" below the king's bust [5–6].

Although base-metal halfpennies and farthings had been introduced in 1672, the Hanoverians were reluctant to issue base coinage, and the vacuum was filled by trade tokens. Not untypical were the heart-shaped tokens, bearing the London arms, issued by Sam Goodakers [7–8]. The first copper pennies and twopences (1797) were the Cartwheels struck by the private Soho Mint in Birmingham [9].

The parlous state of the coinage at the end of the Napoleonic Wars led to the reforms of 1816, re-introducing the sovereign of 20 shillings, much smaller and lighter than the guinea, with a corresponding reduction in the size of the silver coins.

VICTORIAN ERA

Most of the coins of Victoria's long reign portrayed her as a teenager [12] as she came to the throne in 1837, and it came as a shock to the public when the series released in 1887 to mark her golden jubilee showed her as an elderly lady [13]. There were some changes, notably the first attempt at decimalization, which resulted in the florin (1849), and the change from copper to bronze for the smallest denominations (1860), both utilizing more mature portraits [14–15]. The Jubilee bust was unpopular and was replaced by the Veiled Head in 1893 [16].

Benedetto Pistrucci's St George and the Dragon, featured on the gold coins of 1816–25, was revived in 1871 and has occupied the reverse of the gold coins ever since. It was also used for the silver crowns of 1818–23 and 1887–1902 and finally for the crown of 1951 marking the Festival of Britain. The model for St George was a waiter at Brunet's Hotel in Leicester Square, London.

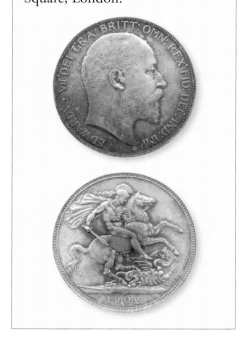

EARLY TWENTIETH CENTURY
The coins of Edward VII followed the pattern of his predecessor, the standing Britannia motif of the florin being a notable concession to Art Nouveau (and inspiring the later Britannia bullion coins). A garlanded crown featured on the reverse of the George V crowns, but an Art Deco version of St George and the Dragon was used for the silver crown of 1935 for the silver jubilee [17]. Pictorial motifs were used on the low-value coins of George VI and Elizabeth II [20], while two different shillings (with English or Scottish heraldic lions) appeared in 1937 [18–19]. Few commemoratives appeared in this period, notably the crown honouring Sir Winston Churchill (1965).

DECIMAL COINAGE
Debated since the 1790s, British decimalization finally reached fruition in 1971. In the run-up to it several of the £sd series were not struck after 1967, while the first decimal coins appeared in 1968, the 5 and 10 new pence being struck in the same sizes as the shilling and florin. The half crown was withdrawn at the end of 1968 and in February 1971 the penny and threepence were superseded by the new ½, 1 and 2 pence coins [21]. In 1969 the 10 shilling note was replaced by the seven-sided 50 new pence. In 1982 the word "New" was dropped from the inscription and the small seven-sided 20 pence was introduced [24]. Two years later the halfpenny was discontinued.

The 50 pence was reduced in size in 1987, and the 5 and 10 pence were likewise reduced in 1990 and 1992 respectively. A nickel-brass circulating pound coin was introduced in 1983 and since its inception the reverse has changed annually [26]. Two pound coins were issued as commemoratives (1988–96) but a bimetallic coin of this value was added to the circulating series in 1997 [22]. The effigy of Queen Elizabeth has been changed four times. A bust by Mary Gillick was used for pre-decimal coinage [23], followed by effigies by Arnold Machin (1969), Raphael Maklouf (1988) [25] and Ian Rank-Broadley (1998). The crown was used for commemoratives and decimalized as 25 pence, but in 1990 it was revalued at £5. The 50 pence coin has often been used as a commemorative medium since 1973 [27].

Above: A crown released in 1981 to celebrate the wedding of the Prince of Wales and Lady Diana Spencer.

IRELAND AND OFFSHORE BRITISH ISLANDS

As well as the United Kingdom, there are four other countries in the British Isles that issue their own coins. The coins of Ireland issued before the Union of 1801 have already been discussed, but after 1928 the Irish Free State (now the Republic of Ireland) issued distinctive coins, while the Channel Islands (Guernsey and Jersey) and the Isle of Man each have a coinage history going back centuries.

Left: Guernsey released a square 10 shilling coin with rounded corners in 1966 to celebrate the 900th anniversary of the Norman Conquest of England, bearing the bust of William the Conqueror, Duke of Normandy. The Channel Islands are the last remnants of the Duchy governed by the British Crown.

JERSEY

Hoards of Armorican Celtic staters from 75–50 BC have been discovered in the Channel Islands, suggesting that they may even have been minted there.

Various bank tokens were issued between 1812 and 1831[1–2], but French currency circulated in Jersey until 1834, when the island switched to British money, and distinctive coins were adopted in 1841. Unfortunately, the money of account was the pre-Revolutionary French sol, tariffed at 520 to the pound. Jersey's largest coin was worth 2 sols – $\frac{1}{260}$ of a pound or $\frac{1}{13}$ of a shilling – hence the values on the early coins: $\frac{1}{52}$ (farthing) [3–4], $\frac{1}{26}$ (halfpenny) and $\frac{1}{13}$ (penny). In 1877 the currency was brought into line with Britain and the coins revalued at $\frac{1}{48}$, $\frac{1}{24}$ and $\frac{1}{12}$ of a shilling [5]. British coins served the higher values until 1957, when the quarter shilling (3 pence) was introduced. Since 1971 the decimal coinage has followed British standards.

GUERNSEY

French coins circulated in Guernsey for centuries, but halfpennies and farthings were imported from England from 1672 along with worn silver coins, which were not recalled until 1817. The vacuum was filled by a wide range of foreign coins and order was not restored until 1830, when the island introduced its own coinage based on

the ancient French *double tournois*, hence "Double" on the Guernsey coins [6–9]. Copper, and later bronze, issues of 8 (penny), 4 (halfpenny), 2 (farthing) and 1 double (half farthing) bore the arms of the bailiwick and the value.

A cupro-nickel threepence featuring a cow appeared in 1958–66 and the square 10 shillings in 1966. Since 1971 the full range of coins has conformed to British standards, the arms occupying the obverse until 1977, when Elizabeth II's profile was substituted. Gold and silver commemoratives have been struck for Alderney, Guernsey's dependency, since 1989.

ISLE OF MAN

Silver pennies modelled on the Hiberno-Norse coins of Ireland, but with blundered inscriptions and a crude portrait, were struck about 1025–35, but otherwise Scottish, English and Irish coins and tokens circulated freely and included Murray's Pence – local tokens declared legal tender in 1673. Distinctive pennies and halfpennies date from 1709, issued under the authority of the Earls of Derby [10–11] and later the Dukes of Atholl [12–13] as Lords of Man, with their emblems. The island was transferred to the British Crown in 1765 but regal coinage was not issued until 1786, with the bust of George III [14–15]. No coins were struck from

Above: The Isle of Man's close ties with Scotland are reflected in the set of four crowns issued in 1996 to mark the bicentenary of the death of Robert Burns, Scotland's national poet.

1813 to 1839, when coppers portraying Victoria were released [16]. Island money was tariffed at 14 pence to the shilling, but the Manx government brought it into line with Britain in 1840 and from then until 1971 British coins circulated. A gold series of 1965 marked the bicentenary of the Revestment Act, while a crown of 1970 featured the tailless Manx cat [19].

Since 1971 the island has issued the full range of coins for general circulation. The reverses often bear the national three-legged emblem and its motto, "Quocunque Jeceris Stabit", which translates as "Whithersoever you throw it, it will stand" [17]. While generally conforming to British standards, the Isle of Man pioneered £1 (1978), £2 and £5 coins (1981) in virenium, a special base-metal alloy [20]. Since 1972 it has been one of the world's most prolific issuers of commemoratives [18] and special issues, often in long thematic sets [21–22].

IRELAND

The first coins, designed by the noted sculptor Percy Metcalfe, appeared in 1928 with a harp (obverse) and various birds and animals (reverse), earning the nickname the Barnyard Series [23–25, 27–28]. The obverse was modified in 1939 when "Eire" (Ireland) replaced "Saorstat Eireann" (Irish Free State). In 1966 the 50th anniversary of the Easter Rising was marked by a 10 shilling coin portraying Padriag Pearse and the

statue of Cuchulainn. Ireland decimalized its currency at the same time as Britain, using the same specifications, but adopted distinctive nickel-bronze 20 pence (1986) and cupro-nickel pound coins (1990). The harp obverse was retained, as well as the horse, salmon and bull motifs on the 20, 10 and 5 pence [29–30], but Hiberno-Norse ornament graced the bronze coins [26], while the pound featured a stag and woodcock, formerly on the farthing, was promoted to the 50 pence. A 50 pence featuring the civic arms celebrated the Dublin millennium in 1998. The Millennium was marked by a pound coin depicting a galley surmounted by a cross, symbolizing the advent of Christianity in Ireland. Ireland adopted the euro in 2002, but medallic pattern ecus signalled the EEC Council Meeting in Dublin in 1990.

Portrait Gallery

One of the most spectacular coins of recent times was the crown released by the Isle of Man in 1987 to celebrate the bicentenary of the American Constitution. The reverse shows the Statue of Liberty surrounded by 11 portraits of US statesmen, from George Washington to Ronald Reagan.

1 2 3 4 5 6 7 8 9 10 11 12 13 14 15 16 17

BRITISH EUROPEAN TERRITORIES

Four Mediterranean countries with long and distinctive histories are grouped here because they came under British rule for many years and their modern coinage was therefore either closely linked to that of Britain or strongly influenced by it.

Left: The traditions of the Knights of St John of Jerusalem are continued to this day by the Sovereign Order of Malta, based in Rome. Since 1967 the Order has produced a large number of medallic pieces, denominated in scudi, illustrating the history of the Knights and raising funds for its charitable works.

CYPRUS

This island was of vital importance to Mediterranean cultures in the Bronze Age as the chief source of copper (from which the island derives its name); imitation cowhides cast in copper rank among the earliest forms of currency. In Greek classical times coins were struck at Amathus, Salamis, Paphos, Idalium and Citium. Typical of these coins was the silver of Evagoras II (361–351 BC) of Salamis [1–2] and Azbaal of Citium in the 5th century BC [5–6]. Coins of Alexander the Great were minted in Cyprus [3–4] from the 4th century BC.

Shown here is a Byzantine coin of Isaac the Usurper (1184–91), struck in Cyprus before he was overthrown [7–8]. Between 1192 and 1324, deniers, obols and gros were issued by the Crusader Guy de Lusignan and his descendants, such as Henry III, who struck large silver gros with facing portraits and cross motifs [9]. Distinctive coinage was revived in 1879 when Cyprus became a British protectorate. The Turkish piastre was tariffed at nine to the shilling, hence there were coins of 18, 9 and 4 piastres as well as smaller coins down to the bronze quarter piastre. These bore the effigy of the British monarch and the value or arms on the reverse. Latterly the reverse featured two lions passant gardant, the emblem of Richard the Lionheart, who seized Cyprus from the Byzantines in 1191.

Decimal currency based on the pound of 1000 mils was adopted in 1955, and pictorial reverses were then selected [10–11]. In 1960 Cyprus became an independent republic and introduced coins with the state emblem on the obverse [12]. The currency was reformed in 1983 and the pound of 100 cents adopted. A few commemoratives have appeared since 1976.

MALTA

Like Cyprus, Malta has a long numismatic history, its earliest coins being attributed to the Phoenicians in the 3rd century BC. Subsequently there was a limited (and very rare) coinage under Greek or Roman influence [13].

The Knights of St John of Jerusalem, having been driven out of Rhodes, occupied Malta from 1530 until they were expelled by Napoleon in 1798, and coins in various denominations from the tiny picciolo (72 to the penny) to the zechino (sequin, or third of a pound sterling) [14–15] were minted under successive Grand Masters from Villiers de l'Isle Adam (1533) to Count von Hompesch (1798) [16–17]. The French garrison produced siege coins in gold, silver and bronze during the British blockade of 1799–1800.

Ordinary British coins circulated from 1800 until 1972 but included third farthings (1827–1913), which corresponded to the copper grano. A decimal system based on the lira or

Gallantry Award

Throughout its long and turbulent history Malta was besieged many times, but its worst ordeal was the incessant bombardment from sea and air during World War II. The fortitude of the islanders was recognized in 1942, when George VI conferred the George Cross, the highest civilian gallantry award, on the island of Malta. Several definitive coins have borne the cross, while the 50th anniversary was celebrated by a £M5 coin featuring the cross and the citation.

pound of 100 cents or 1000 mils was adopted in 1972, with various motifs on the obverse and the value on the reverse [18–21]. In 1982 the tenth anniversary of decimalization was marked by distinctive obverses. An entirely new series with the national arms and pictorial reverses was adopted in 1991 [22–23].

A characteristic of Maltese coins is the use of different shapes – scalloped edges (mils) and octagons or decagons (25 and 50 cents). Gold and silver coins from £M1 to £M100 have appeared since 1972, beginning with a series depicting Maltese landmarks, and a set of 12 £M5 was issued in 1986 tracing the maritime history of the Knights of Malta.

IONIAN ISLANDS

This group of islands in the Adriatic, including Corfu, Cephalonia and Zante, were under Venetian rule until 1798, when they were seized by the French. They were later occupied by the British in 1809 and ceded to Greece in 1864. From 1819 [24–25] onward they had a series of copper

obols and silver 30 lepta coins with the lion of St Mark on the obverse [26] and Britannia on the reverse [27].

GIBRALTAR

The Rock of Gibraltar, captured by Britain from Spain in 1704, used British and Spanish currency, although copper coins of half, one and two quarts appeared in 1842, with a profile of Queen Victoria (obverse) and the key and triple-tower emblem (reverse) [28–29]. Cupro-nickel crowns with the triple tower were issued from 1968 to 1970, mainly for use in casinos.

Gibraltar adopted decimal coinage the following year and switched to a crown-sized 25 new pence with a Barbary ape on the reverse. Otherwise there were no distinctive coins for general circulation until the 1988 series, conforming to British weights and specifications, with the Queen's effigy and pictorial reverses [30–31].

Apart from a set of gold £25, £50 and £100 coins in 1975 to celebrate the 250th anniversary of the introduction of sterling currency, commemoratives began with crowns for the Queen's silver wedding (1972) and silver jubilee (1977). Since 1988, however, commemorative and special issues have been very prolific, ranging from Christmas 50 pence coins to gold pieces marking the Japanese royal wedding (1993) and the centenary of Peter Rabbit (1994). The gold coins are denominated from the tiny 1/25 crown upwards. Gibraltar was also unique in adopting coins denominated in both sterling and ecus (1991), ranging from the cupro-nickel £2 (2.8 ecus) to the gold 140 ecus of 1996 [32–33].

Above: The reverse of the Gibraltar 50 pence shows the value surrounded by candytuft, the national flower.

1
2
3
4
5
6
7
8
9
10
11
12
13

BENELUX COUNTRIES

Belgium, the Netherlands and Luxembourg have a common history dating from the Middle Ages when they formed the duchy of Burgundy, which passed under Habsburg rule in 1494 and later became the Spanish Netherlands. To that period belongs the silver patagon of Charles II [1–2]. The Dutch revolted against Spanish rule in the 16th century, and Belgium later became the Austrian Netherlands. After 1815 the two countries were united under Prince William of Orange-Nassau, who reigned as King William I of the Netherlands and Grand Duke William of Luxembourg. Belgium seceded in 1830, and Luxembourg passed to a junior line of Orange-Nassau in 1890, when Queen Wilhelmina was barred from succession under Salic Law. Close ties resulted in the formation of Benelux in 1945, a forerunner of the European Community.

Left: Francis I (1708–65), Duke of Lorraine and Holy Roman Emperor, whose arms appear on this silver coin struck in Brussels, ruled the Austrian Netherlands with his wife, Maria Theresia. Together they survived numerous disputes with their fellow European powers, including the bloody Seven Years War, during which the Habsburg heiress – rather than her husband – is remembered for her great courage and determination.

BELGIUM

The Celtic tribe known as the Belgae, who inhabited the region in pre-Christian times and struck the staters that formed the first coinage in Britain, gave their name to the country of Belgium. In the Middle Ages, apart from the prolific issues of the Duchy of Burgundy and later of the Spanish Netherlands, the rulers of Brabant [3–4], Hainault and Flanders [5–6] and the bishops of Liege all struck their own coins. Later, Spanish, French and Dutch coins were in use.

The Belgian provinces of the Netherlands broke away from Holland in 1830 and in 1831 elected Prince Leopold of Saxe-Coburg-Gotha as their king, shown here on a pattern 5 francs [7–8]. The country got off to a bad start with its first coin, the 5 centimes of 1831, which was erroneously dated 1811. Other denominations followed in 1832–3, based on the franc. Silver coins portrayed King Leopold with a wreathed value on the reverse. Coins were inscribed in French, but from 1894 both French ("Belgique") and Flemish ("Belgie") versions were produced. Later coins bore the country name in both languages [9] and from 1938 parallel sets had the French or Flemish name first.

Coins portraying a coal miner [10–11] appeared in 1953 and continued until the advent of the euro. Royal portraiture gradually returned to the franc coins from 1969, the reverse showing the date, denomination and country name in French or Flemish [12]. Since the centenary of independence (1930), commemorative coins have marked royal anniversaries and important events, the 20 francs often serving as a medium for precious gold commemoratives[13].

NETHERLANDS

After breaking free of Spain in the 1570s the seven United Provinces issued an enormous range of coins until 1608, when there was some attempt to rationalize the coinage, resulting in gold ducats, silver rijksdaalders [14–15], bronze stuivers and silver klippe double stuivers [16–17] or duits. The French struck coins in the name of Louis Bonaparte as King of Holland (1806–14), but following the establishment of the Kingdom of the Netherlands in 1815 coins based on the gulden of 100 cents were introduced. They continued to be minted at Brussels until 1830, when Belgium seceded, and since then have been struck at Utrecht.

Most Dutch coins have the monarch's profile on the obverse and a crown or the royal arms on the reverse [18–19]. During the long reign of Wilhelmina (1890–1948) five different portraits appeared [20–21], whereas a stylized profile of Queen Beatrix has been in use since 1982. Relatively few commemoratives have appeared since 1979, when the 400th anniversary of the Treaty of Utrecht was celebrated. They are chiefly noted for the avantgarde treatment of the Queen's portrait, at times verging on caricature.

LUXEMBOURG

Originally a county of the Carolingian Empire, Luxembourg became a duchy in 1354. Under the Holy Roman Empire, coins were minted at Antwerp, portraying successive Dukes of Luxembourg [22] with an armorial reverse [23]. The duchy passed under the rule of Burgundy, Spain, Austria and France from 1443 to 1815, when it was constituted a separate grand duchy under the personal rule of the King of the Netherlands.

Dutch and later Belgian currency was used, apart from bronze 2, 5 and 10 cent coins from 1854 to the end of the century, with an armorial obverse and value reverse [26–27]. They were superseded by cupro-nickel coins portraying Grand Duke Adolphe (1901) or William IV (1905–12) [24–25], but higher denominations were only gradually introduced from 1916. Later coins favoured an armorial obverse, the French name of the country being

Anepigraphic Coins

Political correctness in Belgium eventually led to the issue of trilingual coins, with the country name in French, Flemish and German (recognizing the inhabitants of Eupen, Malmedy and St Vith). Alternatively, however, many coins since 1969 have had an anepigraphic obverse with no inscription of any kind, the profile of the king being sufficient identification.

dropped from 1939 in favour of "Letzeburg", although French was later restored to the higher values. Like the Low Countries, Luxembourg was occupied by Germany in World War II; unlike Belgium and the Netherlands, the grand duchy was absorbed into the Third Reich and did not resume its own coinage until 1946. As in Belgium, the language problem has been solved since 1965 by reducing inscriptions to the bare minimum.

A few commemoratives have appeared since 1946, when the 600th anniversary of John the Blind was celebrated. In more recent years most have alluded to Luxembourg's position at the heart of the European Community. A 500 franc silver coin of 1994 marked the 50th anniversary of liberation and featured the US flag on the reverse.

Above: Although modern Luxembourg coins have the denomination in French, the country name in the local German dialect, Letzeburg, has appeared below the arms on the obverse since the 1940s.

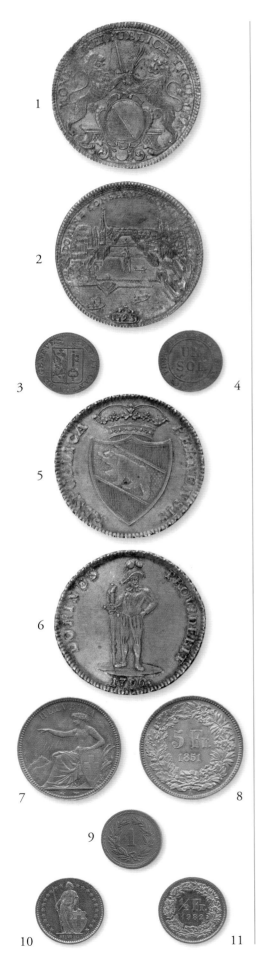

1

2

3

4

5

6

7

8

9

10

11

SWITZERLAND

The Swiss Confederation, consisting of 22 cantons or states located in the Alps, is unique politically, linguistically and culturally: a model of federal union bringing together people of French, German, Italian and Romansch languages and different religious and political backgrounds. The region was successively under the rule of Rome and the Holy Roman Empire, but in 1291 the elders of the remote valleys of Uri and Unterwalden joined forces with Schwyz (from which the modern country name is derived) to form an alliance while recognizing each other's rights to autonomy.

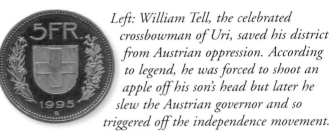

Left: William Tell, the celebrated crossbowman of Uri, saved his district from Austrian oppression. According to legend, he was forced to shoot an apple off his son's head but later he slew the Austrian governor and so triggered off the independence movement.

CANTONAL COINS

Each of the Swiss cantons issued its own coins in a bewildering array of denominations from the early 14th century onwards, including gold from 1411. Even after Swiss independence was briefly suppressed by the French from 1798–1803, when they created the Helvetic Republic (named after the Roman province of Helvetia), the cantons resumed their coinage and continued until 1850, when a federal system based on the franc (frank) of 100 centimes (rappen) was adopted.

The coins used in the individual cantons tended to reflect the currency of neighbouring countries. Thus, those in the Italian-speaking region favoured the franco or lira of 20 soldi or 240 denari (like the British £sd system), whereas the easterly cantons adopted the pfennig, thaler (typified by coins from Zurich [1–2] and Berne [5–6]), kreuzer and haller (heller) and the French-speaking cantons favoured deniers, quarts, sols [3–4], florins and pistols. In many cases the tiny rappen and batzen provided a basic unit, resulting in multiples in odd amounts, such as 21 batzen (Neuchatel) or 39 batzen (Vaud) to fit them into the franc or thaler systems. Most of these cantonal coins had an armorial obverse with the value on the reverse.

FEDERAL COINAGE

War between the cantons, mainly polarized on religious grounds, erupted in 1847, but after a brief campaign law and order were restored and the following year steps were taken to create a federal administration centred on Berne. The cantons agreed to give up their coinage privileges and a decimal system based on the franc was introduced throughout the country.

Probably on account of the confusing plethora of denominations and designs in the cantonal coinage, the federal authorities decided to strike coins that, from the outset, would be universally recognizable and acceptable. The lower denominations of the first series, introduced in 1850, had the name "Helvetia" on the obverse over a shield containing a Swiss cross, while the reverse had numerals within a wreath [9]. No notation of value was included to indicate rappen, centimes or centesimi. Silver coins [7–8] from the franc upwards had allegorical motifs on the obverse and the wreathed value and date on the reverse, although in this case the abbreviation "Fr." could be included to denote "francs", "franchi" or "franken".

The first change came in 1874–5, when a standing figure of Helvetia surrounded by 22 stars standardized the obverse of the 1 and 2 franc coins. In 1878 a female profile replaced the cross on the 5 and 10 rappen, followed by the 20 rappen in 1881 [10–11]. In these coins the country name was rendered in Latin "Confoederatio Helvetica". The seated figure on the 5 franc coin was replaced by a garlanded profile in 1888, with the cross on a shield flanked by the value on the reverse. This type continued until 1922, when the bust of William Tell (obverse) and modified shield (reverse) was introduced. The bronze subsidiary

Shooting Festival Coins

From the late 16th century many German states and free cities issued special coins that were given as prizes at shooting festivals. This tradition spread to Switzerland in 1842, and while it died out everywhere else it continued there until 1939. The coins, variously denominated 4 francs, 40 batzen or 5 francs, usually had armorial or allegorical motifs, with figures of marksmen or crossed rifles as popular images. These handsome silver coins, which were struck for the annual festivals at a different venue each year, were last regularly minted in 1885 but were sporadically revived in the 1930s.

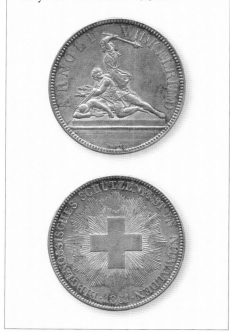

coins had a Swiss cross on the obverse and a wreathed value on the reverse [12–13]. Last, new designs were adopted for the 1 and 2 rappen coins in 1948, with a plain cross (obverse) and a numeral superimposed on an ear of corn (reverse) [14–15]. Apart from the replacement of silver by cupro-nickel in 1968, the Swiss coins have since remained unchanged [16–17].

COMMEMORATIVE ISSUES

Just as the permanent series has been very structured since its inception, so also the approach to commemorative and special issues has been very carefully orchestrated. Beginning in 1936, 5 franc coins were produced for special occasions [18–19], the first such coin publicizing the Confederation Armament Fund. The majority of coins have celebrated historic anniversaries or major current events and organizations, such as the Zurich Exhibition of 1939, the International Olympic Committee [20–21] and the Wine Festival of 1999 [22–23]. Since 1991, however, the chief medium for special issues has been the 20 franc denomination, usually confined to no more than two coins a year.

LIECHTENSTEIN

This tiny principality has had a lengthy association with Austria, whose currency it used until the end of World War I, augmented by the silver and gold vereinsthaler in the 19th century and similar coins in the kronen system from 1900, portraying the ruler (obverse) and princely arms (reverse).

In 1921 Liechtenstein entered a monetary union with Switzerland and adopted its coinage, followed by indigenous coinage of 100 rappen in 1924, portraying John II (1858–1929) or Franz I (1929–38). A series portraying Prince Francis Joseph II appeared in 1946. Since then there have been a few silver or gold commemoratives marking royal weddings, anniversaries [24–27] and the accession of Prince Hans Adam (1990) but Swiss coins are in everyday use.

GERMAN STATES

Within the boundaries of modern Germany there were hundreds of king-doms, principalities, grand duchies, duchies, counties and free cities, which for almost 2000 years produced their own coins, ranging from Celtic and Roman provincial to the prolific Frankish and Saxon issues that preceded the medieval coinage. These coins range from the pilgrim denars of Cologne [1–2] to the regal issues of Otto III (982–1002) [3–4]. Although the number was greatly reduced as a result of mergers and territorial aggrandisement by the more powerful states such as Prussia [5–6] in the course of the 17th and 18th centuries, no fewer than 39 states were, nevertheless, still issuing coins by 1815. Even after the formation of the German Empire in 1871 many states reserved the right to strike coins with distinctive reverses, even if the obverse conformed to the imperial standard – a precedent followed by the European Union's common currency at the present day.

Below: Some of the most spectacular coins ever struck emanated from the Duchy of Brunswick and the Kingdom of Saxony, notably the great multiple thalers of the 17th and 18th centuries. Examples include the 1631 Purim thaler of Erfurt, with Hebrew inscription and radiate sign of Yahweh (left), and the 1661 thaler of the bishopric of Munster showing St Paul above a panoramic view of the city (right).

CURRENCY REFORM

Different systems of weights and measures as well as varying standards of gold and silver meant that each German state was a law unto itself, making interstate trade exceedingly complex. By the late 18th century this had been rationalized to some extent, with distinct patterns emerging in the northern and southern states, whose coinage was largely based on the thaler and kreuzer respectively. Thus, in the north, the thaler was worth 24 groschen, a groschen was worth 12 pfennige and 2 heller equalled a pfennig [7–8], but there was also the mariengroschen, worth 8 pfennige. Meanwhile, attempts to equate the gulden with the thaler resulted in a ratio of 2 gulden to one and a third thalers. In the southern states the kreuzer [9–10] was worth 4 pfennige or 8 heller, but 24 kreuzer Landmunze were equal in value to 20 kreuzer Conventionsmunze, while 120 Convention kreuzer equalled two Convention gulden or 1 Convention thaler ("Convention" refers to an agreement of 1753, which first tried to bring the states into line). A new agreement (1837) reduced the complexity further. In the north the thaler was now worth 30 groschen or 360 pfennige (as recently as the 1960s Germans habitually referred to the 10 pfennig coin as a groschen). In the south the sole unit was the kreuzer.

VARIETY OF SUBJECTS

Several states produced a local coinage for provinces and other administrative subdivisions. Thus the kingdom of Prussia [11–12] also produced a subsidiary coinage for the province of Brandenburg and, within that, coins for Brandenburg-Ansbach-Bayreuth. The most notable of the subdivisions arose in Brunswick, where the practice of dividing a territory among all the sons of the ruler, instead of leaving everything to the eldest son, created a fragmentation resulting in the issue of separate coins for Brunswick-Lüneberg [13–14], Brunswick-Grubenhagen and the numismatically very prolific Brunswick-Wolfenbuttel [15]. Separate coins were also produced by the free cities of Bremen, Hamburg [16–17] (such as the Standing Knight ducat), Hanover [18–19] and Lübeck; in these cases the civic arms replaced royal portraits [22–23].

In the 19th century some states were more apt to strike commemorative coins than others. The most prolific in this respect was Bavaria, which seems to have recorded every event with large silver coins, from the death of the scientific instrument makers Reichenbach and Fraunhofer (1826) to the opening of the steam railway (1836). Several coins featured the various royal orders of chivalry, anticipating the long thematic sets of the present day, and when there was no special occasion to celebrate Bavaria resorted to the magnificent thaler of 1828 entitled "Blessings of Heaven on the Royal Family" whose reverse portrayed the queen and her eight children [20–21].

MONETARY UNION

In 1857 the German states produced the prototype for a single currency, adopting the vereinsthaler ("union thaler") of a standard weight and fineness. Although this became the standard, the states continued to issue their local coins for small change, often attempting to fit them into the Verein system [24–25]. The unification of Germany under the hegemony of Prussia in 1871 did not lead to an immediate streamlining of coinage, and both the thaler and kreuzer systems continued for several years, in the northern and southern districts respectively, before they were replaced by the mark of 100 pfennige.

Although a standard imperial coinage was gradually introduced from 1873 onward, many of the states continued to issue their own gold and silver coins above 1 mark in value. These coins bore the imperial eagle on

Currency Chaos

Coins with values expressed in two ways were frequently issued by the German states. Anhalt-Dessau had coins with "3 pfennige" on one side and "120 Einen Mark" ("120 to one mark") on the other, whereas Anhalt-Zerbst had a coin inscribed "IV Groschen" (obverse) and "LXXX I F. Marck" (reverse) signifying "80 to one fine mark". The 5 kreuzer coins of Arenberg had "CCXL Eine Feine Marck" ("240 to the fine mark"). Conversely, thalers often had their value expressed in local currency, while Hanoverian coins were inscribed in two equivalent values (gutengroschen and mariengroschen) and had three different standards of gold and silver fineness.

one side and, theoretically at least, were legal tender throughout the Reich, though the other side bore the portrait of the local ruler [26–27]. The coins consisted of 10 and 20 marks in gold and 2 and 5 marks in silver. Interestingly, many 3 mark coins were also produced, because this weight was in line with the obsolete thaler. As well as these high-value coins for general circulation many of the states issued commemoratives, mostly celebrating royal weddings and jubilees.

The state coins vanished shortly after the outbreak of World War I (as gold and silver disappeared from general circulation). The last of them appeared in Württemberg in 1916, to celebrate Wilhelm II's silver jubilee, and in Bavaria in 1918, to mark Ludwig III's golden wedding. The concept of a standard obverse with regional reverses has been adopted by the EC for its euro coinage in recent years.

1

2

3

4

5

6

7

8

9

10

11

12

GERMAN REICH

The First Reich was the empire created by Charlemagne in AD 800, uniting most of Christian western Europe. It eventually became the Holy Roman Empire, which was finally dissolved in 1806. The Second Reich was created by the victory of the German states over France in 1871 and was actually proclaimed in the Hall of Mirrors at Versailles. Although it ceased to be an empire in 1918 with the abolition of the monarchies, the term "Deutsches Reich" was retained by the Weimar Republic. In 1933, Adolf Hitler proclaimed the Third Reich, which was to last a thousand years before collapsing in 1945. Thus a unified German Reich existed for a total of only 75 years.

Left: Portrayed on the obverse of the 2 and 5 Reichsmark coins of 1936–9, Paul von Hindenburg (1847–1934) rose to the rank of field-marshal in the imperial army and was a national hero before becoming second (and last) president of the Weimar Republic. He appointed Hitler as chancellor in 1933.

THE EMPIRE

Nothing symbolized the unity of Germany more graphically than the coinage that was introduced in 1873. The obverse, devoid of any inscription, was dominated by the imperial eagle, while the reverse bore the inscription "Deutsches Reich" followed by the date with the value in the centre [1–2]. For all his vanity, Kaiser Wilhelm II never appeared on the imperial coinage (though he was portrayed on the Prussian coins); the imperial eagle alone would be depicted. This concept gives the coins of the German Empire their distinctive character and cohesion. In the early period (to 1889) the eagle was given a generous margin all round but from 1890 onward the size of the eagle was increased to fill the entire obverse of the coins [3–4]. During World War I bronze was replaced by aluminium for the pfennig, while silver coins disappeared after 1916.

Although the German Empire was dissolved in November 1918, its coinage survived for several years: the 5 and 10 pfennige, struck in iron from 1915, lasted until 1922, and the 50 pfennige, which had been discontinued in 1903, was revived in 1919, in aluminium rather than the original silver. In addition there were numerous local

issues of subsidiary coinage, usually including the word *Kriegsgeld* (war money) in their inscriptions. Small-denomination tokens were also widely circulated in lieu of government issues from 1919 to 1921, but they omitted the word *Krieg*.

WEIMAR REPUBLIC

The Kaiser abdicated at the end of World War I and fled into exile in Holland, in November 1918. The other monarchies toppled in his wake. In 1919 a constitutional convention at Weimar in Thuringia proclaimed the republic would ever afterwards be known by this epithet.

Imperial coins continued until 1922 but they were soon engulfed in hyper-inflation, which resulted in millions of marks being needed to buy a box of matches. Workers were paid daily and required wheelbarrows to cart away their wages in paper currency, which lost value overnight. In 1923, Hjalmar Schacht, president of the Reichsbank, performed the economic miracle of restoring the currency, introducing the Rentenmark of 100 Rentenpfennige, whose stability was vested in land [5–6]. Appropriately, the obverse types of this coinage depicted wheatsheaves or ears of wheat. By 1924 it was even possible to reintroduce the silver mark, and the following year a new currency, based on the Reichsmark of 100 Reichspfennige, was adopted. The wheat motifs were retained for the pfennigs [17–18] but from the outset the mark values bore a spread-eagle shorn of its imperial crown and breast shield [15–16].

Designs for coinage with the allegorical bust of Germania on one side and the republican eagle on the other were produced in 1926, but they were never put into production [9–10]. Coins of 3 mark value were issued from 1922 onward, both for general circulation and as a commemorative medium, a hangover from the thalers of an earlier period.

From 1925 onward, 5 mark coins and patterns were also produced to celebrate historic events and people, from the anniversary of the liberation of the Rhineland [7–8] to the pioneering global flights of the Graf Zeppelin in America [11–12] and Egypt [13–14], which also portrayed the zeppelin's commander, Dr Hugo Eckner.

Notgeld

The term *Notgeld*, meaning "emergency money", is usually associated with the prolific issues of paper produced in every German town and city during the hyperinflation of 1922–3, but there were also local coins, mostly struck in aluminium or bronze (sometimes plated to simulate gold). Red stoneware or white porcelain coins were produced at various potteries, notably the Meissen factory, whose coins circulated in Saxony. Unlike the earlier *Kriegsgeld* these pieces attained astronomical denominations, Westphalia producing coins up to 50 million marks in value.

THIRD REICH

Adolf Hitler was appointed Reichs Chancellor by President Paul von Hindenburg in January 1933, not because the Nazis seized power (as is commonly believed) but because at that time they represented the largest party in the Reichstag (the German parliament). The burning of the Reichstag building on February 27, allegedly by communists but actually by the Nazis themselves, gave Hitler the pretext for a general election, which was masterminded by Hermann Göring. Even so, this resulted in only a very slender majority for the Nazi party, but it was sufficient for Hitler to push through an enabling act in March 1933, allowing him to abolish all other political parties. This and the death of the aged president placed absolute power in Hitler's hands. Within weeks of his appointment, therefore, Adolf Hitler had transformed Germany into an absolute dictatorship.

A 4 Reichspfennig coin dated 1932 was struck at Berlin with a new obverse showing the Nazi eagle and swastika emblem – the date was clearly an error rather than an anticipation of Hitler's rise to power in January 1933. This became the standard obverse type for most of the coins issued until 1945 [19–23]. As in World War I, although a reasonable supply of coinage was maintained throughout World War II zinc was substituted in 1940 (1–10 pfennige) [24–25], while aluminium replaced nickel in the 50 pfennige, and the silver mark [26–27] and its multiples ceased to be produced after 1939.

Unlike the Weimar Republic, the Nazi state made very little use of commemorative coins. Among the few exceptions were the 5 mark coins struck for the 450th anniversary of Martin Luther in 1933 and the 175th anniversary of Friedrich Schiller in 1934. Another coin of 1934, showing the Potsdam Military Church, marked the first anniversary of Nazi rule. The same design, minus the date, "21 März 1933", was retained for the general issue of 1934 and 1935 [28–29].

POSTWAR GERMANY

Following its unconditional surrender to the Allies in May 1945, Germany was divided into American, British, French and Russian zones of occupation. The coins that circulated in these zones were either introduced or adapted by the occupying forces. By 1948, Germany had polarized between the three western zones and the five easterly provinces under Soviet control, leading to the establishment of the German Federal Republic (west) and the German Democratic Republic (east). Both East and West Germany adopted the Deutschemark as their currency, although they remained separate entities, subject to different exchange rates. The Deutschemark was also the name of the currency adopted by the unified Germany after the GDR ceased to exist in October 1990.

Left: The silver 5 Deutschemark coin, contrasting with the lightweight aluminium coins of East Germany, was widely regarded as the symbol of West Germany's economic miracle during the Cold War period. This anepigraphic obverse continued until 1974, but from 1975 to 2000 a more stylized eagle was used, with the year inscribed below it.

ALLIED OCCUPATION

A zinc 1 pfennig coin dated 1944 was struck at Munich, presumably in the following year, when the mint was under Allied control, as the eagle motif was divested of its swastika. This set the pattern for the zinc 1, 5 and 10 pfennig coins, which circulated in occupied Germany until 1948 [1].

France occupied the Saar in 1945 and effectively integrated this rich industrial province. West Germany campaigned incessantly for its return and in 1955 France undertook to retrocede the territory to Germany in 1957. French currency was in use until 1954, when coins denominated from 10 to 50 franken (on a par with the French franc), inscribed in German, were adopted as an interim measure. The aluminium-bronze coins showed arms on a background of factories and a coal mine [4–5], while a cupro-nickel 100 franken, issued in 1955, had a more elaborate version of the arms.

FEDERAL REPUBLIC

The Allied powers handed over civil government to the newly constituted Federal Republic in May 1949, but the split between East and West occurred a year earlier, when the currency was reformed and the Deutschemark (DM) was introduced. Coins of 1, 5 and 10 pfennige, in bronze- or brass-clad steel with oak leaves on the obverse, were originally inscribed "Bank Deutscher Lander" (Bank of the German Provinces) [2, 8], but from 1950 they bore the new country name "Bundesrepublik Deutschland" [13]. These inscriptions also appeared on the cupro-nickel 50 pfennige [9], whose reverse showed a girl planting a seedling, and the cupro-nickel 1 [12] and 2 DM featuring the German eagle [6–7]. The 5 DM was struck in silver and had the value on the obverse [3] and eagle on the anepigraphic reverse.

When cupro-nickel replaced silver in 1975 a more stylized design was adopted for the 5 DM. Like the earlier coins of Germany this series was struck at several mints, which were identified by the code letters A (Berlin), D (Munich), F (Stuttgart), G (Karlsruhe) and J (Hamburg).

From 1952 until 1986 the 5 DM [10–11] was the preferred coin for commemoratives, while 10 DM coins, first used to celebrate the Munich Olympics (1972), were used as commemoratives from 1987 until 2000, when the euro coinage was adopted.

Portrait Gallery

From 1957 onwards the 2 DM became more interesting as its reverse portrayed famous Germans. The physicist Max Planck was followed by a series of postwar politicians (clockwise from top left): President Theodor Heuss (dates of use 1970–87), Konrad Adenauer (1969–87), Chancellor Ludwig Erhard (1988–2000) and Dr Kurt Schumacher (1979–93). Also portrayed were Franz Joseph Strauss (1990–2000) and Willy Brandt, Mayor of West Berlin throughout the Cold War (1994–2000). As can be seen, these coins were often in simultaneous production and circulated widely.

DEMOCRATIC REPUBLIC

In the immediate postwar period the coins of the Bank of the German Provinces circulated in the Soviet zone, but economic disparity between the Soviet and Allied zones led to the currency reform of 1948, which recognized the difference between the money in East and West Germany. At this time distinctive coins began to appear in the Soviet zone. They comprised 1, 5 and 10 pfennige in aluminium and were simply inscribed "Deutschland" (Germany), with a numeral obverse and a reverse showing an ear of wheat superimposed on a cog wheel symbolizing industry and agriculture [14–17]. The German Democratic Republic was formally instituted in October 1949 and by 1952 coins bore the emblem of the new state – a hammer and compass on wheat ears – with the country name "Deutsche Demokratische Republik" [18]. The 1 pfennig coin was modified in 1960, the central design now appearing within a border with the legend running around the outside [19–20]. Attempts to introduce higher denominations led to a short-lived 50 pfennig coin (1950 and 1958) [25], although this did not become a regular issue until 1968, followed by the 20 pfennige in 1969 [23–24]. Similarly, 1 and 2 mark [26–27] coins were sporadically produced from 1956 but did not become regular issues until 1973–4. The 1 pfennig was reissued in 1979 and remained in circulation until the switch to West German currency in 1990.

A 5 mark coin showing the Brandenburg Gate was minted in 1971 [21–22] and then annually from 1979 to 1990, but this denomination was mainly used for commemoratives [30–31], beginning with the 125th anniversary of Robert Koch (1968). From 1966, when the 125th anniversary of the architect Karl Schinkel was celebrated, 10 and 20 mark coins [28–29] were also released.

UNIFIED GERMANY

Ironically, the last issue of the GDR was a cupro-nickel 20 mark coin for the opening of the Brandenburg Gate in 1990 – the landmark that, with the breaching of the Berlin Wall, effectively brought the Democratic Republic to an end. The five eastern provinces were formally admitted into the Federal Republic on October 3, 1990.

No change was necessary in the coinage, which was merely extended to the East [32]. However, in 1991 a 10 DM coin marked the bicentenary of the Brandenburg Gate with an inscription signifying "Symbol of German Unity". For 40 years the gate had been the symbol of a divided nation. The commemorative coins issued since then tended to reinforce the concept of unity and a common heritage.

AUSTRIA AND HUNGARY

These two countries of Central Europe were at the heart of the Habsburg dominions, and for centuries they were administered as a single state. In the 19th century the rising tide of nationalism led to the Ausgleich (compromise) of 1867, whereby Kaiser Franz Josef of Austria also became Kiralyi Ferenc Joszef of Hungary. Henceforth, distinctive coins appeared under the Dual Monarchy, denominated in krone (korona) and heller (filler) respectively. The collapse of the monarchy in 1918 led to the establishment of two quite separate countries which, despite the political turmoil of the later 20th century, have retained close cultural and economic ties.

Left: Austria's pre-eminence in European history since the 15th century is reflected in many of the large silver commemorative coins of recent years; the standard obverse has the shields of the nine provinces with the national eagle at the top.

HABSBURG EMPIRE

Small silver coins known as *Wiener pfennige* (Vienna pennies), portraying the Dukes of Austria, were struck in the late Middle Ages, but the Habsburgs' outstanding contribution to numismatics was the development of large silver coins, the guldengroschen and the thaler [1–2] from the late 15th century, while gold ducats [3–4] ranked among the most popular trade coins until the early 20th century.

The circulating coinage of the Habsburg dominions was based on the thaler worth two gulden or 120 kreuzer [5–6], but the currency was decimalized in 1857 to the gulden or florin of 100 kreuzer, with the vereinsthaler worth 1 florin. These coins bore the bust of the emperor (obverse) and double-eagle emblem (reverse), but some of the smaller coins had the imperial arms (obverse) with a value (reverse). They were superseded by the krone of 100 heller in 1892, with arms and a value on the heller coins and the emperor's profile on the krone obverse and the imperial double eagle on the reverse [7–8].

Shooting festival 2 florin coins were struck in 1873 and 1879, while the opening of the Vienna–Trieste Railway in 1857 was marked by a double

vereinsthaler. Both silver and gold coins celebrated the emperor's diamond jubilee (1908). The humble heller and the silver coins vanished after 1916, while iron or zinc alloys were used for the 2 and 10 heller of 1916–18.

Hungary was a major source of both gold and silver in the Middle Ages [18–19], most of it exported to Venice, hence the lengthy series of ducats and florins of the Kremnitz Mint from 1324 onward [20]. After 1526, however, Hungary was claimed by the Habsburgs and thereafter its coinage followed a similar pattern to that of Austria, but inscribed "krajczar" (kreuzer) [21–22] or "forint" (florin). The filler denominations of 1892–1914 featured the crown of St Stephen on the obverse, while the korona coins showed it on the reverse surmounting the value.

AUSTRIA

The krone continued as the unit of currency after World War I but rampant inflation reduced the 100 krone to a tiny bronze coin in 1923–4 [9]. Like Germany in the same period, Austria resorted to *Notgeld* paper money, but, upon the reformation of the currency in 1925 [10], introduced the schilling of 100 groschen. Coins were struck in bronze, cupro-nickel or silver up to the schilling for general circulation, but from 1928 silver 2 and 5 schilling or gold 25, 50 and 100 schilling coins were struck as commemoratives.

Austrian coins were suppressed in 1938, when the country was absorbed into the Third Reich. When distinctive coins resumed after World War II, aluminium or aluminium-bronze were used for the lower values and cupro-nickel for the schilling denominations in general circulation [11–14]. Like their pre-war counterparts, these coins

International Coin

The silver thaler portraying the Empress Maria Theresia, with the date frozen at 1780 (the year of her death), was struck at Vienna until 1937 and also after 1956 to satisfy demand from the Arab countries. It was struck in Milan and Venice in the 19th century, at Rome (1935–9) for use in Ethiopia, and at Paris (1935–57), London (1936–61), Brussels (1937–57), Bombay (1940–1) and Birmingham (1949–55), as well as Prague and Leningrad until 1975. It has been estimated than more than 800 million coins have been struck.

had symbolic or pictorial motifs on the obverse and a numeral reverse. Commemoratives comprised base-metal 20 schilling coins (1982–2000) [15–17], silver 25, 50, 100, 200 and 500 schilling pieces (1955–2000) and gold 1000 schillings (1976–2000). In addition, gold 200 and 2000 schilling coins were struck annually from 1989 to 1999 in support of the Vienna Philharmonic Orchestra.

HUNGARY

Inflation hit Hungary in the aftermath of World War I, but it also suffered foreign invasion and the loss of much territory to its neighbours. A short-lived Soviet republic under Bela Kun was ruthlessly suppressed and Hungary became "a kingdom without a king, ruled by an admiral without a navy".

The currency was reformed in 1925 with the adoption of the pengo of 100 filler, and coins continued to feature the crown of St Stephen with a royal inscription. During World War II steel or zinc replaced bronze and cupro-nickel, while the pengo switched from silver to aluminium. A number of commemorative 2 and 5 pengo coins appeared from 1930, ranging from the silver coin of 1930 marking the tenth anniversary of Admiral Horthy as regent, to the aluminium coin of 1943 celebrating his 75th birthday.

After World War II Hungary suffered the worst inflation of any European country and the currency reform of 1946 restored the forint. The obverse inscriptions reflect postwar political changes: "Allami Valtopenz" (Provisional Government, 1945) "Koztarsasag" (Republic, 1946) [23–24], "Nepkoztarsasag" (People's Republic, 1950) [25–28] and "Koztarsasag" (Republic again since 1990) [30–31]. Most circulating coins under the communist regime were of aluminium, though the 2, 5 and 10 forint were in nickel alloys. The tenth anniversary of the forint was marked by a silver 10 forint in 1956, but 20, 25, 100 or 200 forint coins were the main commemorative medium [29].

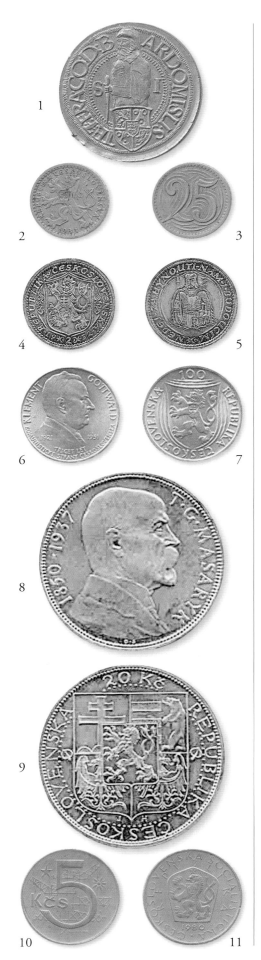

CZECHOSLOVAKIA

Situated in the very heart of Europe, Czechoslovakia was formed at the end of World War I from the historic kingdom of Bohemia, with Moravia, Slovakia and Ruthenia, formerly part of the Habsburg dominions. Ethnically and linguistically Slavonic, these areas were administered under Austria or Hungary, which created an economic and political imbalance leading to dissolution in 1938–9 and again in 1993. The silver mines of Joachimsthal in Bohemia produced the raw material for the large coins that therefore came to be known as Joachimsthalers; the name was soon shortened to "thalers", from which the word "dollar" is derived.

Left: The Pragergroschen, which derived its name from the Latin inscription "Grossi Pragensis" on the original version, was the first of the large coins to circulate in Europe. The coins were originally struck at Kuttenberg (Kutná Hora). The kingdom of Bohemia played a major role in European coinage, its mines producing both gold for the Pragergroschen of the 14th century and silver for the great thalers that were minted from 1519 onward.

KINGDOM OF BOHEMIA

The early denars of Bohemia, struck at Prague in the 10th and 11th centuries, were a curious blend of Anglo-Saxon and German types, reflecting the commercial influences on this important duchy at the heart of Europe. In the 12th century, Bohemia produced bracteates in the German style. The discovery of silver at Kutna Hora in the late 13th century, and the establishment of a mint there in 1298, had a tremendous impact on European coinage thereafter [1].

In the 15th century the kingdom increasingly came under German domination, until in 1526 the throne was claimed by the Archduke of Austria. Thereafter, the Habsburgs ruled Bohemia until 1918, and the later coinage closely followed that of Austria and Hungary. The Prague Mint produced coins for the Habsburg Empire, including the famous Maria Theresia thaler of 1780.

FIRST REPUBLIC

The Czech lands of Bohemia, Moravia and part of Silesia were united with Slovakia and Ruthenia in October 1918 when the Habsburg monarchy collapsed. The coinage, introduced in 1921, was modelled on that of pre-war Austria and Hungary and comprised the koruna (plural *korun*) of 100 haleru. The obverse showed the lion of Bohemia, while numerals and quasi-symbolic motifs occupied the reverses [2–3]. Commemorative silver coins celebrated the tenth anniversary of the republic (1928) or mourned the death of Tomas Masaryk, the first president (1937) [8–9]. Gold ducats (known in Czech as *dukaty*) carried on a Habsburg tradition from 1923 to 1939 [4–5].

The dismemberment of the country began in 1938, when Czechoslovakia was forced to cede the Sudetenland to the Third Reich. Slovakia became a separate state and a fascist ally of Hitler. Carpatho-Ukraine was granted autonomy in March 1939 but was promptly seized by Hungary. At the end of the war, Ruthenia was briefly independent before it was absorbed by the USSR; it is now part of the Ukraine.

On March 15, 1939, Nazi Germany invaded what was left of the Czech lands and proclaimed the Reich Protectorate of Bohemia and Moravia.

Although the general appearance of the coins was similar to the Czech series, the wartime issues of Bohemia and Moravia bore the names of the protectorate in German and Czech.

POSTWAR CZECHOSLAVAKIA

The pre-war coinage was resumed in 1946 but with new reverse designs. It included several silver coins, commemorating the risings in Slovakia and Prague (1947–8), the 600th anniversary of the Charles University (1948) and the 30th anniversaries of independence (1948) and the Czech Communist Party (1951) [6–7].

In February 1948 the communists seized power and Czechoslovakia subsequently became a people's republic, then a socialist republic (1962) and finally the Czech and Slovak Federal Republic (1990) [16]. Within two years, however, the return to democracy led to a break-up, although ties between the Czech Republic and Slovakia have remained close. The coins of 1948–90 reflect the dichotomy between those in general circulation, which are mainly struck in aluminium or brass [10–11], and the prolific issues of silver commemorative coins, from 25 to 500 korun.

SLOVAKIA

Distinctive coins based on the koruna slovenska (Sk) of 100 halierov were struck at Kremnica from 1939 to 1945 [12–15]; zinc, bronze or aluminium was used for the lower values and cupro-nickel for the 50 halierov, and 1 and 2Sk. Despite wartime strictures, the Slovak state even produced a few silver coins marking anniversaries of independence and portraying Monsignor Joseph Tiso, the state president. Their obverse featured the double cross emblem, and this motif has also graced the coins of the republic since its restoration [22].

The present series was introduced in 1993 and has attractive scenic motifs in the background of the numerals on the reverse of the halierov coins [17–19], and images derived from

ancient statuary on the koruna values [20–23]. Silver 100, 200, 500 and 2000Sk and gold 5000Sk coins have also been produced since 1993 to mark anniversaries of independence and pay tribute to famous Slovaks, as well as highlighting environmental problems and nature conservation.

CZECH REPUBLIC

Coins for the Czech Republic were introduced in 1993: the 10, 20 and 50 halierov in aluminium, the 1, 2 and 5 koruna czech (Kc) in nickel-plated steel and the 10, 20 and 50Kc in copper- or brass-plated steel [26]. The top value is a bimetallic coin with a plated brass centre and a copper-plated outer ring. The series has a standard obverse showing the lion of Bohemia [28], while the reverse motifs blend large numerals with symbols (up to 2Kc) [24]. The higher values show the Charles Bridge in Prague (5Kc) [25], Brno Cathedral (10Kc) [27], the equestrian statue of St Wenceslas (20Kc) [29–30] and a panoramic view of Prague. It constitutes one of the most aesthetically pleasing series of modern times. Silver (200Kc) or gold (1000–10,000Kc) coins have provided a rich variety of commemorative or special issues in the same period, including a 2000Kc in gold and silver with a holographic inlay to celebrate the Millennium.

POLAND

In the late Middle Ages, Poland expanded dramatically: at the height of its powers it extended from the Baltic to the Black Sea, encompassing Lithuania, the Ukraine and Belarus, but it declined in the 18th century and between1772 and 1795 it was dismembered by Austria, Russia and Prussia. In 1807, Napoleon reconstituted much of the territory seized by Prussia as the Duchy of Warsaw, which briefly had its own coins portraying Friedrich August of Saxony, whom Napoleon installed as duke [6–7]. The duchy was overrun by Prussia and Russia in 1813 and partitioned between them in an arrangement ratified by the Congress of Versailles (1815), which also created the tiny republic of Cracow and granted the eastern lands to the Tsar as the so-called Congress Kingdom of Poland. The upheavals of World War I and the downfall of the three empires that had partitioned Poland enabled its reconstitution in 1917–18 as a republic.

Left: A 500 zloty coin of 1995 recalled the sufferings of Poland in World War II, when it was again partitioned, Nazi Germany taking the western provinces, including Warsaw, while the Soviet Union grabbed the rest – and retained most of it at the end of the war.

THE KINGDOM OF POLAND

The earliest coins emerged in the 12th century and consisted of bracteates [1–2] as well as small denars of a more orthodox appearance, such as the coin minted by Wladislaw II Wygnaniec [3]. The power and wealth of the medieval kingdom was reflected in the rich diversity of its coinage. This included the first coins with face-to-face portraits since Roman times (Charles I of Hungary and Elizabeth of Poland, 1308) and the coins of Sigismund I featuring the Golden Fleece (1601), after he was admitted as a member of that prestigious imperial order of chivalry. Under Sigismund III Vasa (1587–1632) the coins of Poland reflected Swedish influence, typified by the ort or 6 groschen [4–5].

The designs of the 17th and 18th centuries showed the influence of Germany, Spain and Italy. The coinage was exceedingly complex and included the szostak of 6 groszy and the tympf of 3 szostak, the polturak of 1 grosze or 3 poltura, and the gross of 2 poltura or 3 solidi or schillings. Under the Napoleonic Grand Duchy of Warsaw the basic unit was the talara or zloty (from the Polish word for gold) worth 30 groszy, though 6 zlotych made a reichsthaler and 8 a speciesthaler. The reconstituted kingdom of Poland (1815) rationalized the coinage in 1832 [8–9] and linked it to the Russian system, so that 10 zlotych were worth 1 rouble and 30 groszy were worth 15 kopeks. Under the Grand Duchy and later kingdoms, coins in copper or silver had an armorial obverse and the value in words, but Tsar, as king of Poland, appeared in profile on the higher silver and gold denominations. After 1841, Polish coinage was suppressed and replaced by Russian currency. A crowned eagle obverse and numeral reverse appeared on coins issued in the districts occupied by Austro-German forces in World War I, based on the marka of 100 fenigow.

FIRST REPUBLIC

Because of postwar inflation and the problems of integrating the mixture of Austrian, German and Russian currencies in different parts of Poland, it was not until 1923 that a unified coinage was introduced, based on the zloty of 100 groszy, with the eagle obverse and value reverse [10]. Certain denominations (20 and 50 groszy) had fixed dates and were even restruck during the Nazi occupation, bearing the original date of 1923 but in zinc and iron instead of bronze or nickel. The silver 2 zlotych dated 1924 was originally minted in Paris but was restruck with a fixed date in Birmingham, Philadelphia and the Royal Mint, London, identified by mint-marks. By contrast, from 1932, 2 zloty coins had their designs changed every two or three years [12–13]. A somewhat similar course was adopted with the large silver 5 zlotych, but this was also used as a commemorative medium, with coins for the centenary of the revolution of 1830 and Pilsudski's Rifle Corps (1934). A gold 20 zlotych of 1925 portrayed the medieval ruler Boleslaw I, but this denomination was later reserved for large silver commemoratives.

POLAND RESTORED

The country was invaded from the west by Germany on September 1, 1939, and from the east by the Soviet Union two weeks later. On September 28 Poland was partitioned along the line of the River Bug. In July 1944 the Red Army began to advance into Nazi-held territory and a provisional government was established at Lublin. Postwar Poland lost its eastern provinces to the USSR but was compensated by a substantial part of pre-war Germany. A government of national unity was proclaimed but by 1948 had fallen under communist control.

Coins commenced again in 1949, with a modification of the pre-war types mainly struck in aluminium. The pre-war inscription "Rzeczpospolita Polska" (Polish Republic) continued until 1957 [11, 14], when similar coins with "Ludowa" added to the text belatedly signified the People's Republic. Coins of 2 and 5 zlotych were added to the series in 1958, also struck in aluminium, but were replaced by brass in 1975 [15], reverting to aluminium

Free State

Danzig had been an important Polish seaport, constantly fought over from 1308 to 1919, when it was made a free state. Coins based on the mark and later the gulden of 100 pfennige were issued between 1923 and 1939, when Danzig was incorporated into Nazi Germany. Since 1946 it has been Polish again, under its original name of Gdansk.

in reduced sizes in 1969. Higher values consisted of the cupro-nickel 10 zlotych (1959) [20–21], which went through radically different designs throughout the 1960s [16–19], and 20 zlotych (1973) [22–23]. Both originally had pictorial or symbolic reverses, replaced by plain numerals in 1984. The 10 and 20 zlotych were popular for a wide range of commemoratives, as were the 100 and 200 zlotych (silver) [24–25] and 500, 1000, 2000, 5000 and 10,000 zlotych (gold), although later cupro-nickel [28] and silver were used respectively. Inflation in the 1980s was reflected by astronomical values placed on many of the precious-metal commemoratives, culminating in the massive (70mm/2¾in) 200,000 zlotych coins of 1989 celebrating the tenth anniversary of the papacy of John Paul II.

Poland again became a free and democratic republic in 1990, reflected in the omission of "Ludowa" from the obverse inscriptions, though by that time the smallest denomination was 50 zlotych. The currency was reformed in January 1995, 10,000 old zlotych being equivalent to one new zloty. Brass (1, 2 and 5 groszy) and cupro-nickel (10 groszy to 1 zloty) coins appeared with various dates from 1990 [26–27, 29]. Bimetallic zlotych appeared from 1994.

BALTIC STATES

The republics of Estonia, Latvia and Lithuania have had a very chequered history. Estonia enjoyed less than 20 years of independence between the 13th century and 1918, while its neighbour Latvia fared little better. Both were conquered in turn by German military orders, Swedes, Poles and Russians, and were constantly fought over. By contrast, the Grand Duchy of Lithuania was a major power in the 14th and 15th centuries, extending from the Baltic to the Black Sea, but was united with Poland in 1569 through dynastic marriage, and shared Poland's fate. All three gained independence in 1918 and lost it in 1940 when they were absorbed by the USSR, re-emerging as sovereign nations in 1991.

Left: In 1989 one of the first acts of defiance against the Soviet regime was the linking of hands across the Baltic states to show the solidarity of Estonia, Latvia and Lithuania. The three states later created the road and rail link known as the Baltic Highway. The tenth anniversary was marked by this coin showing three pairs of hands.

LITHUANIA

The most southerly of the Baltic republics, Lithuania had an extensive medieval coinage based on the denier before falling under Polish rule [1]. It then used Polish or Russian coins, and it was not until 1925 that a distinctive coinage was re-introduced. The obverse showed a mounted knight, a revival of the medieval type alluding to the early 15th-century Grand Duke Vytautias.

The vagaries of Lithuanian grammar are reflected in the confusing forms of the denominations: 1 centas, 2 or 5 centai [2], 10, 20 or 50 centu [3], 1 litas, 2 litu, 5 litai and 10 litu in the pre-war series, struck at the Royal Mint in London. Unusually for the period, most of the coins were originally struck in aluminium-bronze (a brass alloy), but switched to bronze in 1936, when the 2 centai was added. The coins up to 5 litai had the value on the reverse with plants or flowers as minor orna-ment. Silver coins of 5 litai (1936) and 10 litu (1938) respectively portrayed Jonas Basanavicius, founder of the modern republic, and President Antanas Smetona, celebrating the 20th anniversary of independence. Both coins had an incuse inscription around the rim instead of the customary grain-ing. The coinage re-introduced in 1991

retains the horseman obverse [4] with a more modern rendering of the values on the reverse [5]. Bimetallic versions of the 2 and 5 litai were introduced in 1998 [8–9]. Apart from a silver 5 litai of 1998 publicizing the work of UNICEF, commemorative and special issues consisted mainly of the cupro-nickel 10 litu and silver 50 litu from 1993 and 1995 onwards respectively, but in 2004 a cupro-nickel 1 litas coin was released to celebrate the 425th anniversary of the University of Vilnius [10–11]. The 75th anniversary of the national bank was celebrated in 1997 with 1 litas coins, struck not only in cupro-nickel for general circulation [7] but also as proofs in pure gold [6].

LATVIA

In medieval times the Latvian capital Riga had an important mint for the Teutonic Knights and later Sweden or Poland, but no distinctive coins appeared until Latvia became an inde-pendent republic. A coinage based on the lats of 100 santimu (centimes) was introduced in 1922, with the national arms and value, the exception being the 50 santimu, which had an allegorical reverse [12–13]. Silver coins of 1 lats (1924) and 2 lati (1926) had the national arms on the obverse [14] and a wreathed numeral of value on the reverse [15]. A dollar-sized silver 5 lati was added in 1929 and depicted a girl in national costume (obverse) and elaborate arms (reverse) The original 1 santims [16–17] of 1922–35 was followed in 1937 with a new design with revised arms (obverse) and wreathed numeral (reverse). No commemoratives were produced in this period.

Coins were revived in 1992 with modernized versions of the arms and numerals on obverse and reverse [18–19, 20–21]. In the higher denominations the reverses feature a salmon (1 lats) or a grazing cow (2 lati). Large 10 latu coins have marked anniversaries and publicized endangered wildlife since 1993, while a few gold coins have celebrated the declaration of independence and the Olympic Games. In 1999 a bi-metallic 2 lati anticipated the Millennium [22–23]. It married a cupro-nickel-zinc central circle with

18 19 20 21 22 23 24 25 26 27 28 29 30 31 32 33

A Chivalric State

Livonia, consisting of much of modern Estonia and Latvia, emerged in the 12th century as a Christian state ruled by the Knights of the Livonian Order. The people were of Finnic or Baltic race with a German ruling class. In 1561 Livonia was absorbed by the union of Poland and Lithuania but the northern portion fell to Sweden in 1620. The coinage of Livonia reflected its strong commercial ties to the Hanseatic League and Russia, hence this silver coin of 1597 tariffed at 96 kopeks. Russia captured Swedish Livonia in the course of the Great Northern War, which ended in 1721.

---

a cupro-nickel outer ring, the two parts of the coin united by the cloud design in the background.

ESTONIA

Until 1721, when it passed to Russia, Estonia was under Swedish rule, yet the people managed to retain their distinctive language and culture. An independence movement developed in the early 20th century and, after the October Revolution, a republic was proclaimed in February 1918, although a state of war with the Bolsheviks continued until 1920.

Coins based on the kroon of 100 marka appeared in 1922 and reflect the influence of Germany and Finland. The standard obverse featured the three lions more commonly associated with England, but also, as here, the emblem of the Knights of the Sword, a crusading order that converted the Estonians to Christianity in the 14th century. The currency was changed in 1928 to the kroon of 100 senti, retaining variations on the armorial theme with the value on the reverse. The kroon values had pictorial reverses showing a Viking longship [24–25] or the fortress at Tompea [26–27], while commemorative coins marked the tercentenary of Tartu University (1932) and the Tenth Singing Festival (1933).

Estonia was occupied by Soviet troops in June 1940 and thereafter only Russian coins were in circulation. Independence was restated in August 1991, and subsequent coins have reprised the pre-war designs [31–33], with a range of commemoratives from the brass 5 krooni of 1993 marking the 75th anniversary of independence [28] and the 75th anniversary of the national bank in 1994 [29–30], to the gold 500 krooni of 1998 for the 80th anniversary. The preferred medium is the silver 10 and 100 krooni, marking the Olympic Games (1992 and 1996), bird conservation (1992) and independence anniversaries. In 1999, Estonia released a tiny gold coin tariffed at 15.65 krooni, the Estonian equivalent of the euro.

RUSSIA

Until the Middle Ages, Celtic, Roman, Anglo-Saxon, Viking and Byzantine coins circulated widely in what is now Russia, and gold Byzantine coins, such as the histamenon of Constantine VIII and Basil II (976–1025) were particularly popular [1–2]. Foreign coins and their imitations continued until the 11th century, when the earliest indigenous coins began to emerge in the Principality of Kiev, such as the cross and bust type struck by Prince Mstislav Vladimirovich [3–4]. Before Peter the Great modernized Russian coinage at the end of the 17th century, foreign gold and silver coins circulated extensively. They were often melted down and cast into ingots known as *grivny* (the name adopted as the unit of currency in the Ukraine). A half ingot was known as a rouble, from the Russian verb *rubit*, "to cut".

Left: The influence of the Byzantine Empire on the development of Russian coinage is shown clearly in the gold-plated coppers of John I Zimisces, ruler of Kievan Rus, in conscious imitation of the gold histamenon that circulated widely in medieval times.

TSARIST EMPIRE

Money of account was translated into actual coins from 1700, when Peter introduced the large silver rouble, often referred to as a "Jefimok" (from Jachymov or Joachimsthal in Bohemia where such large coins originated in 1519). The obverse bore the bust of the ruler [5] with the imperial double eagle on the reverse [6], and this became the standard from the start of the 18th century. The double eagle sometimes alternated with an armorial reverse [7–8], with the Tsar's monogram on the smallest coins, but in 1886 the profile of the Tsar was restored and the eagle relegated to the reverse. This style obtained in the gold and silver coins from then until the collapse of the monarchy in 1917.

The monetary system in the 18th and early 19th centuries was complex: each coin had a distinctive name inscribed on it, from the copper polushka (quarter kopek) and denga or denezhka (half kopek) to the grivna or grivnik (10 kopeks) [9–10], polupoltina (25 kopeks) [11–12], poltina (50 kopeks) and rouble; 10 roubles made an imperial or chervonetz. With such a vast country to supply with coins it is not surprising that production was spread across mints in St Petersburg, Ekaterinburg and Warsaw, as well as smaller units such as Souzan, Kolpina and Anninsk, which often confined their output to the copper coins used as small change.

From 1834 onward, the silver rouble was often used as a commemorative coin, mainly celebrating royal events. Russia also produced the world's first regular coinage struck in platinum, the 3, 6 and 12 roubles of 1828–45.

SOVIET UNION

The ill-fated Tsar Nicholas II was portrayed on the obverse of the coins from 1895 to 1915 [13–14], when the exigencies of World War I drove silver and gold out of circulation. The downfall of the monarchy, followed by the short-lived republic headed by Alexander Kerensky in 1917, and the October Revolution that brought Lenin and the communists to power, occurred at a time when the rouble was hard-hit by inflation. Monetary chaos was aggravated by the wave of civil wars and foreign interventionist campaigns.

In 1921 an attempt was made to re-introduce silver coins, from 10 kopeks to 1 rouble, and the gold chervonetz. These coins bore the hammer and sickle on the obverse, surrounded by the slogan "Workers of the world

Siberian Copper

The city of Ekaterinburg, named in honour of Catherine the Great, was the centre of the Siberian copper mining district. The Ekaterinburg Mint was geared up to refine and coin Siberian copper in 1725–7, and during Catherine's reign it produced very heavy copper coins similar in size to the *plåtmynt* of Sweden. Although much favoured by the monarch, these coins were far too cumbersome for everyday use and were extremely unpopular with the merchant classes for that reason. As a result, they were withdrawn after two years and melted down.

unite", with "RSFSR" at the foot signifying the Russian Soviet Federative Socialist Republic [15–16], which gave way to the Union of Soviet Socialist Republics in 1923. Coins bearing the Cyrillic "CCCP" (USSR) appeared from 1924. A legacy of tsarist times was the wide range of denominations, with coins of 1, 2, 3, 5, 10, 15, 20 and 50 kopeks. Silver was replaced by cupronickel in 1931 and a brass alloy of cupro-nickel-zinc in 1961, with subtly changed designs.

From 1965, when a rouble celebrated the 20th anniversary of the end of World War II, the Soviet Union produced numerous commemorative pieces in denominations of 1, 2, 3, 5, 10, 25, 50, 100 and 150 roubles, culminating in the platinum, gold and

silver coins marking the 1980 Moscow Olympics. Typically these coins had an obverse showing the Soviet arms with the value in the exergue [17], with an image and commemorative inscription on the reverse [18].

As the Soviet Union began to fall apart in 1991, an issue of coins was made by the State Bank in denominations from 10 kopeks to 10 roubles, with a standard obverse showing the Moscow Kremlin and a reverse bearing the value between an ear of wheat and oak leaves for the lower denominations [21–22]. They were struck in copperclad steel (10 kopeks) or cupro-nickel (50 kopeks and 1 rouble), while the higher values were bimetallic. The issue even included a pair of 5 rouble coins for wildlife conservation, depicting an owl or a mountain goat on the reverse, with the value on the obverse. The State Bank also produced special issues such as the series featuring gems of Russian classical architecture [19–20].

Above: Despite the negative experience of issuing very large and cumbersome copper pieces, Russia persevered with comparatively large copper coins, such as this 5 kopek of 1769, with the imperial double-headed eagle on one side and the crowned monogram of the Empress Catherine the Great on the other.

11 12 13 14 15 16 17 18 19 20 21 22

COMMONWEALTH OF INDEPENDENT STATES

The collapse of the communist regime in 1991 precipitated the dissolution of the Union of Soviet Socialist Republics. Mikhail Gorbachev attempted to hold the component republics together in a loose federation known as the Commonwealth of Independent States (CIS), but this concept was short-lived, as the various republics went their separate ways and even fought wars over disputed territory. Nevertheless it is convenient to survey the coins issued since 1992 under this heading. Outside Russia proper, indigenous coinage existed from the beginning of the Christian era in the Caucasus region, crude bronze pieces derived from Greek and Roman models being recorded from Georgia and quite sophisticated coinage in medieval Armenia, emulating the gold and silver of the Byzantine Empire. Although some of the states that briefly emerged in the early 1920s had their own paper money, none had distinctive coins until gaining independence in the 1990s.

Left: Levon, the Lion King of Armenia (1198–1226) allied himself to the Crusaders and married a Lusignan princess, founding a dynasty that expanded its territory in Asia Minor and was for some time a bastion of Christianity against Turkish aggression. Levon was a skilled diplomat, who forged alliances with the German emperors and Pope Celestine III. His westward orientation is reflected in his silver coins, such as this double tram showing him seated on the lion throne, holding the orb and sceptre, with the crowned lion in front of a patriarchal cross on the reverse.

RUSSIAN FEDERATION

By far the largest of the former Soviet republics is Russia, itself a federation of autonomous republics extending from the Baltic to the Pacific. It was hard hit by inflation when the USSR collapsed and a reform of 1992 led to the new rouble worth 10,000 old roubles. Brass-clad steel roubles were introduced that year, with the old double eagle emblem (minus imperial crowns) on the obverse [1–2] and the value on the reverse. Significantly, these and later coins were issued by authority of Bank Rossiya, the new state bank. Smaller coins, from 1 to 50 kopeks, featured St George and the dragon on the obverse [3–4]. The Soviet practice of issuing numerous commemorative coins has continued since 1992, including long thematic sets [5–7], such as the wildlife series of 1995–6. Some tiny 10 rouble gold coins have appeared since 1994.

CAUCASIAN REPUBLICS

As a once powerful kingdom geographically linked to Asia Minor and the Black Sea, Armenia's early coinage was subject to Greek, Roman and Byzantine influences. It struck its own coins from the 3rd century BC to the 16th century, but used Russian coins from 1801. Coins based on the dram (drachma) of 100 luma were introduced in 1994, with a double eagle obverse and value reverse [8–9]. A 5 dram silver coin of 1998, marking the fifth anniversary of the currency, reproduced banknotes on the reverse.

Azerbaijan's currency, based on the manta of 100 qapik, was launched in 1992 with symbols (obverse) and values (reverse) [10–11]. Gold and silver 50 manat appeared in 1996 to honour the national poet Mohammad Fuzuli.

In the 19th century, Georgian silver was mined for imperial Russian coins,

many bearing the Tiflis (Tbilisi) mint-mark [12–13]. Independent Georgia's coinage consists of the lari of 100 thetri; coins from 1 to 20 thetri in stainless steel, and 50 thetri in brass, have a wheel symbol (obverse) and various animals (reverse) [14–16]. A 500 lari gold coin appeared in 1995 to celebrate the 50th anniversary of liberation from Fascism.

WESTERN REPUBLICS

The Ukraine almost rivals Russia in its prolific coinage since 1995. It began with coins of astronomical denominations, but in practice, everyday money consisted of paper and the cupro-nickel 200,000 karbovanetz and silver coins denominated in millions were purely commemorative. The currency was reformed in September 1996, the hryven of 100 kopiyok being worth 100,000 old karbovanetz. Aluminium,

steel or brass coins featured the trident emblem and value [17–20]. Numerous commemoratives from 2 to 500 hryvni in silver or gold have been released.

Belarus (formerly Byelorussia or White Russia) has stuck to the rouble of 100 kapeek and has had commemorative gold, silver and cupro-nickel coins since 1996, while relying on small paper notes for everyday use.

Moldova lies next to Romania and has adopted the currency of that country, the leu of 100 bani, but unlike Romania its lei have not assumed astronomical proportions as a result of inflation. Aluminium coins from 1 to 50 bani [21–22] and clad steel leu and 5 lei pieces were introduced in 1992–3. A few silver 100 lei commemoratives have appeared since 1996.

CENTRAL ASIAN REPUBLICS

If the Ukraine and the Caucasian republics enjoyed a brief existence after World War I, the republics of Central Asia had no political existence before their creation by the USSR. Kyrgyzstan became a Union republic in 1936 and, so far, its only coins (since 1995) have been silver 10 som or gold 100 som commemoratives. Kazakhstan introduced circulating coins based on the tenga of 100 tyn in 1993, with the state emblem and value on obverse and reverse respectively [23–24]. Coins of 20 and 50 tenge (cupro-nickel), 100 tenge (silver) and 1000 tenge (gold) have marked anniversaries of independence and honoured historic figures since 1993 [33–34]. Turkmenistan adopted the manat of 100 tennesi in 1993 and coins with the profile of President Saparmyrat Nyyazow have since been released in plated steel [25–29]. Silver 500 manat coins also circulate [35–36] and since 1996 have featured endangered wildlife.

Uzbekistan alone had distinctive coins before 1994, although these were only the tenga and falus struck in the khanates of Bukhara and Khiva during the last years of the tsarist empire. The contemporary steel-clad coins are based on the som of 100 tyin [30–32].

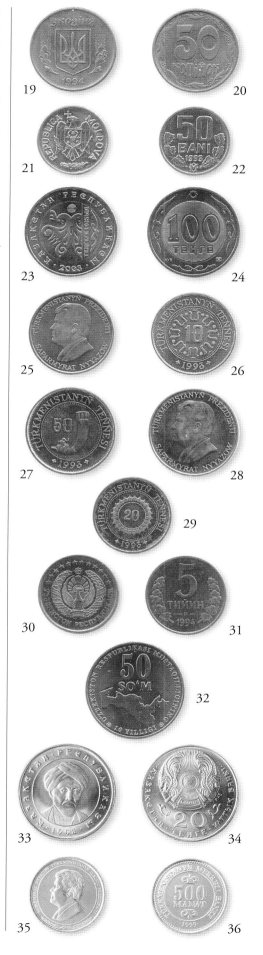

YUGOSLAVIA

The mountainous region of south-east Europe, inhabited by a mixture of ethnic, linguistic, political and religious groups, has been ruled by Greece, Rome, Byzantium, the Ottoman Empire and the Habsburgs. The Balkan mints at Ljubljana, Zagreb, Dubrovnik and Split were significant during the medieval period, producing coinage for local Venetian or Turkish rulers. Serbia was subjugated by the Turks after the decisive battle at Kosovo (1389) and did not regain independence until 1887. Montenegro was alone in precariously preserving its integrity from Turkish domination. As Turkish power waned Russia and Austria carved out spheres of influence, which led to War in 1914, triggered by the assassination of the Austrian Archduke Franz Ferdinand at Sarajevo. Out of the wreckage of World War I emerged the Kingdom of Serbs, Croats and Slovenes, which became Yugoslavia.

Left: Now known as Dubrovnik, in southern Croatia, Ragusa on the Adriatic coast was a major trading centre in the Middle Ages and the origin of the argosy, a large merchant sailing ship. Called the Pearl of the Adriatic, it was noted for the quality of its coinage, especially the silver blasius, named after the patron saint depicted on the obverse. In the 15th and 16th centuries it rivalled Venice in wealth and importance and was an independent republic until 1806, when it was suppressed by Napoleon.

SERBIA AND MONTENEGRO

In the 13th and 14th centuries the rulers of Serbia struck silver dinars as well as imitations of Venetian grossi at Belgrade [1–2]. Coins variously minted in Paris, Birmingham or Vienna were issued sporadically from 1868, based on the dinar of 100 para, with the ruler's profile or the eagle emblem on the obverse and the value on the reverse. After Prince Milan Obrenovich [3–4] assumed the title of king in 1882 coinage was more regularly struck, although under Peter I issues appeared only in 1904 and 1912 [9–10].

The coins of Montenegro, based on the perper of 100 para, began in 1906, with 1, 2, 10 and 20 para with a crowned eagle obverse. Higher values portraying Prince (later King) Nicholas appeared in 1909 with the arms on the reverse [5–6]. Gold and silver coins of 1910 [7–8] celebrated Nicholas's golden jubilee as titular prince-bishop.

YUGOSLAVIA

The Balkan kingdoms were overrun by the Central Powers in World War I, but regained their independence in 1918 and in December that year joined with the southern Slav dominions of the Habsburg Empire, Croatia and Slovenia, to form the Kingdom of Serbs, Croats and Slovenes under Peter I. His son Alexander acted as regent and ascended the throne in 1921. The problems of unifying such a disparate group of territories were immense and were solved only when Alexander assumed dictatorial powers and renamed the country Yugoslavia ("the land of the southern Slavs").

In the face of different languages and scripts (Roman and Cyrillic) the coins introduced in 1920 had an anepigraphic obverse with the royal arms alone, while the reverse had the numerals of value with "Para" in both scripts. Higher denominations, portraying Alexander I, appeared in 1925 [11–12]. When coins were next issued, in 1938, they merely featured a crown on the obverse but were now inscribed with the new country name.

Yugoslavia was overrun by Germany in 1941 and dismembered. Zinc coins with the double-headed eagle were issued in Serbia in 1942, while the puppet fascist state of Croatia issued zinc 1 and 2 kune as well as gold 500 kune in 1941. The half-Croat leader Josip Broz, known as Marshal Tito, eventually drove out the Germans and Italians and restored the country in 1945. Coins now bore the emblem of the Federal People's Republic. They were inscribed in Cyrillic alone [13–14] until the formation of the Socialist Federal Republic in 1963, when the equivalent in the Roman alphabet was added [15–16, 17–18]. From 1965 the denomination was rendered in all four different languages [19–22].

Beginning in 1970 with coins for the FAO "Food for All" programme, Yugoslavia produced commemorative and special issues in denominations from 5 dinara upwards, notably for the Winter Olympics at Sarajevo (1984).

Ancient Warriors

Macedonia, in the heart of the Balkans, has long been the subject of bitter disputes between Serbia, Bulgaria and Greece. It was from here that Philip of Macedon set out to conquer Greece, creating the empire later expanded by Alexander the Great. The Macedonian kingdom of Paeonia was one of the most important sites of ancient coin production and struck silver coins on the Greek model, such as this tetradrachm showing a head of Apollo (obverse) and a Paeonian cavalryman lancing a foot soldier, who is defending himself with shield and spear. Today it forms part of the Republic of Macedonia, which has the epithet "Former Yugoslavia" at the insistence of Greece, whose most northerly province is also called Macedonia.

DISINTEGRATION

After Tito's death in 1980 the six component republics began to drift apart, culminating in the break-up of 1990–1. The secessionist movement began in Croatia and swiftly spread to Slovenia, these republics having formerly been part of Hungary and Austria respectively. Macedonia [23] and Bosnia-Herzegovina also declared their independence, despite strenuous protests from Greece regarding the former and the rivalries of Croatia and Serbia over the latter. In the mid-1990s Serb Orthodox, Croat Catholic and Bosnian Muslim factions fought each other. The Serbs of southern Croatia even formed their own Serbian Republic of Krajina. Serbia and Montenegro alone maintained the fiction of Yugoslavia and coins thus inscribed appeared until 2002, latterly assailed by inflation, which witnessed coins up to 100,000 dinara. The currency was reformed three times in 1992–4 as ten, then a million and latterly a billion old dinara were revalued at one novi dinar [24–25].

Croatia had emerged as a fascist state in 1941 and introduced the kuna (from the word for a marten, reflecting the use of fur as currency in the Middle Ages). On regaining independence Croatia tariffed its kuna of 100 lipa at 1000 old dinara. Coins from 1 lipa to 25 kuna have the numerals of value superimposed on the national emblem on the obverse, with birds, animals and flora on the reverse [26–27]. Commemorative silver or gold coins of 25, 100, 200, 500 or 1000 kuna have appeared since 1994 [28]. Slovenia adopted the tolar (dollar) of 100 stotinov and has aluminium or brass coins with the value (obverse) and fauna (reverse) [29–30]. Many special issues from 5 to 500 tolarjev have appeared since 1991. Macedonia has had coins featuring wildlife since 1993, based on the denar of 100 deni [31–33]. Despite political divisions within the Croat-Muslim Federation of Bosnia and Herzegovina and the Serb Republic, a common currency is used [34–35].

ALBANIA, BULGARIA AND ROMANIA

These three countries lie in the southern Balkans, but apart from geography they have very little in common. Ethnically, culturally and linguistically, they are each unique. Distinctive coins appeared in the regions as far back as the 5th century BC, reflecting the successive influence of the Greek, Roman, Byzantine and Venetian worlds. Bulgaria was a major power until it fell under Turkish rule in 1395. In modern times, all three countries were kingdoms before World War II and people's republics from the 1940s until the collapse of communism in the 1990s. In the 1890s both Bulgaria and Romania issued gold coins that conformed to the French 20 franc piece, which was the standard in the Latin Monetary Union.

Left: During the 5th and 4th centuries BC the Greek colony of Olbia, a thriving port on the Black Sea, produced large coins cast from copper mined locally. Many of these curious pieces depict leaping dolphins and quasi-religious symbols. Quite unlike the usual Greek coins, they are believed to have originated as votive offerings to Apollo.

ALBANIA

The earliest coins in this area were struck at Apollonia (near modern Pojani), a colony founded in 588 BC by Greeks from Corfu. It struck its own coins until 229 BC, when it was annexed to the Roman Republic.

A Turkish province until 1912, Albania was fought over during the Balkan Wars and World War I. It was successively a principality (1914), a republic (1925) and a kingdom (1928). Coinage was not adopted until 1926, based on the lek of 100 qindar. The higher values portrayed President Ahmet Zogu, who later became King Zog I. The bronze or nickel coins were mostly struck in Rome and apart from the double-headed eagle on the 5 qindar and the half lek, motifs drew heavily on those of ancient Rome. The 20 franga of 1922 [1–2] had a reverse showing the Albanian double-headed eagle, but it was superseded in 1926 by a coin portraying medieval hero George Castriota Skanderbeg [3] with the winged lion of St Mark (a Venetian symbol) on the reverse [4]. In 1937–8

gold coins with King Zog facing right [5] had armorial reverses that celebrated the 25th anniversary of independence, the king's marriage and 10th anniversary of his reign [6], shortly before he fled the country. Victor Emmanuel III graced the coins issued in 1939–41.

Enver Hoxha led the partisans during World War II and emerged as head of the People's Socialist Republic, whose aluminium or zinc coins appeared from 1947 [7–9]. Steel or brass coins since 1995 have had various pictorial images on the obverse and a wreathed value on the reverse. Silver and gold coins proliferated from 1968, beginning with a series honouring Castriota Skanderbeg.

BULGARIA

The towns on the Black Sea coast of what is now Bulgaria struck Greek-style coins from the 4th century BC. Chief among them was Apollonia Pontica, which struck drachmae in 450–400 BC showing the Gorgon and maritime motifs such as a crayfish and an anchor [10–13]. Distinctive coins appeared in

Thrace from the 3rd century BC. Handsome drachmae were minted at Odessus (now Varna) in the period of the Mithridatic Wars with Rome (127–70 BC) with the head of Alexander and seated Zeus [14–15], and coins were minted at Serdica as a Roman and then a Byzantine province.

Straddling the northern Aegean and Black Seas, the area was settled by the Bulgars in the 7th century and flourished in the Middle Ages, striking its own coins from the early 13th century [16–17]. It became a principality in 1878, nominally under Turkish control, but joined forces with Eastern Roumelia in 1885 to form Bulgaria. Prince Ferdinand of Saxe-Coburg was appointed ruler in 1887 and proclaimed himself king in 1908.

Coins based on the lev of 100 stotinki were adopted in 1881 [18], with an armorial obverse. The silver (from 1891) and gold (from 1894) portrayed Ferdinand until 1916. Some 1 and 2 leva coins appeared between 1923 and 1941–3, but there were no other coins until 1951 when brass or cupro-nickel pieces from 1 to 25 stotinki were released by the people's republic, which abolished the monarchy in 1946 [19–22]. Further issues appeared in 1962 [23] and 1974 [24].

The return to democracy in 1992 was signalled by new coins from 20 stotinki to 50 leva, with obverses featuring ancient sculpture. In July 1999 the currency was reformed, 10,000 old leva being worth 1 new lev, and brass or cupro-nickel coins from 1 to 50 stotinki had a standard obverse. Numerous gold or silver commemoratives have been minted since the 1960s.

ROMANIA

The Roman province of Dacia bordering the Black Sea has retained the Latin influence in its language as well as its name, although the Christian principalities of Moldavia and Wallachia in the eastern Danube valley were under Turkish rule until 1877. A wide variety of coins was produced in this area from the 3rd century BC, long before the

Reflected Glory

Romania harked back to the time of Michael the Brave (1601) and Ferdinand I in World War I, portrayed alongside King Michael in the gold 20 lei coin of 1944 celebrating the restoration of territories formerly lost to Hungary and Russia. The reverse bore the arms of all 11 provinces, grouped around the crown.

arrival of the Romans. In the Middle Ages the princes of Moldavia and Wallachia struck coins, before and after the area came under Turkish control. Transylvania, now part of Romania, was successively under Hungarian or Habsburg rule, and an independent principality at various times. In each period, it produced distinctive coins.

The ruler of the Danubian principalities, Alexander Cuza, was ousted in 1866 and Prince Karl of Hohenzollern-Sigmaringen was appointed in his place. Karl (Carol) proclaimed himself king in 1881. Coins based on the leu of 100 bani, with the arms of the Danubian principalities and inscribed "Romania", were introduced in 1867 [25], followed by a series portraying Carol I (obverse) and the arms (reverse) [26–29]. Few coins below 50 bani were issued for general circulation between 1906 and 1952 [30–31]; in the interim Romania was ravaged by two World Wars, suffered inflation and ceased to be a monarchy in 1947. In the 1950s coins of the people's republic had the communist emblem and the value on the obverse and reverse. A new series in clad steel appeared in 1965–9, marking the change to a socialist republic, and since 1989 coins have reverted to the original title of Romania [32–35] with arms or symbols on the obverse.

GREECE

The cradle of Western civilization and a major contributor to the origin and development of democracy, the arts, architecture and, of course, coinage, Greece fell under the domination of the Roman Empire in the 2nd century BC and was part of the Byzantine Empire until 1453, when it came under Turkish rule. Thereafter coins were struck in various parts of what is now Greece, by the crusader Dukes of Athens [1–2], the Princes of Achaea, and under the auspices of the Knights of St John in Rhodes (until 1522), such as Grand Master Dieudonné de Gozon, who rebuilt the Kingdom of Rhodes in the 14th century [3–4]. Venetian and Genoese trading companies also struck coins in a number of Frankish principalities. Greece retained its distinct language and culture under Turkish rule and a revolt in 1821 triggered off the nationalist movement that led to the creation of a Greek state by 1827. In 1833 the European Powers recognized the sovereignty of Greece, choosing Prince Otto of Bavaria as its king.

Left: Many modern Greek coins use images from coins of ancient Greece: this brass 100 drachma piece of 1990–2000 portrayed Alexander the Great as king of the Macedonians – part of the ongoing propaganda campaign against the independent Republic of Macedonia.

FIRST KINGDOM

The newly independent state revived the ancient coinage system of the drachma of 100 lepta. Copper 1 and 5 lepta appeared in 1828 with a cross above a phoenix, symbolizing the rebirth of the country. Other denominations soon followed, with silver coins portraying King Otto in 1833 [5–6]. Otto was deposed in 1862 and in his place the Powers elected George, second son of King Christian of Denmark [7–10]. He reigned from 1863 to 1913, when he was assassinated during a state visit to Salonika, recently acquired as a result of the Second Balkan War. During his long reign his portrait was extended to the smaller coins. New types appeared in 1912, including holed 5, 10 and 20 lepta with the first essays in pictorialism, reviving the owl [11–12] and Athena motifs from ancient coins.

Relatively few Greek coins portrayed the reigning monarch, so the revolts and factiousness of the ensuing decade are not reflected in the obverses. Constantine I was forced to abdicate in World War I for his pro-German sympathies. Restored to the throne, he was driven out again in 1922 following a disastrous campaign to seize the seaboard of Asia Minor from Turkey. He was briefly succeeded by his son, George II, but he too was ousted, and Greece then became a republic.

FIRST REPUBLIC

The monarchy was overthrown by Eleftherios Venizelos, who had worked closely with the British and French during World War I. The republic lasted until 1935, when George II was restored to the throne. During this period Greece abandoned royal symbolism on its coins; instead the country looked back to the glories of ancient Greece for inspiration, using the helmeted Athena from Corinthian coins for the series of 1926 from 20 lepta to 2 drachmae. In 1930 a nickel 5 drachma coin featured the phoenix derived from the coins of 1828 [13–14], while 10 and 20 drachmae revived ancient types respectively showing Demeter the corn goddess and an ear of wheat or Poseidon the sea god with the prow of a galley. The 5 drachma coin was struck in London and Brussels, distinguished by dots in the berries on the reverse.

MONARCHY RESTORED

Discontent with the republic led to a plebiscite on November 3, 1935, which voted in favour of restoring the monarchy. King George II returned to Athens and was formally restored to his throne on November 25. This was celebrated by gold and silver 20 and 100 drachma coins showing the king and the date of his restoration, although the coins themselves were not actually minted until 1940 [15–16]. The republican coins remained in general circulation and it is remarkable that, apart from these commemoratives, no further coins were issued until 1954 [17–18].

Greece was occupied by Nazi Germany in World War II and suffered inflation for many years, making coinage impractical. George II went into exile in 1941 but was restored for a third time in 1946 and succeeded the following year by his brother Paul, whose profile appears on the middle values of 1954–65 [19–20], though Selene the moon goddess was reserved for the 20 drachmae. Constantine II's reign began auspiciously in 1964 with

Blend of Ancient and Modern

The best example of the way in which modern Greece identifies with its ancient past is seen in the 10 drachma coins since 1976: the portrait of the philosopher Democritus (c. 460–370 BC), who devised the atomic system, is linked to a reverse showing a symbolic representation of an atom.

a 30 drachma silver coin showing the conjoined busts of the young king and his bride, Anne-Marie of Denmark. The permanent series bore his profile and the national arms [21–22].

SECOND REPUBLIC

When a military junta seized power in 1967 Constantine attempted a counter coup. It failed and he fled to Rome. The dictatorial regime of the Greek colonels deposed the king and abolished the monarchy in 1973. Ironically, new coins appeared in 1971 with Constantine's profile (obverse) and the phoenix emblem. Two years later a series appeared with the figure of a soldier superimposed on the phoenix, but the figure was soon removed [24]. The reverse of the series took motifs from ancient coins [23], including the owl and Pegasus, the winged horse [25]. The 1 and 2 drachma coins were inspired by the wars of independence, with portraits of Konstantinos Kanaris and Georgios Karaiskakis [26–7] on the obverse and various motifs symbolic of that period on the reverse [28], but the higher values reverted to classical motifs with Democritus, Pericles, Solon and Homer on the obverse and appropriate pictorial images on the reverse [29–30]. In the 1990s the circulating coinage became a medium for profiling Greek personalities of more recent times [31–32]. Classical motifs, however, have been used for the Greek versions of the euro coinage.

Commemorative coins from 50 to 1000 drachmae (silver) and 2500 to 20,000 drachmae (gold) proliferated from 1975 onward; many had sporting themes, from the Pan-European Games (1981) to the Chess Olympics (1988). For the Athens Olympic Games in 2004 Greece produced a prolific series showing Athenian landmarks and Olympic sports harking back to the Ancient Games. It included a 500 drachma piece portraying Pierre de Coubertin, father of the modern Games, alongside Demetrios Vikelas who organized the first modern Olympics at Athens in 1896 [33–34].

ITALY

The history of coinage in Italy goes back to the cumbersome cast copper coins of the 3rd century BC [1–2], but under the influence of the Greek colonies gold staters [3–4] and silver drachmae were struck in various parts of the Italian peninsula from the 4th century BC. As a political entity, Italy dates only from 1861. After the fall of the western Roman Empire in 476, the Italian peninsula was divided into petty kingdoms, city states and papal dominions, each with its own distinctive coins. In the Middle Ages Milan and Florence took a leading role in the revival of realism in coin design, while Venice created a great commercial empire in the Adriatic and eastern Mediterranean, and its coinage was a major influence in that area. Italy was finally unified under Victor Emanuel II of Piedmont, Savoy and Sardinia.

Below: In 1922 Benito Mussolini seized power in Italy and created the world's first Fascist country. While Mussolini wielded dictatorial powers as Il Duce ("the leader"),

Victor Emanuel III continued as king. After the annexation of Abyssinia (Ethiopia) in 1936 Victor Emmanuel was styled as King and Emperor and the coins of this period bore dates in the Fascist era as well as the Christian calendar.

ITALIAN STATES

The Kingdom of Naples and Sicily emerged by 1130, but was under the rule of Spain or Austria from 1502 until 1733, when the Bourbon Prince Carlos became king [5–6]. It was sometimes called the Kingdom of the Two Sicilies, as on coins of Joachim Murat, styling himself Gioacchino Napoleon (1808–15) [12–13]. Sardinia was alternately ruled by Pisa and Genoa before falling to Aragon in 1297. It remained under Spanish rule until 1720, when it became part of the dominions of the House of Savoy and the nucleus of the future Kingdom of Italy.

Powerful families, such as the Sforzas of Milan, the Gonzagas of Mantua and the Medicis of Florence created city-states in the medieval period that came to wield enormous commercial influence and produced attractive gold and silver coins, such as this Florentine half tallero of Cosimo III (1670–1723) [7]. From the 16th century, however, the Italian city-states began to fall under the sway of France, Spain and Austria, and only the Republic of Venice maintained its independence until 1798. A silver ducat of 1676–84 shows the Doge of Venice kneeling before St Mark, the city's patron saint [8–9]. Napoleon Bonaparte briefly redrew the map of Italy in the 1790s, first creating a series of republics and then a kingdom under his personal rule (1804–14). Under Napoleon, coins bore his left-facing profile (obverse) and the crowned and mantled arms of his Italian kingdom (reverse) [10–11].

The Congress of Versailles of 1815 awarded Lombardy and Venetia to Austria; coins with the Lombard crown or the Austrian eagle, based on the scudo of 6 lire, 120 soldi or 600 centesimi, were issued from 1822 until 1866, when the kingdom fell to Italy. Naples and Sicily had a complex coinage based on the ducato or tallero (dollar) [14–15] of 100 grana, but 120 grana were also worth a piastra, 6 tari, 12 carlini or 240 tornese, while 6 cavalli made a tornese. In 1813 the currency was reformed and the franco or lira of 100 centesimi was adopted.

The Duchies of Parma, Modena and Tuscany, as well as the States of the Church, each had distinctive coinage. Piedmont and Sardinia each had their own currency systems, based on the doppia of 2880 denari or the doppietta of 1200 denari respectively, but from

1816 the lira of 100 centesimi was in use and it eventually extended to the whole of Italy.

KINGDOM OF ITALY

The campaign of 1859–60 known as the Risorgimento, led by Giuseppe Garibaldi, resulted in the unification of Italy under the House of Savoy, and coins portraying Victor Emanuel II were introduced in 1861 [16–17]. The Pope, under French protection, held out until 1870, but on the withdrawal of the French garrison Rome finally became the capital of a united Italy.

The reverse of the coins showed the value, but from 1908 onward, a more allegorical treatment was adopted, often using images that harked back to the Roman Empire [18–22]. Exceptionally, between 1894 and 1936, the 20 centesimi had either a crown, a Roman profile or the royal arms on the obverse. The use of imperial imagery increased from 1936 onward, with the rebirth of an empire that Mussolini hoped would encompass the Mediterranean [23]. Italy pioneered stainless steel as a coinage metal (1939) and bimetallic coins (1982).

REPUBLIC

During World War II, Italy was originally allied to Nazi Germany, but it changed sides in 1943 when Mussolini was overthrown, later to be captured and executed by partisans. Umberto II succeeded his father as king in 1946, but by referendum the monarchy was abolished and Italy declared a republic.

After the welter of wartime coins as the currency became depreciated, postwar Italy had a relatively stable coinage, with aluminium 1, 5 and 10 lira coins [24–25], aluminium-bronze 20 lire coins [26–27], stainless steel 50 and 100 lire and silver 500 lire. Allegorical portraits and imagery derived from classical motifs predominated. The size of the coins was reduced in 1951 and cupro-nickel was substituted for stainless steel in the 50 and 100 lira coins in 1993–6. A 200 lire in aluminium-bronze was introduced in 1977 and a

---

Vacant See

Distinctive coins are issued by the Vatican during the period between the death of a Pope and the election of his successor. These coins, inscribed "Sede Vacante" (Latin for "empty chair"), follow a tradition going back many centuries.

---

bimetallic 500 lire was adopted in 1982 [28–29]. Coins of this denomination continued to be minted in silver as collector's pieces. The 100, 200 and 500 lire were often struck as commemoratives from 1974 onward.

SAN MARINO AND THE VATICAN

The tiny mountain Republic of San Marino, which had been independent since AD 350, began issuing small bronze coins in 1864 and silver in 1898, but Italian coins predominated. Since 1972, San Marino has revived its coinage, producing a different series annually, mainly as tourist souvenirs but also including commemorative gold and silver scudi.

Papal coinage was suppressed in 1870 but revived in 1929, when the Vatican City State was created under the terms of the Lateran Treaty. These coins generally portray the Pope, with religious, allegorical or symbolic motifs on the reverse.

Above: A coin of Pope Pius XI from 1931, showing the papal arms and the Virgin Mary.

FRANCE

The Gaul of Roman times, France became the kingdom of the Franks and, under Charlemagne in the 9th century, the leading power in Europe. Central power weakened in the Middle Ages, with the rise of petty kingdoms such as Brittany and Navarre, and it was not until the early 17th century that France emerged as a highly centralized state. It attained its greatest power under Louis XIV, who came to the throne in 1643 at the age of five [1–2], but the autocratic monarchy was unstable and collapsed in the Revolution of 1789, which led to the First Republic in 1792. This was followed by the Napoleonic Empire (1804–14), the restoration of the monarchy (1814–48), the Second Republic (1848–52), the Second Empire (1852–71), the Third Republic (1871–1940), the fascist Vichy state (1940–4), the Fourth Republic (1944–58) and the Fifth Republic instituted by President Charles de Gaulle, which continues to this day.

Left: Louis Napoleon Bonaparte, nephew of Napoleon I, was elected president of the Second Republic but engineered a coup in 1852, restoring the Bonapartist Empire and taking the title of Napoleon III. On coinage his profile acquired victor's laurels in 1861, following a series of French victories in the campaign for the unification of Italy. France flourished under his rule but the monarchy collapsed as a result of the disastrous war with Germany in 1870–1.

MEDIEVAL COINAGE

Coin production was devolved to the towns and districts of medieval France. Many of the nobility struck their own coins, creating an immense field of study [7–9]. Anglo-Gallic coins were struck in the regions under English rule during the Hundred Years' War.

The regal coinage was reformed by Louis XI (1461–83) after he defeated the English and broke the power of the nobility. Separate coinage continued in Brittany and Navarre until Henry of Navarre took the throne as Henry IV in 1589. The third son of Antoine de Bourbon, Henry established a royal dynasty that was to rule France for the next two centuries.

REVOLUTION AND EMPIRE

In the period prior to the Revolution, French coinage became increasingly complex. The mouton d'or [3–4], a 14th-century gold coin, depicted the lamb of God, and was followed by the ecu d'or [5–6]. Others followed, including the angel, angelot, teston

[10–11], pavillon d'or, louis d'or and pistole. Latterly the currency was based on the gold livre of 20 sols or 240 deniers [12–13].

Following the abolition of the monarchy in 1792, some livres and sols were struck in 1793–4 with republican motifs. The transition of power is reflected in the coins portraying Louis XVI but with a reverse showing the

---

A Record of Longevity

The standing figure of Marianne as a sower of seed was adopted for the silver coinage in 1898 and continued until 1920, but following the currency reform of 1958 she was restored and continued until the advent of the euro.

Above: Marianne, the personification of the French Republic, has been a popular obverse motif. Some of her many guises are shown here on coins of 1872, 1849, 1904 and 1931.

Phrygian cap, fasces and Gallic cock flanking an angel writing a new constitution, with the date expressed as year 5 of Liberty [14–15] in the revolutionary calendar. In this period money rapidly collapsed and coins were replaced by paper currency known as assignats and mandats. In 1794 the currency was reformed and coins based on the franc of 10 decimes or 100 centimes were introduced. These had the head of Marianne, the allegory of Liberty, on the obverse while the reverse bore the value and the date expressed as *L'an* (the year) followed by a number from 4 to 9 (1793–1808).

Although Napoleon had proclaimed himself emperor in 1804, three years elapsed before the first coins bearing the initial N appeared [16–17]. Silver coins portrayed him as first consul and later as emperor.

LATER COINAGE
The Bourbon dynasty was restored in 1814 and silver and gold coins portraying Louis XVIII appeared in 1816 [18–19], followed by those portraying Charles X (1824–30) [20] and Louis Philippe (1830–48) [21–22]. No bronze coins for small change appeared until the overthrow of the monarchy in 1848. After this, Marianne was again portrayed. Silver 1 and 2 francs appeared in 1852, with Louis

Napoleon Bonaparte as president, but from 1853 Napoleon III (obverse) and the imperial eagle (reverse) were the norm [23–26]. After the downfall of the empire, the female allegory Liberty, in various guises, was restored.

France was the driving force behind the creation of the Latin Monetary Union in 1865, which created a coinage standard for Belgium, Italy and Switzerland that endured until 1927. The circulating coins of the French Republic rank among the most artistic in the world and from the 1870s reflected a gradual change from Neoclassicism [27–28] to Art Nouveau in the 1890s and Art Deco after World War I. There have also been a wide variety of base-metal alloys, from bronze and nickel before World War I, through the aluminium of the Vichy era and the postwar period before the advent of the "heavy franc" in 1958, to chrome steel, aluminium-bronze and nickel-brass. Many commemoratives have appeared in recent years, often in base metal for general circulation.

MONACO
The tiny principality on the French Riviera has had its own coinage since the late Middle Ages. Modern coinage, based on the French decimal system, dates from 1837, when 5 centime coins were cast in brass or struck in copper along with silver 5 franc pieces. Gold 20 and 100 francs appeared in the 1880s, but lower denominations were not released until the 1940s, conforming to the French specifications [29–30]. Coins were minted sporadically from then until 1974, but since then dates have been changed annually. Some high-denomination commemoratives have appeared in recent years.

Above: Prince Rainier III and the crowned arms of the Grimaldi family.

IBERIAN PENINSULA

The most south-westerly part of Europe was fought over and conquered by Phoenicians, Carthaginians, Greeks and Romans. Silver coins were struck at Gades (now Cadiz) on Greek lines [1–2] and copper denarii appeared before the beginning of the Christian era [3]. The Visigoths and Moors also left their mark on the coinage, but by the 12th century Christian kingdoms were beginning to emerge [4–5]. In the late 15th century the regions of Aragon and Castile were united by the marriage of their rulers, Ferdinand and Isabella [7–8], and the Moors were driven out in 1492 – the very year that Columbus set sail for the New World, whose mineral wealth would make Spain the richest and most powerful nation in Europe. Spain was also one of the major components of the Habsburg Empire in the 16th and 17th centuries and exerted a major influence on its coinage. Portugal was one of the kingdoms to emerge in the 12th century and managed to resist the encroachment of Spain, apart from the period 1581–1640. Both countries won and lost vast colonial empires, followed by political instability, the downfall of monarchy and the rise of fascist dictatorships before the establishment of democracy in the 1970s.

Left: The silver peso a ocho reales, or "piece of eight", featured the Spanish royal arms on one side and a depiction of the Pillars of Hercules (the Straits of Gibraltar) on the other, for which reason it is often known as the Pillar Dollar.

SPAIN

The silver and gold of the Americas flooded Europe from the 16th to the late-18th centuries and transformed the Spanish peso a ocho reales into the world's most popular coin and a role model for the dollar currencies ever since [6]. The gold escudo was worth 16 silver reales, while 34 copper maravedis equalled a silver real. This system was replaced by decimal coinage in 1848 based on the real of 10 decimos or 100 centimos, changed to the escudo of 100 centimos in 1864 and finally to the peseta of 100 centimos in 1868.

In the monarchical periods the obverse portrayed the reigning king or queen, with an armorial device on the reverse. Intermittent coinage during the 1870s [9–10] meant that the first republic (1873–4) came and went without note. Alfonso XIII, born after his father's death, was king from 1886 to 1931, and the early coins of his reign portrayed him successively as a baby and in various phases of childhood.

After the monarchy was overthrown in 1931 a few coins inscribed "Republica Espanola" appeared in 1934–7. In the early years of the nationalist regime, coinage was equally meagre, and it was not until 1947 that something like a regular series was adopted [11–12], with the portrait of General Franco as El Caudillo ("the leader") on the obverse [13] and national arms on the reverse. Although Spain was technically a kingdom from 1949, it was not until the death of Franco in 1975 that its monarchy was restored in the person of King Juan Carlos, grandson of Alfonso XIII.

Spanish coins often have a fixed date, the actual year of production being indicated by tiny numerals within an eight-pointed star, the mark of the Madrid Mint [14]. Conversely, letters after the date are those of mint officials. In recent years some handsome commemoratives have been released, notably for the World Cup football championship (1982) and the Barcelona Olympics (1992) [15].

PORTUGAL

Like that of Spain, the currency of Portugal [16–17] was originally based on the silver real, but higher values were covered by *moeda ouro* (literally "gold money"), hence the term *moidore*. Portugal's commercial power was largely derived from the gold of the Guinea Coast, exemplified by this 4000 reis of João V, 1720 [18–19]. The monarch subsequently received the title "King of Portugal and Guinea".

As Portugal declined in uwealth and importance in the 18th century the value of the real fell to the point at which it vanished altogether. The smallest copper coin was the 3 reis (the Portuguese form of *reales*) but its multiples included the 10 reis [20], vintem (20 reis) [23], pataca (40), tostão (100), cruzado (480), escudo (1600) and the 8 escudo (6400) such as this coin of Carlos IV [21–22]. This cumbersome system continued until the overthrow of the monarchy in 1910, when the escudo of 100 centavos was adopted.

In the closing months of the monarchy, large silver coins celebrated the centenary of the defeat of Napoleon in the Peninsular War or honoured the Marquis de Pombal, the 18th-century statesman who rebuilt Lisbon after the earthquake of 1755. There was a great variety of types in the reis coinage, with the royal effigy or crowned shield (obverse) and value, arms or a cross (reverse). The same approach was adopted in the republican decimal coinage, on which various effigies of Liberty facing left or right [25] replaced the regal portraits. At first the reverses showed either the arms, minus the royal crown, or a wreathed value, but a more pictorial style gradually developed in the 1930s, notably in the silver coins that featured the flagship of the navigator Vasco da Gama [24].

While Portugal's circulating coinage has remained relatively conservative in style and treatment, the commemorative and special issues have escalated in recent years, recording anniversaries of numerous historic events, from the medieval explorations to the revolution of 1974 [26–7].

ANDORRA

The tiny principality of Andorra in the valleys of the Pyrenees is a feudal anachronism: the Counts of Foix (in France) and the Bishops of Urgel (Spain) have ruled it as co-princes since 1278. As a result, French and Spanish currency has circulated freely ever since. Since 1982, however, distinctive coins based on the diner (denier) of 100 centims have been struck, mainly as tourist souvenirs [28–30], along with silver and gold coins aimed at the numismatic market. Some of these coins bear the bust of the Bishop of Urgel (the role of the Comte de Foix has now passed to the President of France), but most feature the arms of the principality. Andorra even produced ecus, but now uses the euro.

Above: Recent motifs on coins of Andorra have ranged from wildlife (such as this Pyrenean goat) to historical figures such as Charlemagne, who granted the valleys their first charter.

AFRICA

Historically regarded as the Dark Continent, Africa is today home to many of the Third World's poorest countries. Exploited by the rest of the world for centuries and now hampered by colossal debt and unfair trade, it has experienced political turmoil, tyranny and corruption.

NORTH AFRICA

The portion of the continent on the southern shores of the Mediterranean came into contact with the civilizations of Greece and Rome, but long before that period the coastal regions were dominated by Egypt and colonized by the Phoenicians, who created the great power of Carthage, which challenged the might of Rome in the 3rd century BC. Coins struck to Greek standards date from the 6th century BC at Cyrene, such as the horned head of Karneios, counterpart of Apollo [1–2], and from about 410 BC at Carthage, bearing the profile of Tanit, the Carthaginian counterpart of Persephone (obverse) and a horse's head (reverse) [3–4]. Later coins featured entire horses or lions, and both gold and electrum pieces were also struck. The large silver coins, up to 12 drachmae, were heavily influenced by those of Sicily. By 146 BC, Carthage had been conquered and thereafter Roman coins were in use [5–6]. Some coins were also struck by the Berber kingdoms from the third century BC. In the Dark Ages Carthage was overrun by the Vandals but a Byzantine mint flourished briefly, and from the 8th century Islamic coinage was in use. After the death of Haroun al Rashid the power of the Caliphate was divided, and thereafter Ifriquiyah (Africa) became increasingly separate, with its own dynasties issuing Islamic coins in their own names, such as an 8th-century dirham in the name of Haroun's successor [7–8]. By the 14th century the Barbary states (Algeria, Morocco and Tunisia) were emerging; though continuing with the basic Islamic types, they gradually introduced their own distinctive features.

Left: Obverse and reverse of a silver coin of Juba I, king of Numidia in the first century BC. Juba, of Phoenician descent, ruled over Numidia, Mauritania and Libya. In pursuance of his ambitions to create an empire in North Africa he allied himself with the Roman Senate in their struggle against Julius Caesar and struck vast quantities of these coins to finance his campaign.

ALGERIA

The important city and seaport of Algiers was founded in 950 on earlier Phoenician and Roman settlements. Nominally subject to the sultans of Tlemcen, it achieved autonomy in the 15th century and became a commercial centre following the expulsion of the Jews and Moors from Spain in 1492. Although part of the Ottoman Empire from 1518 the Turks gave the Barbary corsairs a free hand, which is reflected in the distinctive coins struck at Timilsan (modern Tlemcen) by Murad III [9–10].

It was to suppress piracy that the French invaded in 1830, annexing Algeria in 1848. Coins modelled on Turkish weights and values were struck at Algiers and Constantine, and also at Mascara and Taqident during the revolt of Abd-el-Kader (1834–47). Latterly

Libya

Nominally part of the Ottoman Empire until 1911, the region of North Africa west of Egypt fell to the Italians in 1934, and they named it "Libia", the Latin name for the territory. Under Turkish rule the pashas, or governors, had struck copper and billon coins for small change, but it was not until 1952 that coins were adopted by this newly created kingdom, with the bust of Idris I on the obverse. The monarchy was overthrown in 1969, and Libya was declared a socialist people's republic, but coins with the republican emblem were not produced until 1975.

the coinage was based on the silver budju of 24 muzuna or 48 kharuba, along with the gold sultani and its subdivisions. French coins were normally circulated, but during World War I token coins were issued by the chambers of commerce. Coins with the head of Marianne, corresponding to the French style but inscribed "Algerie" on the reverse, were introduced in 1949–50. Independence was proclaimed in July 1962 and coins of the Algerian Republic appeared in 1964, based on the dinar of 100 centimes [11–12]. A new series, from the aluminium quarter dinar to the bimetallic 100 dinar coin, was adopted in 1992. A number of commemoratives have been issued since the tenth anniversary of Algerian independence.

MOROCCO

Of immense strategic importance at the western end of the Mediterranean, Morocco was successively ruled by Phoenicians, Romans, Vandals, Visigoths, Byzantines and Arabs.

Around 1062 Berber tribes, migrating northwards from Senegal, established themselves at Marrakesh. The Almoravids were so named from the Arabic for "those from the frontier posts". By 1086 they had extended their rule from Algiers to southern Spain. Various dynasties rose and fell, such as the Murabitid [13–14], but the Sharifs of Tafilat gained power in 1660 and have ruled ever since. From this period belongs the dirham struck at Madrid for issue in Marrakesh [15–16]. European rivalries resulted in the partition of Morocco into Spanish and French protectorates in 1912, but sovereignty was regained in 1957.

Coins, struck at Fez, Rabat, Tetuan and Marrakesh, conformed to Islamic styles, although from the early 19th century onward Solomon's seal (a five-pointed star) was a prominent feature [17]. The currency was reformed in the 1890s, based on the rial of 10 dirhams or 500 mazunas, with inscriptions entirely in Arabic except for a date of the Muslim calendar in western numerals. In 1921 the coinage was changed to the dirham of 100 francs, the only decorative feature being a five-pointed star. Following the resumption of independence portraits of Muhammad V appeared on the higher values [19–20]. The currency was changed in 1974 to the dirham of 100 santimat [18].

TUNISIA

The suppression of the Barbary pirates virtually bankrupted Tunis and enabled the French to establish a protectorate in 1881. Previously, successive beys (governors) had issued coins in the name of the Turkish sultan [21–22]. Similar coins, with the Paris mintmark, were struck until 1891, when the franc was adopted. Thereafter, coins were inscribed in Arabic (obverse) or French (reverse). Tunisia became a republic in 1957 and introduced a coinage based on the dinar of 1000 millim [23–26], showing a tree or President Bourguiba on the obverse. A few commemoratives have been issued since 1976.

EGYPT AND SUDAN

Pharaonic Egypt had a sophisticated weighed-metal system, which did not require round pieces of metal but relied on standard weights of silver for certain transactions. Athenian tetradrachms were circulating in Egypt by the 5th century BC. Pharaoh Nectanebo II (359–343 BC) struck a gold stater inscribed "Neft Nub" ("good gold") in hieroglyphics and a few silver tetradrachms with indigenous inscriptions are known from around the same period. A distinctive coinage on Greek lines was adopted by Ptolemy I, one of Alexander the Great's generals, who in 304 BC established the Hellenistic kingdom that ended with the suicide of Cleopatra in 30 BC. Greek influence is clearly seen in the tetradrachms of Ptolemy I [1–2] and Ptolemy VI [3–4] of the 4th and 2nd centuries BC. Under Roman rule, Egypt was allowed a subsidiary coinage for local circulation, the output of these coins from the imperial mint at Alexandria being very prolific [5–8].

Left: Ali Bey al Kabir, born in the Caucasus (now Abkhazia), seized power in 1760 and established the Neo-Mamluk Beylicate, repudiating allegiance to the Turkish sultan. Distinctive coins of this period bear Arabic inscriptions on both sides.

BYZANTINE PERIOD

At the division of the Roman Empire Egypt passed under eastern control and Alexandria continued to strike copper nummia until 646 – some years after Egypt fell to the Arabs in 642. These coins were produced in unusual multiples of 3, 6, 12 and 33 nummia. Gold coins were minted sporadically, but later in some abundance towards the end of Byzantine rule, under Heraclius (610–41). The motifs conformed to Byzantine standards, with facing portraits of the emperor and his son Constans on the obverse and the stepped cross or a standing figure on the reverse. Coins portraying Heraclius flanked by the sun and moon were actually struck by Khusru II during the Sasanian occupation of 718–28.

ISLAMIC PERIOD

The Alexandria Mint was one of the casualties of the Arab conquest. When distinctive coins emerged under the Caliphate in the 9th century, coins of the Tulinids [9–10] and Ikshidids [11–12], independent governors in Egypt in the 9th and 10th centuries respectively, were struck at Cairo [13–14], Alexandria and other places.

In 969 Egypt fell to the Fatimids, who struck coins in entirely new designs at Cairo until the province was conquered by Saladin in 1171. Thereafter, coins followed the Ayyubid pattern until 1250, when Egypt became the realm of the Mamelukes [15–16]. They were in turn overthrown by the Turks in 1517. Thereafter the coinage followed the Turkish pattern. Ottoman control of Egypt declined in the late 18th century.

KINGDOM OF EGYPT

Though nominally khedive (viceroy) of the sultan, Mehemet (Mahmud) Ali created a dynasty that lasted from 1808 to 1953. The son of an Albanian tobacco merchant, he came to prominence in 1798 when he headed the Albanian–Turkish force despatched by the sultan to counter the French invasion. After the French were ousted by the British he became viceroy. He destroyed the Mamelukes (1811), conquered much of Arabia (1818) and annexed Nubia (1820). He extended his empire to Crete and Morea in Greece (1821–8) and Syria (1831) respectively, but his wish to become sultan of Constantinople was thwarted by the Quadruple Alliance (1840).

The coinage was reformed in 1835 and British coin presses were installed at the Cairo Mint. Nevertheless, the coinage continued to be very similar to the prevailing Turkish types, with the *toughra* on the obverse and elaborate Arabic inscriptions distinguished by the word "Misr" (Egypt) inscribed above the date on the reverse. The currency was based on the guerche or piastre of 40 para, but in 1885 it was extended to the pound of 100 piastres.

Egypt was under British military occupation from 1881 and formally became a British protectorate in 1914, following Turkey's entry into World War I on the side of the Central Powers. It became an independent sovereign state in 1922, when Fuad I was proclaimed king. Illustrated here is a silver 10 piastre coin with dates in both Muslim and Common Era calendars [23–4], struck by the Heaton Mint in Birmingham on behalf of Sultan Ahmed Fuad in 1920, two years before he was elevated to the kingship. Egyptian coins were dated according to the Muslim calendar until 1916, when the currency was reformed and based on the piastre of 10 milliemes; thereafter, dates were given in Arabic according to both calendars [17]. From 1924 onward the obverse bore the bust of the ruler [18–22].

Postman as National Emblem

The image on the Sudanese coins of 1956–71 is that of an Arab postman mounted on a camel, derived from the postage stamps issued from 1898 onward. So familiar was this motif (designed by Colonel E.A. Stanton during the re-conquest of the Sudan) that it became a national icon.

REPUBLIC

King Farouk reigned from 1937 until he was deposed by a military junta in 1952. He was briefly succeeded by his infant son Fuad II, but the monarchy was abolished in July 1953. The Sphinx replaced the bust of Farouk on the obverse of coins, which continued to be inscribed entirely in Arabic, the text reading "Jumhuriyya Misr Al Arabiyya" (Arab Republic of Egypt). Following union with Syria in the form of the United Arab Republic in 1958, the eagle emblem was adopted on the obverse. Syria left this union in 1961 but a decade elapsed before Egypt abandoned the grandiose title and styled itself once more as the Arab Republic of Egypt; the inscriptions on the coinage were suitably amended from 1971 onward [25–26]. The *toughra* was revived as an obverse type in 1984 [31] while higher denominations had a central hole [30], but a more pictorial approach was adopted for the circulating coins in 1992 [27–29]. Many commemorative coins have appeared since the 1960s, often harking back to the Pharaonic period.

SUDAN

This vast country south of Egypt was conquered by Mehemet Ali, seceded in 1881 during the Mahdist revolt, and was re-conquered in 1898. Gold and silver piastres were struck by the Mahdi at Khartoum (1885) and at Omdurman by his successor, the Khalifa (1885–98). From 1898 until 1954 it was an Anglo-Egyptian condominium. Autonomy was followed by the grant of full independence in 1956. Egyptian coins were used until then and the same currency, based on the pound of 100 ghirsh or 1000 millim, was retained. A democratic republic was proclaimed in 1969, signalled on the coins from 1971 by an eagle replacing the original camel motif [32–33]. Most of the special issues since 1972 marked anniversaries of independence or the 1969 revolution. The currency was reformed in 1992 and the dinar of 100 dirhems introduced [34–35].

SOUTH AFRICA

This large country at the southern tip of the continent was for centuries the most European part of Africa in its population and political character. Although the Portuguese first explored it in 1498 it was not colonized until the Dutch arrived there in 1652. The hinterland of the Cape of Good Hope fell to the British during the Napoleonic Wars and was formally annexed in 1814 as the Cape Colony. Discontent with British rule induced many of the Afrikaners (the Dutch settlers) to trek northward and establish independent republics. The subsequent discovery of gold and diamonds in these states led to friction between the Boers (Dutch farmers) and those they defined as Uitlanders (foreign incomers), culminating in the Anglo-Boer War of 1899–1902. Most South African gold was exported and had little effect on the indigenous coinage, and it was not until 1923 that a branch of the Royal Mint was established in Pretoria to produce sovereigns with the SA mint-mark [1–2].

Left: Jan van Riebeeck, portrayed on the obverse of the coins of the South African Republic (1961–9) led the expedition by the Dutch East India Company that founded Cape Town in 1652. His ship, the Dromedaaris, *was depicted on the reverse of the bronze halfpennies and pennies of 1923–60.*

EARLY COINAGE

Ordinary Dutch or British coins were used widely in southern Africa in the 17th and 18th centuries. The first distinctive pieces were issued by the Revd John Campbell, head of the mission station at Griquatown in the territory known as Griqualand, between the Kalahari Desert and the Boer republics. They consisted of copper farthings and halfpennies and silver 5 and 10 pence, depicting a phoenix on the obverse with the name of the mission and numerals of value on the reverse. They were undated but circulated in 1815–16 and are extremely rare. A pattern penny with the profile of Queen Victoria (obverse) and dove (reverse) was produced in Berlin in 1889 [3–4].

Distinctive coinage was first attempted in the South African Republic (Transvaal) in 1874, when gold pounds portraying President Thomas Burgers were struck. Only a few hundred of these Burgersponds were struck. Regular coinage, struck at Pretoria and bearing the bust of President Paul Kruger, was introduced in 1892 [11–12]; it consisted of the bronze penny, silver 3 and 5 pence, 1 shilling [13–14], 2 and 5 shillings [5–6] and gold pound [7–10]. Apart from the smaller silver coins (which showed the value in a wreath), this series bore the arms of the republic on the reverse.

UNION OF SOUTH AFRICA

British coins were in use from 1900 onward, extending from Cape Colony and Natal to cover the former Boer republics, now renamed Transvaal and Orange River Colony. Although the Union of South Africa was proclaimed in 1910 – the former colonies becoming provinces – a distinctive coinage was not introduced until 1923. This series, following British weights and specifications, ranged from the bronze ¼ penny (farthing) to the 2 shillings [15–18]. A curious feature of the 3 and 6 pence from 1925 onward was the depiction of three or six bundles of brushwood on the reverse to denote the value. The obverse portrayed the reigning monarch, with Latin titles, while the reverse was inscribed in English and Afrikaans. A silver 5 shillings was introduced in 1947 to celebrate a royal visit [19]. These coins, with a Springbok reverse, were minted on a regular basis thereafter, as well as appearing in commemorative versions. From 1923 British gold sovereigns and half sovereigns were minted at Pretoria, identifiable by the SA mint-mark, followed by distinctive half pounds and pounds in 1952.

REPUBLIC OF SOUTH AFRICA

The rise of Afrikaner nationalism after World War II, and the implementation of the racially divisive policy of apartheid ("separateness"), led to South Africa becoming a republic in May 1961 and its expulsion from the Commonwealth the following October.

A new currency, based on the rand of 100 cents, was adopted and Jan van Riebeeck replaced the royal effigy [20]. The large brass subsidiary coins [22] were replaced by small bronze 1c [21] and 2c [24] coins in 1965. In 1989, as concerns mounted over costs, three series – red, white and yellow [28–29] – of steel-plated coins were introduced, the colour depending on the usage of copper, nickel and/or tin. Depictions of South African fauna and flora were used on the high denominations [23], while the arms of the republic [25] replaced Van Riebeeck in 1970, interspersed by coins portraying the latest state president [26–27]. The blue crane – the national emblem and a threatened species – appears on the 5c [30].

Above: The rand, named after the reef containing one of the largest gold deposits in the world, started life as a small gold coin in 1961, switched to silver in 1965, then nickel from 1977, to 1990, and finally nickel-plated copper later the same year. For 45 years, however, the reverse design has remained constant, showing a springbok. The protea (right) is the floral emblem of South Africa and has appeared on coins since 1965.

Biblical Allusion

From 1923 the farthing had a reverse motif of two sparrows, an allusion to the rhetorical question posed by Christ (Matthew 10:29): "Are not two sparrows sold for a farthing?" This motif was retained for the reverse of the half cent (1961–83) and extended in 1965 to the cent, where it has continued, in various guises, to this day.

Although South Africa took its doctrine of separateness to the extent of creating four black "homelands" in the 1970s, these territories continued to use South African currency. Bophuthatswana alone produced gold nkwe or platinum lowe bullion pieces in 1987 to mark the tenth anniversary of independence.

The apartheid regime ended in 1994 with the first free elections for all the people of South Africa. In the Afrikaner period, coins had been mainly inscribed bilingually, although some were released in distinctive English or Afrikaans versions. Since 1996, however, coins have been inscribed in Zulu, Venda, Ndebele, Tsonga, Tswana, Sotho, Swati and Xhosa, or other languages indigenous to the country.

The silver rand was a popular medium for commemorative issues from 1967 onward, although a tiny gold rand appeared in 1997 to mark the 30th anniversary of the world's first successful heart transplant, by the South African surgeon Christiaan Barnard. More recently, 2 rand coins have been used as commemoratives. South Africa pioneered modern bullion coins, launching the gold Krugerrand in 1960, followed by the Protea (1986) and Natura (1994) series.

SOUTHERN AFRICA

This term encompasses the countries bordering South Africa (including Lesotho, which is entirely within the boundaries of that country). Three of them were formerly British High Commission territories and the fourth was a German colony, subsequently mandated to South Africa under the name of South West Africa and now called Namibia. They now form a common currency area, with all currencies pegged to the rand.

Left: Although Namibia has a largely pastoral economy, it has considerably developed its offshore fishing industry in recent years. Appropriately, this 5 cent coin, issued as part of the UN Food and Agriculture Organization coin programme in 2000 to celebrate the dawn of the new century, depicts a horse mackerel with the exhortation to "Eat More Fish".

NAMIBIA

Formerly German South West Africa, this vast territory was occupied by South African troops soon after the outbreak of World War I and in 1920 South Africa was granted a mandate by the League of Nations. In 1948 the South African government approached the United Nations with a proposal to annexe South West Africa, but this was turned down. In 1950, when South Africa refused to allow a UN trusteeship, the matter was resolved at the International Court of Justice in the Hague, which ruled against South Africa. The UN terminated the mandate in 1966 but South Africa refused to comply and continued to occupy and govern South West Africa illegally and, moreover, to use it as a base for incursions into Angola. This situation continued until 1988, when South Africa and Cuba withdrew their forces from Angola and steps were finally taken towards independence as Namibia, granted in March 1990.

German currency was used in the colonial period. Namibia continued to use South African currency until 1993, when the Namibian dollar was introduced, on par with the South African rand. Coins from 5 cents to $5, with the republican arms on the obverse and fauna and flora on the reverse, are now in circulation [1–9]. The fifth and tenth anniversaries of independence (1995 and 2000) were celebrated by coins with a multicoloured reverse, and this has been extended to a few other special issues, notably the wildlife series of 1996.

BOTSWANA

Formerly the British Protectorate of Bechuanaland, Botswana became an independent republic in September 1966. Ironically, the first president was Sir Seretse Khama, who had been deposed as Paramount Chief of the Bamangwato and banished following his marriage to an Englishwoman, Ruth Williams, in 1948. He was permitted to return as a private citizen in 1956, entered politics and became the first prime minister (1965) and president a year later. His profile appeared on gold and silver coins celebrating independence and also its tenth anniversary.

Botswana switched from South African currency to the pula of 100 thebe in 1976, remaining on par with the rand. Coins showing the national arms (obverse) and wildlife (reverse) [10–15] consist of the aluminium thebe, bronze 2 and 5 thebe and cupro-nickel higher values. The 25 and 50 thebe coins switched to nickel-clad steel in 1991, while the pula in 1991 and 2 pula in 1994 switched to nickel-brass. A bimetallic 5 pula was added to the series in 2000 and shows a caterpillar devouring a leaf – a message to farmers to be vigilant in pest control [16–17]. A few special issues, including a series devoted to wildlife conservation, have appeared in recent years. Silver and gold coins have also marked the Commonwealth Games (1986), a papal visit (1988) and the International year of Disabled Persons (1991).

LESOTHO
Previously Basutoland, the tiny country of Lesotho is entirely surrounded by the territory of South Africa. A sparsely populated region, it was occupied by refugees from tribal wars, led by Moshoeshoe (1787–1870), who founded a dynasty and established his capital at Thaba Bosiu ("mountain of the night"). Originally named Lepoqo ("disaster", because the region was then famine-stricken), he earned his later name ("shaver") because he dispensed with the beard of an adversary. He withstood the territorial ambitions of Shaka, the mighty Zulu leader, and united the Basotho people through his conciliatory approach to rival tribes. Boer encroachment from the 1830s onward induced Moshoeshoe to seek British protection in 1868 and for a time Basutoland was part of Cape Colony, but from 1884 it was administered by a British high commissioner.

Self-government was granted in 1959, leading to complete sovereignty in 1966. Distinctive coins based on the loti (plural *maloti*) of 100 lisente were introduced in 1979 [18–25]. Moshoeshoe II was twice king (1966–90 and 1995–6), but his meddling in politics infuriated the prime minister, Leabua Jonathan, and resulted in two spells of house arrest, exile (1970) and deposition in favour of his son Letsie III. Moshoeshoe II was restored in 1995 but was killed in a car crash the following year. He was portrayed in military uniform, but during the period when he was deposed the royal arms appeared instead. During the political crises of 1970 and 1990, and also for a few months after Moshoeshoe's death, Ma Mohato (his wife and Letsie's mother) acted as regent. Many of the commemorative coins portrayed Moshoeshoe I on the obverse [22].

SWAZILAND
By contrast with the turbulent politics of Lesotho, Swaziland has been one of the most stable countries in Africa. Sometimes called the Switzerland of Africa because of its mountainous terrain, it lies between the Transvaal, Natal and Mozambique. Though small, it is rich in minerals. Zulu raids induced King Mswati to appeal for British protection and from 1881 independence was guaranteed by Britain and the South African Republic (Transvaal). After the Boer War Britain assumed full responsibility and Swaziland became a High Commission territory. Its independence was granted in 1968.

South African currency was in use until 1974 when a distinctive series, based on the lilangeni (plural *emalangeni*) of 25 luhlanga or 100 cents, was adopted [26–27]. A wide range of circular, polygonal and scalloped shapes made each denomination distinctive, the obverse portraying Sobhuza II [30] and reverses often showing fauna and flora [28–29, 31]. King Makhosetive (Mswati III) has appeared on the coins since 1986 [32–35]. The relatively few special issues include silver and gold coins celebrating the 75th and 80th birthdays of Sobhuza II as well as his diamond jubilee (1981). An unusual feature of some of these coins was a serial number stamped on the reverse.

Africa's Longest-reigning Monarch
King Sobhuza II, born in 1899, ascended the throne in 1921. The year after his diamond jubilee (1982) he stepped down in favour of his grandson Mswati III who was crowned in 1986. In the intervening period, Queen Dzeliwe acted as regent.

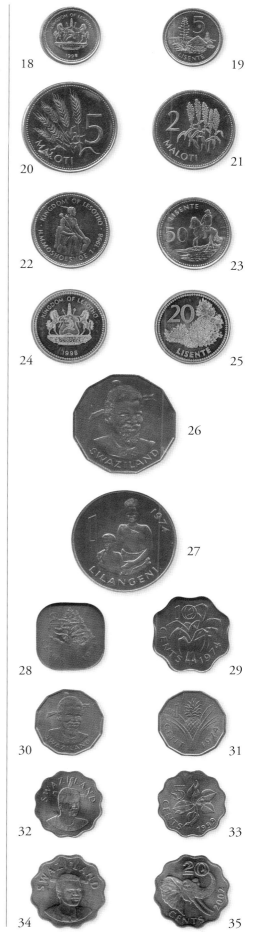

CENTRAL AFRICA

The area of Central Africa, south of the Equator, consists of the two former Portuguese colonies of Angola and Mozambique, the former Belgian Congo and the territories mandated to Belgium by the League of Nations, and the former colonies and protectorates that made up British Central Africa. These countries were carved out by the various European powers during the "scramble for Africa" in the 19th century.

 Left: A brief attempt to weld the colony of Southern Rhodesia and the protectorates of Northern Rhodesia and Nyasaland into a single dominion is recalled by the coins of Rhodesia and Nyasaland, which were issued between 1955 and 1963.

FORMER PORTUGUESE TERRITORIES

Coins for specific use in Portuguese Africa were minted from 1693 onward, while coins struck at Goa in Portuguese India, such as the 1000 reis of José I [1–2], were produced for circulation in Mozambique from 1725. Decimal coins inscribed "Republica Portuguesa" on the obverse, with the name of the territory on the reverse, were introduced in Angola in 1921 [3–4] and in Mozambique in 1936, gradually replacing the coins of the mother country, whose national emblems had given the colonial issues a degree of uniformity.

Both of Portugal's "overseas provinces" were in revolt from 1960 onward, but they gained their independence as people's republics only after the collapse of António de Oliveira Salazar's regime, and the advent of democracy, in Portugal in 1974. Following independence, Mozambique adopted the metical of 100 centimos, and Angola chose the kwanza of 100 lwei (1979). While Angola featured its national emblem on the obverse and numerals on the reverse of its coins [5], Mozambique chose the profile of President Samora Machel and various plants.

Both countries subsequently reformed their currencies. Mozambique switched from centimes to centavos in 1980, while Angola introduced the "re-adjusted" kwanza of 100 centimos, the equivalent of 1000 old kwanzas, in 1995.

FORMER BELGIAN TERRITORIES

Leopold II, King of the Belgians, was granted the Congo in 1885 and governed it as his personal property. This was reflected in the inscription on the coins introduced in 1887, which proclaimed him as Sovereign of the Congo Free State. Revelations of misrule led to it being annexed by Belgium in 1908 and renamed the Belgian Congo [7, 11]. The star emblem of the Free State was replaced by a profile of the king and crowned arms. A palm replaced the latter in 1920 [6], while an elephant replaced the portrait in 1944.

The Democratic Republic of the Congo gained independence in 1960 but was immediately plunged into civil war. Coins issued by the national bank appeared in 1965 [10]. The country's name was changed to Zaire in 1971 and the zaire of 100 makuta was adopted. In the ensuing period, coins portrayed President Mabotu [8–9], but following a civil war in 1997 the country reverted to the previous name and adopted coins featuring a lion (obverse) and various fauna (reverse). Rectangular or triangular coins (2000) publicized the campaign for animal protection.

During the civil war of 1961, bronze coins were struck in the breakaway southern province of Katanga, featuring bananas (obverse) [12] and the bronze crosses [13] used as money before the advent of coinage [14].

Belgium was granted a mandate over Rwanda-Urundi, formerly part of

German East Africa. Congolese coins were used there until 1952, when a series with these names was released. When the Congo gained independence in 1960, coins inscribed "Rwanda Burundi" were adopted. Separate issues in each country appeared in the Kingdom of Burundi (1965) [15–16] and the Republic of Rwanda (1964) [17–18]. Rwanda adopted a new series in 1974–7, with the national arms on the obverse and millet, coffee or bananas on the reverse [19–22]. In 1966, ,Burundi abolished its monarchy and replaced the portraits of Mwambutsa IV with the republican arms.

FORMER BRITISH TERRITORIES
British and South African coins circulated in the vast territories of the British South Africa Company headed by Cecil Rhodes. Rejecting incorporation in the Union of South Africa (1923) the territory was broken up into the

Above: Pictorial reverses of the 20 ngwee of Zambia, 1985 (left) and 1968–88.

colony of Southern Rhodesia and the protectorates of Northern Rhodesia and Nyasaland.

Distinctive silver coins were adopted in 1932 [23–24], followed by holed cupro-nickel halfpennies and pennies in 1934. Coins bore the head of the reigning monarch [25], with pictorial reverses [26–28]. Coins inscribed for use in the Federation of Rhodesia and Nyasaland (1955–64) followed a similar pattern. On the break-up of the federation, Nyasaland became Malawi and Northern Rhodesia became Zambia, both introducing distinctive coins in 1964. Both countries adopted a decimal system based on the kwacha [35–36], comprised either of 100 tambala (Malawi, 1971) [29–30] or 100 ngwee (Zambia, 1968) [31–32].

The former Southern Rhodesia dropped the adjective and then unilaterally declared independence in November 1965. Although the regime, headed by Ian Smith, was declared illegal, its coins continued to portray Elizabeth II until 1970, when a republic was declared and an armorial obverse was adopted. In 1978, Smith signed a pact with moderate African leaders and the country adopted the name Zimbabwe Rhodesia. No coins bearing the double name were ever issued, and in 1980 the country became the Republic of Zimbabwe. Coins thus inscribed, with the emblem of a bird carved from soapstone on the obverse, were issued that year [33–34].

While Malawi and Zimbabwe have produced very few special issues, Zambia has been prolific in releasing large silver coins, often multicoloured and in unusual polygonal or upright oval shapes.

Coins in Two Currencies
The coins issued by Rhodesia from 1964 to 1968 were denominated in both sterling and decimal currencies, on the basis of the pound of 20 shillings or 2 dollars. Thus the shilling of 12 pence was also worth 10 cents. Cupro-nickel coins, which ranged from the 3 pence (2 cents) to the 2 shillings (25 cents), were accompanied by gold coins solely denominated 10 shillings, £1 or £5.

EAST AFRICA

The countries of East Africa were formerly in the British or German spheres of influence and were created as a result of a series of pacts and treaties between these European powers and the various tribal rulers. The area included the offshore islands of Zanzibar and Pemba, governed by the Al-Busaid dynasty, originally from Muscat in Arabia and for centuries the centre of the Arab-dominated slave trade of Africa. The first regular coinage in this region consisted of the bronze pice and silver annas and rupees issued by the British East India Company at Mombasa in 1888–90 [1–6].

Left: Coins of the lower denominations of East Africa had a central hole, with the value and elephant tusks on the reverse and a crown on the obverse. They bore the names and titles of British monarchs, and thus had the distinction of being one of the few issues to be inscribed with the name of King Edward VIII, who ascended the throne in January 1936 and abdicated the following December.

ZANZIBAR

Coins were struck by various seaports along the Swahili Coast from the 11th century, and these remained in use until the arrival of the Portuguese in the 16th century. The sultans of Zanzibar had distinctive coinage in the 19th century. Barghash ibn Sa'id (1879–88) introduced silver ryals and copper pysa in 1882, with Arabic inscriptions on both sides [7–10]. The pysa, however, also featured scales on the reverse, copying the coins of the British East India Company. The rupee of 100 cents was adopted in 1908 and bronze or nickel coins of 1, 10 and 20 cents had a palm tree reverse. Otherwise the sultanate used the coins of the East African Monetary Union. A large silver medal marked the Zanzibar Exhibition in 1905 [11].

FORMER GERMAN EAST AFRICA

Germany obtained trading rights in Dar es Salaam and Witu in 1884 and declared a protectorate in 1891. Six years later the territory was proclaimed a German colony. At first the rupee of 64 pesa was used, and a copper pesa was released in 1890–2 with the name of the German East African Company with the imperial eagle on the obverse and an Arabic reverse. Coins inscribed "Deutsche Ostafrika" were introduced in 1904, based on the rupee of 100 heller, and featured the imperial crown and a wreathed value (heller denominations) or the bust of Kaiser Wilhelm II (rupees). During World War I, German troops fought a skilful guerrilla campaign to the very end, and even produced emergency coins inscribed "D.O.A."

Under the name of Tanganyika, the territory was mandated to Britain in 1920 and became an independent republic in 1961. In 1964 it joined with Zanzibar (where the Arab sultanate had been overthrown) and adopted the name of Tanzania in October that year.

EAST AFRICAN MONETARY UNION

Instituted in 1906, the Union provided a common currency in five territories: British East Africa (the colony and protectorate of Kenya), Uganda, British Somaliland, Zanzibar and latterly Tanganyika. Coins inscribed "East Africa & Uganda Protectorates" were introduced: the low values had a central hole and a crown (obverse) [13], and elephant tusks (reverse) [12, 14], while the silver 25 and 50 cents bore the crowned bust of the monarch (obverse) and a lion and mountains (reverse) [15–16]. Similar coins appeared from 1921 based on the shilling of 100 cents. This pattern continued until 1966, when it was replaced by the coinage of the component states as they gained independence.

INDEPENDENT REPUBLICS

Uganda was granted independence in 1962, followed by Kenya (1963) and Tanganyika (1964). Meanwhile the British Somaliland protectorate had joined with the former Italian colony to form the Republic of Somalia. Initially, the three republics within the Commonwealth continued with the coins of East Africa, but separate issues were adopted when the Union was dissolved in 1966.

The subsidiary coins of the Bank of Uganda retained the Union's ivory tusk motif but the higher values replaced the royal effigy with the arms of the republic [17], while a crested crane superseded the lion on the reverse [18]. The composition of the coins was changed in 1976, with copper-plated steel replacing bronze in the lower denominations and cupro-nickel plated steel taking the place of cupro-nickel in the higher values. A new series in stainless or copper-plated steel (1987) had numerals in a floral reverse [19–20]. Inflation in the ensuing decade led to the 1998 series of 50 to 500 shillings, featuring wildlife on the reverse.

Kenya opted for a series with an armorial obverse and a bust of President Jomo Kenyatta on the reverse. In 1968 the reverse inscription was altered but Kenyatta's effigy stayed until 1978. After his death, the portrait of his successor, Daniel Arap Moi, was

Above: Imprisoned by the British during the Mau Mau campaign, Jomo Kenyatta became Kenya's first president.

Wartime Gold
In 1916 gold from the Kironda Mine at Sekengi in German East Africa was coined as 15 rupee pieces, popularly known as Tabora Sovereigns (from the railway workshop where they were struck). The dies were engraved by a Sinhalese prisoner of war, and German regulations decreed that they could be issued only to "residents of the better class."

substituted [21–22], and bimetallic coins from 5 to 20 shillings were added to the series between 1995 and 1998. The very few special issues have commemorated Kenyatta's 75th birthday (1966), the 25th anniversary of independence (1988), the tenth anniversary of Moi as president (1988) and the silver jubilee of the Central Bank (1991).

Julius Nyerere was portrayed on the coins of Tanzania from their inception [23, 25], with mammals, birds and fish on the reverse [24, 26]. As in other parts of East Africa, plated steel has replaced cupro-nickel in recent years [27–28]. The basic circulating series originally ran from the bronze 5 senti to 1 shilingi [29–30]. From 1974, a number of gold or silver high values, up to 2,500 shilingi, marked anniversaries of independence and the Central Bank of Tanzania or publicized wildlife conservation. A polygonal 5 shilingi, released in 1971 to mark the tenth anniversary of independence and contribute to the FAO coin programme, showed agricultural products grouped around the value. This motif was retained for the permanent coins of this denomination. Bimetallic circulating coins of 10 shilingi were introduced in 1987 and 20 shilingi in 1992; both portray Nyerere (obverse) and the national arms (reverse).

HORN OF AFRICA

The north-east corner of the continent, bounded by the Red Sea and the north-western part of the Indian Ocean, is described as the Horn of Africa. This region was predominantly in the Italian sphere of influence, since Eritrea and Somalia were Italian colonies or protectorates, while Ethiopia was under Italian occupation from 1936 to 1941. The French controlled the port of Djibouti and its hinterland, while the British established a protectorate over the area on the southern shore of the Gulf of Aden.

Left: Italian coinage was in use in Ethiopia from 1936 to 1941, but coins portraying the Emperor Haile Selassie, dated 1936 in the Ethiopian Era (1944), were issued following the country's liberation. They were struck in Philadelphia, Birmingham or London between 1945 and 1975.

ETHIOPIA

Formerly known as Abyssinia, this large country south of Sudan is the oldest independent nation in Africa, tracing its origins back to the 4th century BC, when it was founded by Menelik I, son of Solomon and the Queen of Sheba. The powerful kingdom of Axum was probably the first country south of the Sahara to issue coins, from the 2nd century AD, including exquisite little gold coins such as the tremissis of about AD 450 [1–2]. Brass or billon coins called mahallak were struck at Harar from 1807 to 1892.

Under Menelik II (1889–1913) Ethiopia emerged from centuries of isolation and rapidly modernized, adopting western-style coinage in 1892 based on the silver talari (derived from the Maria Theresia thaler) of 20 gersh (piastres) or 40 besa. In 1903 the talari was re-tariffed at 16 gersh or 32 besa. A decimal system based on the birr (dollar) of 100 santeems or matonas was adopted in 1931. Coins bore the effigy of the monarch (obverse) and the Lion of Judah (reverse) [3–4].

Haile Selassie was deposed in 1974 and the country became a people's democratic republic in 1976. Coins had a lion's head (obverse) and aspects of agriculture (reverse) [5–6]. A few gold or silver coins of more recent years have marked UN events, such as International Year of the Child (1980) or Decade for Women (1984).

ERITREA

The region on the south-west coast of the Red Sea was annexed by Italy in 1889, and merged with Ethiopia in 1936 to form Italian East Africa. Silver coins from 50 centesimi to 5 lire appeared in 1890, with the crowned profile of Umberto I on the obverse. A silver tallero (dollar) of 1918 showed an allegorical female bust (Italia), with the crowned arms of Savoy (reverse).

The area was under British military administration from 1941 to 1952, when the United Nations declared it an autonomous state federated with Ethiopia, whose coinage it used. This union, unpopular from the start, led to a long-running guerrilla war. By 1991 the Eritrean People's Liberation Front controlled most of the country and the independent republic was recognized in 1993. A series of coins based on the dollar of 100 cents was introduced in 1997, featuring wildlife (obverse) and soldiers with the flag (reverse) [7–16]. Cupro-nickel or silver coins with a camel and dhow on the obverse have proliferated since 1993, celebrating Eritrea's independence or promoting the "Preserve Planet Earth" campaign.

DJIBOUTI

French interest in the Red Sea resulted in trading concessions at the port of Djibouti in 1839. The same year, the British secured the port of Aden on the opposite side of the Bab el Mandeb strait. A protectorate was established in 1884 and the colony of the French Somali Coast proclaimed in 1896.

French coins were generally used, but a series of tokens was issued at Djibouti in 1920–1. Distinctive coins were introduced in 1948 and bore the effigy of Marianne (obverse), with a lyre antelope [17–18] or an Arab dhow and ocean liner (reverse), reflecting the growing importance of Djibouti as a port of call for cruise ships. The name was changed to the French Territory of the Afars and the Issas in 1967, and coins with this inscription but similar motifs (as well as high values depicting camels) were introduced in 1968–9. In June 1977, the country attained its independence as the Republic of Djibouti. Coins retain the reverse motifs of earlier issues but have the national shield and spears emblem on the obverse [19–22].

SOMALIA

Indigenous coins date from the 14th century and were struck at Mogadishu by Arab traders, conforming to strict Islamic standards. Of particular interest are the undated brass tokens, which were extensively used as small change by Somali Muslims crossing the Red Sea on pilgrimage to Mecca, including types issued by the Italian colonial authorities between 1895 and 1914 [23].Whereas British Somaliland used Indian rupees and coins of East Africa until 1961, when it was united with the former Italian Somaliland, the latter had distinctive coins from 1909. The rupia of 100 bese bore the effigy of Victor Emmanuel III, with the value in Italian and Arabic on the reverse.

Coins in the Italian currency system were planned, but only the silver 10 lire of 1925, with a crowned bust of the king, was issued. The resumption of Italian rule in 1950 was signalled by coins depicting an elephant or lioness from 1 centesimo to 1 somalo [24–25].

Following the unification with British Somaliland in 1960, to create the Somali Republic, the currency changed to the scellino (shilling) of 100 centesimi [26–27] with an armorial obverse and inscriptions in English and Arabic. Gold coins portraying President Abdulla Osman celebrated the fifth anniversary of independence (1965). After a military coup in 1969, however, Somalia became a democratic republic. Apart from some gold coins of 1970 marking the tenth anniversary of independence and the first anniversary of the revolution, the previous coinage continued until 1976, when the shilling of 100 senti was adopted, with an armorial obverse and various animals on the reverse [28–31]. Although in general circulation, this series was conceived as part of the FAO coin programme. Paradoxically, as true democracy was restored in the 1990s the word "Democratic" was dropped from the inscription. Since 1998 numerous bimetallic coins with multi-coloured centres have been produced in sets with such themes as wildlife and world shipping.

Somalia has been wracked by civil war. The Somali National Movement controlling the former British Somaliland seceded in 1993, and began issuing coins inscribed "Republic of Somaliland" in 1994. The obverse shows a Somali stock dove, both a symbol of peace and the national emblem of the breakaway republic [32–33].

Unique Calendar

Ethiopia has its own Amharic characters to denote numerals, and a calendar that began seven years and eight months after the Common Era (AD). Dates are expressed by separate figures up to ten, then in tens to a hundred, using a combination of multiplication and addition to produce a five-digit date, as shown on the 1969 series.

21

22

23

24

25

26

27

28

29

30

31

32

33

1 2

3 4

5 6

7 8

9 10

11 12

13

14 15

16 17

WEST AFRICA

The countries surveyed here are located to the north of the Gulf of Guinea. Four of them were in the British sphere of influence and are now republics within the British Commonwealth, while the fifth, Liberia, was settled by freed slaves returned from the United States and is nominally English-speaking, with close ties to neighbouring Sierra Leone.

Left: Because the low-value coins of British West Africa did not portray the monarch, it was relatively simple to engrave new dies in 1936 bearing the name of Edward VIII as King and Emperor of India. This penny was one of the few coins issued in his name.

BRITISH WEST AFRICA

As in East Africa, a currency board, set up in 1912, provided the coinage in use throughout the British colonies and protectorates of West Africa. Previously, however, coins thus inscribed had been introduced in Nigeria in 1906 and had the distinction of including one of the world's first aluminium coins, the ⅒ penny with a Star of David about a central hole (obverse) and a crown over the value (reverse) [1–2]. From 1908 subsidiary coins were struck in cupro-nickel [3–4]. Coins from 3 pence to 2 shillings were initially minted in silver but switched to brass in 1920. On these denominations a crowned effigy of the reigning monarch (obverse) and an oil palm (reverse) were used for the shilling values [5] and a wreathed value for the 3 and 6 pence denominations [6]. Coins portraying Elizabeth II were in use from 1954 until the four countries achieved independence.

GHANA

The Gold Coast had a silver coinage based on the ackey of 8 tackoe, produced by the Royal African Company between 1796 and 1818. A copper proof tackoe of the first year of issue is shown here [7–8]. It was the first colony to attain independence, together with the mandated territory of Togoland, emerging in February 1957 as the sovereign nation of Ghana, which revived the name of an ancient

West African empire. Pence and shillings, introduced in 1958, portrayed Kwame Nkrumah, first the prime minister and later (1960–6) president, of the republic. The currency was reformed in 1965, based on the cedi of 100 pesawas, retaining similar motifs [9–11]. After Nkrumah's overthrow, cocoa beans replaced his image [12], with the national arms dominating the reverses [13–15]. Some coins since 1979 have featured a cowrie, alluding to the currency of earlier generations.

THE GAMBIA

This tiny state along the banks of the River Gambia was purchased by London merchants in 1588 and thus became England's first colony in Africa. Originally a centre for the slave trade, it later became a base for its suppression. It gained independence in 1965, with Elizabeth II as head of state, hence her bust on the coinage [16], whose reverse featured fauna, flora and a sailboat [17]. It became a republic within the Commonwealth in 1970 and new currency, based on the dalasi of 100

Above: The cupro-nickel shilling of the Gambia has an effigy of Elizabeth II (obverse) and an oil palm (reverse).

bututs, appeared the following year, with the effigy of the former prime minister, now president, Sir Dawda Jawara on the obverse, and the republic's arms on the reverse [18].

NIGERIA

The first indigenous coinage of Nigeria (1959) was modelled on that of British West Africa, with the Star of David on the holed coins [19–20] and the crowned bust of the queen on the higher values, with agricultural themes on the reverse [21–22]. Nigeria became a republic in 1963 but the coinage remained unchanged until 1973, when the naira of 100 kobo was introduced. The series featured the republican arms, with pictorial reverses alluding to the country's mineral wealth and diverse agriculture [23–26]. Place of honour on the reverse of the naira was reserved for Herbert Macaulay (1864–1946), regarded as the father of independence.

In 1967, the eastern region broke away and proclaimed the Republic of Biafra. Aluminium coins from 3 pence to 2 shillings, with the palm tree emblem, appeared in 1969. A few silver and gold pieces were struck at the same time to celebrate the second anniversary of independence [27–28], although Biafra ceased to exist in January 1970 following a bloody war.

SIERRA LEONE

An important centre of the slave trade in the 17th and 18th centuries, Sierra Leone was chosen for the first experiment in returning freed slaves to Africa, the aptly named Freetown being established in 1787 [29–30].

Modern coinage, based on the leone of 100 cents, dates from 1964, three years after Sierra Leone achieved independence. Sir Milton Margai, prime minister and, later, the first president, appeared on the obverse with various fauna and flora on the reverse [31–32]. A leone produced for general circulation (1987) used an unusual octagonal format, which was originally applied to bicentennial coins issued to mark the anniversary of Freetown.

Earliest British African Coins
The Sierra Leone Company, set up to settle freed slaves, produced the earliest British colonial coinage issued anywhere in the African continent: the bronze cent (below) and penny; and silver coins from 10 cents to the dollar of 1791. All showed the lion and mountain (from which the country derives its name) on the obverse, and hands clasped in friendship (reverse).

LIBERIA
The country whose name means "the land of the free" was first settled in 1822 by the American Colonization Society, with the aim of repatriating freed slaves. Various settlements combined in 1839 to form the Commonwealth of Liberia, which became a republic in 1847.

A copper cent produced in 1833 showed a man planting a symbolic tree of Liberty, and this was the forerunner to the series of coins of 1896 with the head of Liberty on the obverse and a palm tree on the reverse. Coins were produced very sporadically prior to 1960 and many issues since then [33] exist only in proof sets.

Conversely, Liberia has produced numerous special coins since 1993, often in lengthy thematic series, such as the prolific Pioneers of the West, aimed principally at the American collector market. Other long-running sets since the 1990s have portrayed world statesmen, from Churchill and Roosevelt to Nelson Mandela, Formula One racing drivers, famous baseball players, from Babe Ruth to Reggie Jackson and even the leading characters in the *Star Trek* television series.

SAHARA AND EQUATORIAL AFRICA

Much of this vast region was formerly part of the French colonial empire, and was administered as French West Africa and French Equatorial Africa. To this day the common currency in these regions is issued by the West and Central African States, although some countries have their own distinctive coinage. Although most of the Equatorial region was in the French sphere of influence, both Spain and Portugal managed colonies here, and their successor states likewise now issue their own coins.

Left: Leopold Sedar Senghor, dubbed "the black de Gaulle", was a distinguished teacher, writer and poet who was prominent in the political development of French Africa after 1945, becoming the first president of Senegal (1960–80).

CENTRAL AFRICAN STATES

Ordinary French coins were used in French Equatorial Africa (Middle-Congo, Ubangi-Shari, Chad and Gabon) until 1942, when the region adhered to Charles de Gaulle and the Free French, and coins bearing a Gallic cock (obverse) and the Cross of Lorraine (reverse) were introduced. In 1948 a new type, with the head of Marianne (obverse) and a Loder's gazelle (reverse) was adopted [1–2].

Following the break-up of the French colonial empire in 1958–9, an attempt was made to form a political union comprising Chad, Congo, the Central African Republic and Gabon. Although this failed, an outcome was the monetary union known as the Equatorial Customs Unit, to which Cameroon acceded in 1961. Coins were struck by the authority of the Central Bank of the Equatorial African States, with a standard obverse of three giant eland and a wreathed value reverse [3–8]. The name was changed in 1974 to the Bank of the Central African States. Coins with the new title retained the original motif but from then until 1996 a letter was included to denote the country in which a coin was originally issued: A (Chad), B

(Central African Republic), C (Congo), D (Gabon) and E (Cameroon). Equatorial Guinea, a former Spanish colony, issued its own coins in 1969 [9] before joining the Central African States. Conversely the former French Guinea refused to join, and has issued its own coins [10–11] since 1962.

The bank also produces 100 franc coins with the great eland obverse and inscriptions signifying use in the Central African Republic [12–13], Chad, the Congo People's Republic and Gabon. All four have also produced distinctive commemoratives, notably Chad [14] which, in 1970 alone, honoured both Kennedy brothers as well as Martin Luther King, de Gaulle and President Nasser of Egypt.

WEST AFRICAN STATES

French West Africa comprised Dahomey, French Guinea, French Sudan, Ivory Coast, Niger, Senegal and Upper Volta, using French coins until 1944, when a series featuring Marianne and a horn of plenty was introduced. From 1948 to 1958 coins used the Marianne and Loder's gazelle motifs of Equatorial Africa, with the obverse inscription modified. The former mandated territory of Togoland (for which

Odd Man Out

Mauritania only became part of French West Africa in 1920, gaining autonomy in 1958, and becoming the Islamic Republic of Mauritania in 1960. It withdrew from the French Community in 1966 and left the West African monetary union in 1973. It has since issued coins based on the ouguiya of 5 khoums. These have an obverse showing the crescent and star of Islam with palms and the value, while the reverse bears inscriptions in Arabic.

separate coins were issued in 1924–6 and 1948–56) joined the French West African monetary union in 1957, and 5, 10 and 25 franc coins then included Togo in the inscription [15–16].

The coins of the West African States adopted a standard obverse showing an Ashanti gold weight [17], with wreathed values [18–19] or a Loder's gazelle [20] on the reverse.

Since 1980–1, the 10, 25 and 50 franc coins have had reverses showing food production, issued as part of the Food and Agriculture Organization coin programme [21–22]. These coins circulate in Dahomey (now Benin), Senegal, Upper Volta (now Burkina Faso), Ivory Coast, Mali, Togo and Niger [23–24]. Guinea had a currency based on the syli of 100 cauris from 1971 to 1985, when the Guinean franc was adopted [25–26].

In addition to the common currency, several member countries have issued their own coins. Sporadically, coins have been produced by Ivory Coast (1966), Niger (1960), Togo (1977) and Mali (1960–7). Mali's issue of aluminium 5 [28–29], 10 and 25 "francs maliens" underlined the nation's

new indepedence from France the previous year, and from the French-backed franc. Dahomey (Benin) and Senegal, meanwhile, have issued quite a number of gold and silver coins [27].

FORMER PORTUGUESE AND SPANISH TERRITORIES

In colonial times, the scattered possessions of Spain and Portugal in the Saharan and Equatorial regions used the coins of their mother countries, but since independence they have produced their own. In the north-west, the former Spanish Sahara was partitioned between Mauritania and Morocco in 1975, but after a long war of independence the Saharawi Arab Republic emerged in 1992. Coins from 1 to 100 pesetas have an armorial obverse and a camel reverse. There is also a prolific output of commemoratives aimed mainly at the Spanish market.

Distinctive coins are issued in the islands of Cape Verde [30–31] and São Tome and Principe, off the west coast of Africa, and in Guinea-Bissau (formerly Portuguese Guinea) on the mainland. São Tome issued coins in 1813, but both territories began issuing decimal coins in 1929–33 with the allegory of the republic and "Republica Portuguesa" (obverse) and arms with the name of the colony (reverse). The word "Colonia" was omitted during the 1960s when they became overseas provinces. In 1975 they became independent republics and have issued their own coins since 1977. All three began with modest series promoting the FAO coin programme but have since moved on to lengthy issues, often of little cultural relevance to their own countries, but aimed primarily at the overseas numismatic trade.

Above: The bronze 20 centavos (1962) of São Tome and Principe, with the Portuguese arms on the obverse.

17 18 19 20 21 22 23 24 25 26 27 28 29 30 31

ASIA

This vast continent, which stretches from the Mediterranean to the Pacific, was the birthplace of coinage. Scholars may argue as to whether it was the inhabitants of Asia Minor (modern Anatolia) or China who first adopted metallic currency, but there is no argument that this is where it all began.

TURKEY

Ancient Lydia, in the territory of modern Turkey, produced the first coins of the western world in the 7th century BC. By the time of King Croesus (561–545 BC) its coins had a lion and bull motif (obverse) and rectangular incuse marks (reverse) [1–2]. After Lydia's conquest by the Persian Cyrus the Great, tiny quarter-sigloi were struck under Darius I [3–4].

Although politically classed as a European country, Turkey lies mostly in western Asia, and from medieval to relatively modern times its coinage owed more to its Asiatic and Islamic background than to European influence. Under Ottoman rule the land of the Turks grew into a mighty empire, which stretched from the Danube to the Persian Gulf and from the Caspian Sea to the Barbary Coast of North Africa. The Ottomans controlled the trade routes between Europe and China and dominated the Mediterranean until their naval power was checked by the Battle of Lepanto in 1571. A century later they even besieged Vienna, but from 1700 their power gradually waned. The Ottoman Empire collapsed in the aftermath of World War I, and the republic that succeeded it was confined to Anatolia and a wedge of territory in eastern Thrace, the last remnant of Turkey in Europe.

Left: Out of an obverse type in which the Arabic letters of the ruler's title were interwoven developed the elaborate calligraphic toughra, *or sign-manual of the sultan, a device that continued to be used on Turkish coins from the 11th to the 20th centuries.*

HELLENISTIC AND ROMAN TURKEY

The Persian Empire declined in the 4th century BC under a succession of weak rulers. Asia Minor was invaded first by Philip of Macedon and then by his son Alexander the Great, who defeated the Persians and annexed the empire, ushering in a period of Greek settlement and rule. After his death, his generals divided his empire among them and struck coins bearing his effigy, such as the tetradrachm struck by Mithridates at Smyrna [5–6]. Under Roman rule (from 63 BC) local issues continued [7–8], latterly in the name of the emperor, such as this early 3rd century bronze coin portraying Severus Alexander [9–10].

MEDIEVAL TURKEY

Anatolia (Asia Minor) formed part of the Byzantine Empire and used its coins [11–12] but from the 10th century onward, it was frequently invaded and overrun by Mongols [13–14] and Turkmens, who established separate dynasties. The Seljuqs of Rum ("land of the Romans") [15], whose capital was the Byzantine city of Nicaea, the Qaramanids, Ilkhanids and others struck coins that were based on Byzantine models but inscribed in Arabic, and sometimes in Greek.

OTTOMAN EMPIRE

In 1453 the Ottoman Turks conquered the city of Constantinople and overthrew the Byzantine Empire. In the ensuing centuries the empire expanded dramatically, from the Caucasus to the whole of North Africa, but by 1914 Turkish dominions in Europe had shrunk to the hinterland of Istanbul (Constantinople), while alliance with Germany and Austria in World War I hastened the end of the empire.

The coins of the Ottoman Empire were struck in copper, silver and gold in a bewildering array of denominations based on multiples of the para, from 3 (*akce* or *asper*) to 240 (*altilik*). In the 17th century, Suleiman II introduced the kurus or piastre, originally a large silver coin worth 40 para. By the 18th century low-grade silver was being used for coins ranging from 1 para upwards, but between 1808 and 1840 the size and fineness of the coins were progressively reduced on eight different occasions as the economy collapsed [18–21]. The gold coinage was infinitely more complex, with numerous coins in different weights and fineness, each distinguished by its own name and issued simultaneously.

The coinage was reformed in 1844 by Abdulmejid, who introduced the gold lira (pound) of 100 silver piastres or kurus; the smaller coins, from 5 para upwards, were struck in bronze [22]. Large bronze piastres bore the Arabic numerals for 40, signifying their value in para. In this series the toughra of the sultan appeared on the obverse, with plain or elaborate surrounds, while the reverse bore the name of the sultan with a regnal year at the top and the date in the Muslim calendar at the foot. Gold coins [16–17] were produced in two types, for trade and mainly for jewellery respectively, the latter being generally thinner and pierced for adornment.

TURKISH REPUBLIC

The Greek invasion of Anatolia in 1921 provoked a resurgence of Turkish nationalism under Mustapha Kemal, who proclaimed a republic at Ankara in 1923 and overthrew the sultanate. The republic adopted the piastre of 100 para, omitting the toughra and

Currency Reform

The Turkish currency was reformed in January 2005, when the yeni (new) lira of 100 yeni kurus replaced a million old lira.

introducing the first pictorial elements: an ear of wheat (obverse) and a spray of oak leaves (reverse), with the crescent and star emblem at the top. These coins continued to be inscribed entirely in Arabic until 1934–5, when the lira of 100 kurus was inscribed in the modified Roman alphabet and the date appeared in the Western calendar [23–24]. In the early versions of the lower denominations the star appeared above the crescent, but from 1949 onward the emblem was rotated so that the star appeared on the left side. Silver coins bore the profile of Kemal Ataturk ("father of the Turks") and a wreathed value [25–26]. Gold coinage was resumed in 1943, with Kemal's effigy (obverse) and an elaborate Arabic inscription (reverse).

INFLATION

Turkey was overtaken by inflation in the 1980s; in the space of 20 years the 50 lira piece was reduced from a large silver coin to a tiny aluminium-bronze piece. In the 1990s base metal coins of 500, 1000, 1500, 2500 and 5000 lira briefly appeared, followed by coins denominated in *bin lira* (thousands of lira). By the end of the 20th century the 100,000 lira was a small aluminium coin [27–34].

In the same period commemorative coins appeared in gold or silver, culminating in the coin issued to celebrate the 700th anniversary of the Ottoman Empire (1999), which was denominated 60,000,000 lira.

PALESTINE, ISRAEL AND JORDAN

The region known as the Middle East forms the land bridge connecting Asia and Africa, and has therefore been an important crossroads of commerce since time immemorial. For the same reason, it has frequently been fought over and, indeed, remains an area of conflict to this day. Palestine (the land of the Philistines) was conquered by the Jews 3000 years ago. Since then it has been successively invaded and occupied by the Assyrians, Persians, Egyptians, Greeks, Romans, Byzantines and Arabs. For four centuries Palestine was part of the Ottoman Empire, before it came under British rule in 1917–18, following the demise of the empire. Britain was granted mandates by the League of Nations to administer the territories of Palestine and Transjordan. These mandates terminated in 1948 and resulted in the emergence of the State of Israel and the Hashemite Kingdom of Jordan.

Left: The Jewish Kingdom of Judaea was under Greek and later Roman rule, but rose in revolt on several occasions. The first Jewish revolt (AD 66–70) was suppressed by the Roman emperor Vespasian, who issued coins to celebrate this victory. He appears on the obverse. The reverse, inscribed "Judaea Capta", shows two Jews under a palm tree, symbolizing their defeat.

JEWISH KINGDOMS

For most of the period before the Common Era, the biblical lands of Judah and Israel used the coinage of foreign invaders and conquerors: the darics and sigloi of Persia, minted locally at Samaria [1–2]; the staters and tetradrachms of Alexander the Great and his successors, such as this coin depicting the goddess Athena but with a Samaritan–Aramaic countermark [3–4]; the Ptolemies of Egypt, exemplified by this tetradrachm of Ptolemy II, struck at Gaza [5–6]; and the Seleucids of Syria.

In 167 BC the Jews under Judas Maccabaeus rose in revolt against the Seleucid emperor Antiochus IV. At one time Jewish coins were attributed to this period, but it has now been proved that they belong to the first rebellion of the Jews against Rome in AD 66–70 [7–8]. In the interim, however, copper pruta circulated as small change and bore a Hebrew inscription on one side and twin cornucopiae on the other [9–10]. During the 1st century BC, Alexander Jannaeus assumed the kingship, and he and his successors struck bronze coins bearing various symbols, such as an anchor, wheel or stars. Although some coins were inscribed in Hebrew, most bore Greek titles. The coins of Herod the Great (37–4 BC) are particularly interesting, as they show increasing Roman stylistic influence. In AD 132–5 the Jews again rose in rebellion, led by Simon Barcochba ("son of the star"), hence the star symbols found on many of the coins of this period. After the revolt was crushed the Romans dispersed the Jews, beginning the Diaspora that continued until the early 20th century.

ISLAMIC RULE

Roman and Byzantine coins were used thereafter, but the encroachments of the Arabs were reflected in coins based on Byzantine models with Arabic inscriptions and motifs [11–12]. Islamic influence began in the 6th century AD, when the Sasanian Khusru II overthrew Byzantine rule. Byzantine gold and copper coins continued to be used in the region until supplies ran out. In the 10th century, Arab mints were established at Iliya Filistina (Jerusalem), Tiberias and Akka (Acre), striking Ikhshidid dinars [13–14]. By the end of that century the concentric designs of the Fatimids were prevalent, as seen in this gold bezant of Acre [15–16], and their coins were copied by much of the Islamic world.

KINGDOM OF JERUSALEM

By the end of the 11th century, the Fatimids had been overthrown by the Christian Crusaders. They established the Kingdom of Jerusalem, which initially extended over much of what is now Egypt and Lebanon. Typical of the Crusader coinage is a denier showing the Tower of David on the reverse [17–18]. The kingdom expired with the fall of Acre to the Mameluks in 1291. While Palestine remained under the rule of the Mameluks and later of the Ottomans, Syrian and Egyptian coins were in use.

BRITISH MANDATE

Under British rule coins inscribed in English, Hebrew and Arabic were issued in Palestine from 1927 to 1948. Those that did not have a central hole

---

Microprocessor Background
Since 1984 a number of definitive and commemorative Israeli coins portraying famous people, such as Theodor Herzl (below right), have had backgrounds formed by the continuous repetition of their names printed by microprocessor.

---

bore an olive branch on the reverse [19–25]. Technically the mandate included Transjordan, so Palestinian currency circulated there as well, even though politically it was administered separately. In 1921 the British installed the Emir Abdullah, and in 1923 the lands to the east of the River Jordan became an autonomous state, although they remained under British mandate until 1948.

ISRAEL

The British mandate terminated in May 1948 and the State of Israel was proclaimed on May 14. Coins bearing dates according to the Jewish calendar were introduced, their motifs derived from the coins of the Jewish revolts [26–34]. The currency was originally based on the Palestinian pound of 1000 mils, but in 1949 the lirah israelit (Israeli pound) of 1000 prutah was adopted. Following the monetary reform of 1958 the lirah was divided into 100 agorot. Continuing inflation led to the reform of February 1980 that introduced the sheqel of 100 new agorot (worth 1000 old agorot), but since September 1985 the currency has been stabilized on the basis of the sheqel chadash (new sheqel) worth 1000 sheqalim. In all of these series the biblical themes have continued.

Israel has been a prolific producer of special coins, partly commemorative and partly didactic, upholding the image of the modern state with its roots in ancient Jewish traditions.

JORDAN

The coinage of the Hashemite Kingdom of Jordan, commencing in 1949, is based on the dinar of 10 dirhems or 1000 fils, with inscriptions in Arabic (obverse) and English (reverse) [35–36]. Non-figural motifs were used exclusively until 1968, when a profile of King Hussein appeared on the obverse. In 1996 the currency was reformed and the dinar divided into 100 piastres [37–38]. The few commemoratives since 1969 have mainly marked anniversaries of the kingdom.

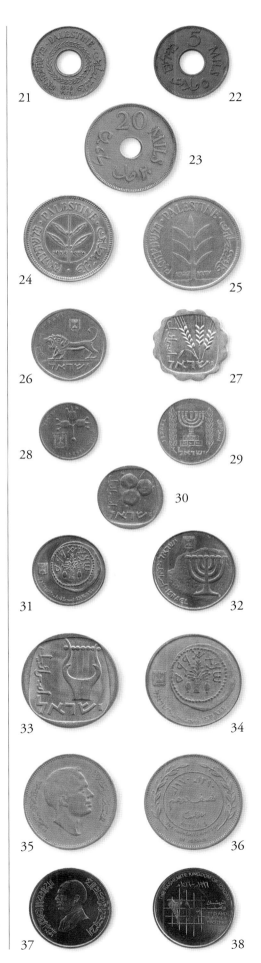

LEBANON, IRAQ AND SYRIA

This group of Middle Eastern countries did not exist until the 1920s, and yet the region has a numismatic history that goes back many centuries. It was successively conquered by the Persians, Alexander the Great, the Romans, Byzantines, Arabs and Crusaders, each of whom left their mark on the coinage of the area. For 400 years the territories remained under Turkish rule, until they were liberated by the Allies during World War I and mandated to the British or French by the League of Nations.

Left: The obverse of the 25 and 100 dinar coins of 2004, the only Iraqi issues since the fall of Saddam Hussein, features a map of Iraq – the historic Mesopotamia, or land between the two rivers, Tigris and Euphrates, which the Arabs styled Al Jazira ("the island") – with dates according to the Western and Muslim calendars.

ANTIOCH

Seleucus I Nicator, who founded the city of Antioch, naming it after his father Antiochus, was one of Alexander the Great's generals. After Alexander's death the generals divided his empire between them and Seleucus gained the territory of Syria and built the Seleucid Empire. Successive Seleucid kings struck coins on Greek models, typified by these tetradrachms of Antiochus II (261–246 BC) [1–4] and Antiochus IV (175–164 BC) [5–6].

No fewer than 12 towns or cities called Antioch struck coins in the classical period [7–8], but of these the most important was Antioch on the Orontes, the capital of the western Seleucid Empire and later of the Roman province of Syria (modern Antakiyah, transferred from Syria to Turkey in 1939). In the Roman and Byzantine periods it ranked third in importance after Alexandria and Constantinople [9–10]. The city was devastated by an earthquake in 526 and rebuilt under the name of Theopolis. It produced a large number of light-weight gold solidi [11–12] in the reigns of Justin II and Maurice Tiberius in the late 6th century.

In the early Islamic period Syria fell under the rule of the Umayyads and Abbasids and struck silver dirhams, notably under Caliph al-Malik, who struck coins at his capital, Damascus, as well as Basra [13–14]. Antioch was liberated in 1098 during the first Crusade and became the capital of a principality that flourished in the 12th century. In this period copper folles [15–16] were struck by Roger of Salerno. Its fall to the Mameluk sultan Baybars in 1268 marked the end of an era that left a rich legacy of copper and billon coins [17–18].

MEDIEVAL DIVERSITY

Antioch was only one of several Crusader kingdoms and principalities that struck gold, silver and base-metal coins in the 12th and 13th centuries, modelled mainly on French deniers, and coins may also be encountered from Acre, Tripoli and Edessa, such as this follis of Baldwin II [19–20]. Meanwhile, Turkic tribes were migrating from Central Asia into the Near East. The Artuqids settled at Hisn Kayfa, while the Zengids occupied Mosul and Aleppo. Their coins are remarkable for their obverses, which bear astrological symbols [21–22] or are derived from classical Greek models [23], while the reverses conform to the Islamic style.

In the 11th century Tughril Beg, leader of the Seljuqs, advanced westward and made himself master of Baghdad. He and his successors extended their empire to the Caucasus and Anatolia. Islamic coinage was struck in many towns in and around Mesopotamia by Seljuqs, Urtuqids,

Royal Portraiture

Unusually for the period, the coins of Iraq portrayed the reigning monarch on the obverse and followed the British custom of profiles facing alternately to the right (Faisal I, 1931–3), then to the left (Ghazi, 1933–9).

Abbasids and Zengids. In the epoch of the Ottoman Empire, from 1516 onwards, coins were struck at Dimishq (Damascus) and Halab (Aleppo), in what is now Syria, and at Mardin, Al-Ruha and Amid in what is now Iraq. The rich variety of coins surviving from this period ranges from the 16th-century gold sultani of Mehmed III, struck at Dimishq [24–25] to the silver dirhams of Haroun al Rashid struck at Basra and the coins of the Zengid Atabegs of Mosul.

IRAQ

Mesopotamia was freed from Turkish rule in 1917 by the British, who were granted a mandate to govern the territory in 1920. It became an independent kingdom in 1921 under Faisal I, whose profile appeared on the coins introduced there in 1931 [26–29]. Similar coins portrayed Ghazi (1933–9) and Faisal II, who was murdered in 1958 when the monarchy was toppled in the first of several military coups. The reverse of the royal coinage, denominated in fils, dirhams, riyals and dinars, bore the value and inscriptions entirely in Arabic. Under the republic, royal effigies were replaced by a motif of palm trees. The relatively few commemoratives issued since 1970 have celebrated such events as peace with the Kurds (1971), oil nationalization (1973) and various anniversaries of the army or the ruling Ba'ath Party.

SYRIA

The League of Nations conferred a mandate on France to rule the Levantine states of Syria and Lebanon. A series of revolts in the 1920s led the French to concede an autonomous republic in Syria (1930), leading to complete independence in 1944. Faisal was briefly king before the French ejected him and the British placed him on the Iraqi throne, and in this period a gold dinar was minted.

Under the French protectorate piastres were inscribed in French and Arabic [30–32]. From 1948 onward, coins bore the eagle emblem of the republic, with Arabic values on the reverse. Subtle changes in inscriptions signified the United Arab Republic (1959–60) and the Syrian Arab Republic (since 1962).

LEBANON

Although the French had a mandate to govern Syria and Lebanon together, they were quick to distinguish between the predominantly Christian Sanjak of Lebanon and Muslim Syria, and as early as September 1920 established the former as the Etat du Grand Liban (State of Greater Lebanon). Coins thus inscribed were adopted in 1924; those without a central hole bore the cedar emblem on the obverse. Some coins from 1929 onward were inscribed "République Libanaise" (Lebanese Republic) although full sovereignty was not granted until 1946 [33, 36]. Few coins were struck during the prolonged civil wars of the 1970s and 80s; those issued since 1968 bear the name of the Banque du Liban (Bank of the Lebanon) [34–35]. A handful of gold and silver coins marked the Lake Placid Winter Olympics of 1980.

Above: Palm trees replaced royal portraits on the coins issued by the Iraqi Republic.

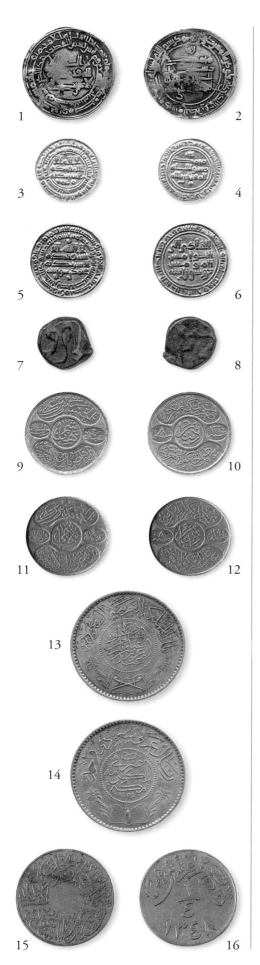

ARABIA

A geographical, rather than a political, entity, Arabia is a great peninsula of more than 2.5 million sq km/1 million sq miles between the Red Sea and the Persian Gulf, stretching from the Mediterranean in the north to the Indian Ocean in the south. At its core lies the kingdom of Saudi Arabia; to the south lies the Yemen, while along its eastern and northern borders are a series of smaller countries and petty states whose wealth and importance far exceed their size, as a result of the oil reserves that lie beneath them. Arabia was the cradle of Islam in the 7th century AD, and its language, alphabet, literature, arts and sciences have spread across the world, from Spain and north-west Africa to South-east Asia and the East Indies.

Left: The silver dirham (drachma) evolved in AH 79 (AD 698) and was to become the standard coin of the Islamic world for five centuries. The design of both obverse and reverse was composed entirely of Arabic inscriptions surrounded by circles and annulets. The obverse bears the Muslim declaration of faith while the reverse has a Qur'anic quotation surrounded by the prophetic mission.

CENTRE OF ISLAM

In September 622 Muhammad bin Abdallah fled from Mecca, his birthplace, where he was being persecuted by those who objected to his prophetic mission and teachings on monotheism, to join his followers at Yathrib, later renamed simply Medina ("the city"). This dramatic event was the Hegira or Hijra, from which Muslims date their calendar. Over the ensuing century the followers of Muhammad would create a movement that spread across the known world like wildfire and remains a potent force to this day.

Muhammad led his followers in war on Mecca, in which they were eventually victorious. He consolidated his rule over a unified Arabia, but when he died in 632 he left no son to succeed him. Instead, his powers were divided among two of his fathers-in-law and his two sons-in-law. To the senior father-in-law, Abu Bakr, fell the title of Caliph ("follower"), the spiritual head of Islam.

Arabia was an arid region inhabited by nomadic pastoralists, yet by the 8th century the Arabs had conquered the whole of North Africa and penetrated the Iberian Peninsula. They struck north, south and east, spreading the doctrines of Islam wherever they went. Inevitably as Islam spread, the centre of the religious and temporal power moved away from Mecca and Medina, and by the 9th century Arabia had reverted to the cluster of petty tribal states that had existed before the rise of Muhammad.

RIVAL CALIPHATES

Under the early caliphs, Arabia relied heavily on the gold and silver coins brought to Mecca and Medina by the faithful. By the 9th century, the Abbasids were striking coins at Sana'a and Aden in the Yemen as well as at Makka (Mecca), mostly silver dirhams [1–2]. They were followed by other dynasties such as the Rassids, who minted some beautiful gold dinars at Sana'a [3–4] and even larger coins at Sa'da about 910 [5–6].

Other dynasties that were prolific producers of gold and silver coins included the Ziyadids and Najahids of Zahid, the Sulayhids and the Fatimids. Constantly at war with each other, they fell easy prey to the invading Osmanli Turks who, by 1516, were in firm control. Thereafter Arabia was part of the Ottoman Empire. During this period, however, base-metal coins intended for small change were also struck by local *sharifs* (governors). They were pretty basic pieces, with simple motifs and mint-marks, such as this coin from Mecca [7–8].

SAUDI ARABIA

By the beginning of the 20th century Ottoman power was more nominal than real. From the late 18th century onward Arabia was in the British sphere of influence, the agents of the East India Company having concluded commercial treaties with local rulers from Aden to the Persian Gulf. In the 19th century a power struggle developed between rival factions, and the Turks supported the Rashidis against the Saudis. By 1887 the latter had lost most of their lands and went into exile in Kuwait. But in 1901 Abdul Aziz ibn Saud recaptured Riyadh, capital of the Sultanate of Nejd. He proclaimed himself sultan in 1905 and captured the Turkish province of Al Hasa in 1913.

Ibn Saud struck Hashimi gold dinars of good quality in AH 1334 (1915) [9–10]. Backing the British against the Turks in World War I, he embarked on the conquest of the Hejaz in 1925 and seized most of Asir the following year. To this period belongs the dinar minted in 1923 [11–12]. In 1932, Ibn Saud merged Hejaz and Nejd and founded the Kingdom of Saudi Arabia.

Countermarked coins were used at first, notably the Indian rupee and the Maria Theresia thaler, but a regular coinage based on the dinar of 5 riyals or 100 piastres was adopted in 1916, followed by similar coins, inscribed entirely in Arabic, for Hejaz and Nejd [13–16] and then the series of Saudi Arabia, distinguished by the palm tree and crossed swords emblem, from 1937 onwards [17–19].

A new currency, based on the riyal of 100 halala, was adopted in 1963. The innate conservatism of Saudi Arabia is demonstrated by the strict adherence to Qur'anic teaching and the total absence of any image, human or animal, on the coins [20–23].

United Yemen

In May 1990 the Yemen Arab Republic, also known as North Yemen, joined its southern neighbour to form a single nation state, the Republic of the Yemen. Coins depicting the eagle emblem, modern buildings and the ancient bridge at Shaharah were introduced in 1993.

YEMEN

Coins based on the imadi riyal of 40 buqsha or 80 halala were struck at Sana'a, the capital, from 1902 [24–27], the Mutawakelite Kingdom finally breaking free from the Ottomans in 1916. 1962 the imam was deposed and the socialist Yemen Arab Republic was proclaimed. There was little change in the coinage, other than the Arabic inscriptions, but in 1974 the currency was decimalized, introducing the rial of 100 fils, with an eagle emblem on the obverse [28–29]. A number of gold or silver coins since 1969 have commemorated such disparate subjects as the *Mona Lisa* and the Apollo landing.

The coins of the British East India Company and later of India circulated in British-ruled Aden prior to 1959, when it formed the core of the Federation of South Arabia and adopted the dinar of 100 fils. The reverses of these coins featured crossed *jambiyas* (curved daggers) or a dhow [30–31]. Following a revolution in 1970 the country became the People's Democratic Republic of Yemen, and its coins were subsequently inscribed in Arabic and English [32–33].

1
2
3
4
5
6
7
8
9
10
11
12
13
14
15
16
17
18

GULF STATES

This is the collective term for the small countries on the fringes of Arabia, along the western and southern shores of the Persian Gulf. They were inhabited by Arab tribes, the subjects of Persia or the Ottoman Empire at various times. They were first penetrated by the Portuguese in the 16th century but the British East India Company established trading posts in the early 19th century and in the wake of commerce came treaties of protection with Britain. These relations with the sheikhdoms and emirates of the Gulf terminated in the 1960s, leading to full independence a decade later.

Left: The 100 baisa bimetallic coin of Oman, issued in 1991, celebrated the centenary of coinage in the sultanate. The copper half-anna of 1891, showing a view of the port of Muscat, was reproduced on the reverse. The Arabic numerals signify AH 1411.

BAHRAIN

This country, ruled by the Al Khalifa family, consists of a cluster of islands that, prior to the discovery of oil in the 1930s, depended on pearl fishing. Revenue from oil has been wisely used to create an ultra-modern state and a major communications and commercial centre. Bahrain attained complete sovereignty in 1971 but introduced its own coins in 1965, with a palm tree obverse and value reverse based on the dinar of 1000 fils [1–2]. A new series, released in 1992, has the values in Western numerals on the reverse [3–10]. A few commemoratives have appeared since the UN Food and Agriculture Organization issue of 1969, including several silver coins portraying the ruler in Arab dress.

KUWAIT

Fearing Turkish encroachment, Sheikh Mubarak of the ruling Al Sabah family, who struck this Kuwaiti baisa in 1887 [11–12], sought British protection in 1899. The agreement was terminated in 1961 and Kuwait became a fully independent country.

Thanks to oil revenue, the Kuwaiti dinar is the world's strongest currency, fully backed by gold. The coins from 1 to 100 fils, introduced in 1961, feature a *sambuke*, or two-masted Arab dhow, with double dates (Christian and

Muslim) in Arabic numerals, while the obverse bears the value with the name of the country in Arabic and English [13–16]. A few commemoratives have appeared since 1976, when a silver double dinar celebrated the 15th anniversary of independence with portraits of Abdullah ibn Salim (1950–65) and his successor Sabah ibn Salim (1965–77) side by side. Gold and silver coins of 1981 marked the 1500th anniversary of the Hegira.

OMAN

Although the mint at 'Uman (Oman) operated only occasionally in the 10th century, both gold and silver coins were struck by the Wajihid governors of the province. The dirhams shown here were struck by Ahmad bin Hilal [17–18] and Muhammad bin Yusuf [19–20] between AH 299 and 310, but after about AH 350 coins were supplied from the Yemen.

In 1508 the Portuguese captured Muscat, the capital and chief seaport of the sultanate, in the first European penetration of the Gulf region. In 1650 they were ejected by the Persians, who ruled until 1741, when Ahmed ibn Sa'id seized power and established the dynasty that has reigned ever since. Muscat and Oman was the most powerful state in Arabia until the mid-19th century, when it was weakened by

Prolific Output

Immediately before the Federation of Arab Emirates was formed, many distinctive coins were produced in Ajman, Fujairah, Ras al Khaimah, Sharjah and Umm al Qiwain, a parallel to the unduly prolific stamp issues of the same period and likewise aimed at collectors. Subjects ranged from the World Cup to champions of sport. Sharjah's 5 rupee coin of 1964 was the first in the world to mourn the death of John F. Kennedy.

nomadic attacks. In 1798 it signed a treaty with Britain, which subsequently played a major role in its defence. Sultan Sa'id was overthrown in 1970 by his son Qabus, who dropped "Muscat" from the country's name.

The first coins were quarter and twelfth annas, struck in 1893. They had a pictorial reverse but the following year an all-Arabic non-figural type was adopted. The coinage was reformed in 1945, adopting the Saidi riyal of 200 baisa, with the national emblem, a dagger over crossed swords, on the obverse and Arabic inscriptions on the reverse. Qabus reformed the currency in 1972, adopting the Omani riyal of 1000 baisa. As well as a modified obverse inscription reflecting the change of

name, this series has the value in Arabic numerals on the reverse [21–24]. A conservative policy with regard to special issues was followed until 1995, when a lengthy series of 20 silver coins depicting Omani forts was released.

QATAR

This emirate was under Ottoman rule from 1872 until 1916, when the Turkish garrison was withdrawn. Sheikh Abdullah bin Qasim promptly sought British protection, which continued until 1971. The first coins were issued in 1966 and bore the names of Qatar and Dubai, with a gazelle on the reverse [25–26]. A plan to unite with Bahrain and the Trucial States was abandoned and since September 1971 Qatar has been fully independent. Separate coins were introduced in 1973 based on the riyal of 100 dirhem, with Arabic values (obverse) [27] and a dhow and palm tree (reverse).

UNITED ARAB EMIRATES

The sheikhdoms of Abu Dhabi, Ajman, Dubai, Fujairah, Sharjah and Umm al Qiwain [28–29] formed the Federation of Arab Emirates in December 1971, after the withdrawal of British protection over the area formerly known collectively as the Trucial States. In February 1972 Ras al Khaimah joined the federation, which became the United Arab Emirates and began issuing coins thus inscribed in 1973. Its coins are comparatively conservative, with Arabic values (obverse) married to reverses depicting date palms, dhow, gazelle, Mata Hari fish [30–32] and an offshore oil rig.

Above: The diamond-shaped 20 baisa of AH 1359 (1940) was struck by Oman specifically for Dhofar Province.

IRAN AND AFGHANISTAN

The Persian Empire embraced the lands now occupied by both modern Iran and Afghanistan, and at its height extended from Asia Minor to the north-west frontier of India, from the Caspian Sea to the Bay of Bengal. In its heyday, more than two millennia ago, it was one of the greatest civilizations and played a major role in the development of early coinage.

Left: Since 1994 Iranian coins of the higher denominations have been struck in bimetallic combinations. Their reverse motifs are derived from ancient art forms featuring stylized flowers.

ANCIENT PERSIA

The art of coinage spread eastward from Lydia, in modern Turkey, in the mid-6th century BC. The Greek historian Herodotus suggested that Darius Hydaspes (521–486) was the first ruler to strike coins, hence the name "daric" applied to the gold piece, equivalent to 20 sigloi (shekels) of silver. Both bore the kneeling figure of an archer – the king himself – on the obverse. These coins were roughly oval in shape and remained unchanged until the fall of the Persian Empire to Alexander the Great in the 4th century BC.

After Alexander, Persia was ruled by various satraps, or governors, who struck silver coins in abundance. In the mid-second century the Parthians overcame their Seleucid (Greek) masters and created a new empire in Persia. Silver coins on the Greek standard portrayed Arsakes, founder of the dynasty, exemplified by this coin of Osroes II dating from AD 190 [1–2]. Latterly, coins had inscriptions of corrupt Greek mingled with Pehlevi, the indigenous language.

The Kushans, a tribe originating in Xinjiang, China, created an empire that flourished from AD 105 to 250 and stretched from Tajikistan to northern India. At its height it produced gold and copper coins [3–4] but virtually no silver. The Kushan Empire declined early in the 3rd century AD, and much of its territory was absorbed by the Sasanians. Ardashir defeated the Bactrians and Parthians and established the Sasanian Empire, which ruled all of Western Asia and originally struck coins with a strong Kushan influence [5–6]. Gold and silver coins were modelled on Roman solidi and Greek drachmae respectively, the latter noted for their very wide, thin flans, later copied by the Arabs. Shown here are a gold solidus of Peroz I (459–84) [7–8] and drachmae of Khusru V (631–3) [9–12]. More orthodox in appearance were the billon tetradrachms of Elymais [13–14], a semi-independent kingdom in what is now south-western Iran, which was conquered by Ardashir.

MEDIEVAL PERSIA

In the 13th century the Mongols, under Genghis Khan, swept across Asia. The Ilkhans of Persia produced spectacular coins in gold [15–16], silver and copper at Tabriz, with the Shia creed of Islam (obverse) and the khan's title in Mongol (reverse). Shah Rukh introduced a new type of dirham, which remained popular from the 15th to the early 18th centuries [17–18] and provided the model for the thin silver coins, which later became smaller and thicker [19–20]. These coins were remarkable for their inscriptions and extensive use of rhyming couplets.

Regal coinage, confined to silver and gold, was struck at numerous provincial mints identified by Arabic abbreviations of their names. Many towns, however, produced their own copper falus, usually featuring animals or birds on the obverse, which serve to identify their origin.

MODERN COINAGE

The bewildering array of weights and values in the Persian coinage was rationalized in 1835 and the currency was based on the toman of 10 krans, 200 shahis or 10,000 dinars. The coins of Persia were consolidated by Shah Nasr al Din in 1876. All the branch mints were shut down and western machinery was installed at Tehran. Coins featured the radiate sun or lion and sunrise emblems [21–22] but from 1897 onward the portrait of the shah was often used.

In 1925 Reza Pahlavi overthrew the Qajar dynasty and proclaimed himself Reza Shah. He reformed the coinage in 1931, creating the toman of 10 rials, 1000 dinars or 5000 shahis. The name of the country was changed to Iran in 1935. In Reza Shah's reign coins reverted to the lion motif with the value in Arabic script [23–24]. His successor, Muhammed Reza Shah, had his profile on coins from 1966 until 1979, when he was overthrown [25–26]. Since then, the coins of the Islamic republic have eschewed portraiture, and mosques, tombs and other landmarks have appeared instead.

AFGHANISTAN

This remote country between Iran and India has been fought over for countless centuries. Distinctive coinage was produced in the area from the 4th century BC onward, notably the issues from the kingdoms of Bactria and Kabul. Lying between the Hindu Kush and the Oxus, Bactria occupied what is now northern Afghanistan and struck coins on the Greek standard, such as this gold stater of 250–230 BC [27–28]. Rectangular copper coins, such as the type by Menander of about 155 BC [29–30], were also produced.

The Kingdom of Kabul, ruled by the White Huns (5th century) and the Turko-Hephthalites (8th century) also minted coins. Afghanistan as a sovereign state developed only from 1747 under the Durrani dynasty, whose coinage aped that of the Mughal Empire, with the same fondness for

The Tyranny of the White Huns

The Hephthalites or White Huns were a nomadic people who invaded the Sasanian Empire in the 4th century. They captured Shah Peroz, ransomed him, then used the millions of Sasanian silver coins paid to them as the basis of their own coins, derived from Sasanian, Kushan and Greek types.

poetic couplets [31–32]. Copper coins were struck by hand in numerous provincial mints, while gold and silver pieces often appeared in the name of rival contenders for the throne.

A national mint was established at Kabul in 1891 and machine-struck coinage was adopted in a system based on the Kabuli rupee of 2 qiran, 3 abbasi, 6 sanar, 12 shahi, 60 paisa or 600 dinar. These coins bore the state emblem and an Arabic text. In the 1920s coins based on the afghani of 100 pul were struck bearing the *toughra* of Muhammed Nadir Shah. Following the overthrow of Zahir Shah in 1973, coins were issued with a wreathed eagle emblem.

Afghanistan became a democratic republic in 1979, and this regime, under Soviet protection, continued until 1989. In this period, coins with communist-style emblems were struck in Cuba. When Russian forces withdrew, Afghanistan descended into chaos as the Mujahideen fought the Taliban, who established a fundamentalist Islamic state in 1994. The most recent coins of the Islamic Republic of Afghanistan, denominated in afghanis, feature a mosque [33–34]. The date on the reverse is 1383, which approximates to the year 2004.

BURMA, PAKISTAN AND BANGLADESH

These countries were at one time part of British India, acquired by the Honourable East India Company by conquest in the course of the 18th and 19th centuries. Apart from this, the regions had little in common. Britain fought a long series of wars between 1824 and 1885 to subjugate Burma, which had its own long-established culture and political structure. The territory that is now Pakistan was a major component of the Mughal Empire. It had close ties with Afghanistan, and a coinage with a long and complex history dating back to the pre-Christian era.

Left: The independent Kingdom of Burma was renowned for its distinctive coinage, which had a peacock motif on the obverse and continued until 1885, when it was replaced by Indian coins. Highly prized were the silver kyats, which were subsequently decorated with coloured enamels to make a fashionable form of jewellery at the end of the 19th century.

BURMA

The Kingdom of Arakan struck coins based on Indian designs from the late 7th century, the conch being a popular motif [1–2]. In the Middle Ages, coins of the neighbouring Muslim sultans in Bengal were in use, but Arakanese coins were revived in the 16th century and continued until the 1790s; this 17th-century tanka bears the title "Lord of the White Elephants" used by the Arakan kings [3–6]. In southern Burma, influenced by Malaya, there was a tradition of tin coins from the 17th to 19th centuries [7–8].

Under the last kings, Mindon (1853–78) and Thibaw (1880–5), coins were struck in various denominations (kyat of 5 mat or 10 mu, 20 pe or 80 pyas), the silver kyat corresponding to the Indian rupee and the gold kyat to the mohur. Burma is one of the few countries in relatively modern times to have struck coins in lead for small change; the eighth and quarter pya of 1869 with a hare on the obverse. The quarter pe was struck in different metals: copper (1865), iron (1865), copper again (1878) and latterly brass. Higher denominations featured a lion or peacock on the obverse, with the wreathed value inscribed in words on the reverse [9].

In 1937 Burma was detached from India and granted autonomy, though it continued to use Indian currency. In 1948 it attained independence and left the Commonwealth. Cupro-nickel or pure nickel coins denominated in pyas or pe appeared in 1948–9, followed by the decimal kyat of 100 pyas from 1952. All these coins had the image of a *chinthe* (mythological lion guardian) on the obverse and the value in Burmese script on the reverse. Ironically, in 1966 a new series portrayed national hero Aung San, whose daughter Aung San Suu Kyi, winner of the Nobel Peace Prize, has been under house arrest by the ruling military junta, beginning in 1989. The country changed its name in that year to Myanmar (actually a more accurate phonetic rendering of the indigenous name) and coins with that name in European lettering have been issued since 1999 [10–11], but the new name and government have not been internationally recognized.

PAKISTAN

The area that was Pakistan was ruled in turn by Parthians, Kushans and Hephthalites (White Huns), the last-named striking silver coins in the 5th century [12–13]. Later came the

Sasanians and the Ghaznavids, who introduced Islam and struck coins at Lahore derived from Afghan types. From Afghanistan the Mughals conquered much of the Indian subcontinent. Multan, where this gold mohur was struck [14–15], was an important mint from the 16th to late 18th centuries. The Punjab was conquered in the mid-18th century by the Sikhs, who produced silver rupees at Lahore [16–17] and Peshawar [18–19] until the mid-19th century, when the region came under British rule.

When the British left India in 1947, the subcontinent was divided into the predominantly Hindu Dominion of India and the Muslim Dominion of Pakistan. Coins inscribed "Government of Pakistan" appeared in 1948, with a *toughra* or crescent and star motifs. The rupee of 16 annas gave way to the rupee of 100 paisa in 1961.

The Islamic Republic of Pakistan was proclaimed in 1956, and at first there was no change in the inscription, but English was dropped in 1964 [20–21]. A few 50 paisa or rupee coins have appeared since 1976, mainly to commemorate anniversaries of Jinnah, founder of the state [22–23], or the 1400th anniversary of the Hegira (1981). Gold, silver and cupro-nickel coins of 1977 publicized the Islamic Summit Conference. A set of three large coins in gold or silver appeared in

1976 to promote wildlife conservation. Pakistan has been under military rule for many years, punctuated by brief periods of parliamentary democracy, but political instability has not been reflected by any changes in the coinage.

BANGLADESH

Situated on the Bay of Bengal, between India and Burma, Bangladesh was formerly the province of East Pakistan. Although sharing the Muslim faith of West Pakistan, it was culturally and historically distinct. In the 2nd and 3rd centuries AD, local Bengal kings issued beautiful Kushan-style coins [24–25]. There were significant developments in the late Gupta period, notably under Sasanka, King of Gauda c. 600–30 [26–27], while the silver coins of the Akara dynasty of Bangla Desh in the 10th–11th centuries [28–29] are particularly noteworthy.

In the medieval period, coins reflected Indian, Burmese and Islamic influence. The Ghorids (also dominant in Afghanistan) struck coins, as did the sultans of Bengal. Sultan al-din Iltutmish revived the horseman motif in gold and silver tankas. Chittagong and Dacca (Jahangirnagar) were prolific mints in the Mughal period, while the East India Company struck traditional gold mohurs for circulation in the Bengal Presidency [30–31].

East Pakistan's sense of neglect by the more affluent West Pakistan led to an independence movement. Its people used the techniques of civil disobedience developed by Gandhi in India, provoking massive military retaliation. In support of East Pakistan India went to war with West Pakistan in 1971, and as a result the East declared independence as Bangladesh. Pakistani currency continued until 1973, when the taka of 100 poisha was introduced. Coins feature the *shapla* (lily) national emblem and various symbols of agriculture [32–33]. Significantly, many coins have been issued in connection with the FAO programme and since 1991 a few silver coins have celebrated anniversaries of independence or global concerns such as conservation.

Family Planning

The population of Bangladesh is increasing at an alarming rate, and even coins are harnessed to the government campaign for family planning. Several coins since 1975 have depicted the ideal nuclear family in an attempt to get this message across.

EARLY INDIA

One of the world's largest and most populous countries, India is regarded as a subcontinent, bounded by the Arabian Sea and the Bay of Bengal, and it gives its name to the ocean that lies to the south. It is home to civilizations and religions that date back several millennia and it is probable that coinage originated there quite separately from that of Asia Minor or China, although it very quickly came under Greek influence.

Left: Typical of Indo-Greek coinage is this silver drachm of Radhasinha II (AD 305–13). It combines the sculptural and punch-mark techniques characteristic of the period.

EARLIEST COINAGE

Some of the earliest money in circulation in India consisted of gold discs with a central hole, which doubled as jewellery [1–2], but lead coins were struck by the chiefs of Karnataka in the second century AD [3]. Indian coinage developed along distinctive lines, consisting of pieces of silver or copper, often square or rectangular in shape, with flat surfaces into which various symbols or marks were punched on both sides [4–5].

During the period 600–300 BC, various petty kingdoms and states were producing distinctive coins that drew heavily on the Greek influences of the same period in their weight and style [6–7]. By the 4th century BC, if not earlier, both square and circular coins [8–9] were being cast in copper, with somewhat similar, though less diverse, symbolism. It is clear, from later discoveries of hoards, that these coins circulated all over India.

The empire created by Alexander the Great extended to the Indus and beyond, and the provinces of Parthia and Bactria (lying in what is now Iran) exerted a great influence on the development of Indian coinage, both the copper coins of numerous petty states and the tiny silver hemidrachms, which were rich in mythological symbolism. In the 2nd century BC the Greeks of Bactria encroached on north-west India and struck a wide range of portrait coins. The Greek inscriptions gradually gave way to Prakrit or became very corrupt, and the gods of classical Greece were supplanted by Indian deities, reflecting the rise of the Indo-Scythian kingdoms and the great Kushan Empire, which flourished in the north-west from the 1st century AD and whose coins were apparently influenced by Roman models [10–11]. The Kushans' prolific gold and copper coinage was notable for inscriptions in Persian but written in a corrupt Greek form [12–13]. Portraits of rulers vied with images of the deities pertaining to all the religions of the period, in a style that endured for over 1000 years.

A great number of different types of coinage flourished in the various parts of India. In western India, satraps of Persian origin ruled from the 1st century BC and produced an abundant supply of silver coins featuring a bust of the ruler, down to the time of Swami Rudrasimha III, the last of the satraps of western India [14–15], who ruled in the late 4th century. The western satraps were overthrown by the Guptas, who began to imitate their silver. The Guptas originated in eastern India and spread northward. Their coins were elegant and often adapted Kushan designs [16–20], notably the Lakshmi and lion-slayer types of Chandragupta [21–22]. The White Huns swept aside the Gupta and other Indian civilizations in the 6th century but produced coins modelled on Kushan, Sasanian and Gupta types [23–24].

In central and southern India the Andras struck coins in lead around the beginning of the Common Era; later dynasties in the same area struck

gold coins: these usually depicted the dynastic emblem [25–26], such as the elephant of Malabar or the boar favoured by the Chalukyas of the Deccan, who also produced punch-marked gold pagodas in the 11th and 12th centuries [27–28]. The Chola dynasty struck coins with a standing figure of the ruler on the obverse and the same figure seated on the reverse, a style that was widely copied.

Coinage declined in southern and eastern India in the 6th century, though kingdoms close to Bombay continued to mint coins for some time. A seated figure of Lakshmi was a popular motif for the Kalachuri gold coins of Tripuri [29–30].

MUGHAL EMPIRE

Islam spread to north-west India in the 8th century, but apart from some coins struck in what is now the Indo-Pakistan border area it was not until Mahmud of Ghazna conquered the Punjab in the 11th century that the new culture had much impact on Indian coinage. In 1193 Muhammad bin Sam conquered northern India and established a devoutly Islamic dynasty that lasted until 1399, when Tamerlane sacked Delhi. He created a great Mongol Empire, which stretched from the Mediterranean to the Ganges. As this disintegrated, the Mughals built up an empire that embraced much of modern Afghanistan but gradually spread over the whole of India. The coins of the first Mughal rulers, Baber and Humayun, accorded with the prevailing types of Central Asia [31–32]. However, new designs, sizes and weights were adopted by their successors, notably Jahangir, whose gold coins are among the most splendid in their artistic calligraphy as well as their poetic inscriptions. Square rupees continued under Akbar until the early 17th century [33–34].

Gold was struck only sporadically in the 15th and 16th centuries; there were brief experiments with brass coins but billon was preferred. Under Sher Shah (1539–45) there was a profuse issue of good silver coins, bearing the Kalima (the Islamic confession of faith) and the names of the Four Caliphs, and this set the style for the gold and silver coins that continued until the Mughal Empire was swallowed up by the French and British in the 18th century.

In 1613 Shah Jahangir commissioned the production at Agra of five gold coins with a value of 1000 mohur. These massive coins had a diameter of 203mm/8in and weighed over 12kg/26lb. Their value in modern currency would be £250,000–300,000/ $440,000–525,000. Not intended for general circulation, they were presented to various foreign ambassadors. Gold 500 mohurs are mentioned in Jahangir's autobiography, while an electrotype of a 200 mohur is preserved in the British Museum in London. A 100 mohur coin, struck by Jahangir in 1639, had a diameter of 97mm/3.8in and weighed 1094g/2.4lb [35]. Aurungzeb (1658–1707) replaced the Islamic confession of faith with the name of the mint and the date, and this style prevailed until the end of Mughal rule.

Above: A gold coin issued in the reign of Muhammad bin Sam, Sultan of Delhi in the late 12th century.

1

2

3

4

5

6

7

8

9

10

11

12

13

14

15

16

17

18

19

20

21

22

INDIAN PRINCELY STATES

As the Mughal Empire declined from 1700 onward, many local dynasties sprang up, carving out independent principalities and often warring with each other or seeking alliances with one or other of the European powers gaining control in India. Although the Mughal Empire continued in name until 1857, by 1800 its powers had largely passed to the British East India Company, which exercised control to a greater or lesser extent over the princely states. After the suppression of the Sepoy Mutiny most of India came directly under British rule, but the rest was ruled indirectly through the medium of more than 1000 autonomous states. Even as late as 1947, when India gained independence, no fewer than 675 principalities remained. By 1950 the last of them had been abolished. At least 125 states produced their own coinage, mainly in the period from 1800 to 1900, though a number continued to issue coins until the 1940s.

Left: This gold mohur bearing the crowned bust of Victoria as Empress of India was struck at the Calcutta Mint in 1885. Copper and silver coins of this type were also issued from 1877 onward and were issued by the states of Alwar, Bikanir, Dhar and Dewas. Before she was proclaimed Empress of India in 1877, coins in the name of Queen Victoria had been struck in India from 1862.

MONETARY CONFUSION

Virtually every state had its own currency system, a situation complicated by the fact that there was very seldom a fixed ratio between copper, silver or gold. Values tended to vary according to the decrees of the local potentate, which could not have facilitated trade between the states. Certain denominations were widespread, such as the gold mohur, the silver rupee and the copper paisa, based on the coins of the Mughal Empire. Indeed, many coins included the name of the Mughal emperor in their inscriptions, presenting a nominal semblance of unity and adherence to the imperial principle. This silver rupee of Jaipur names the Mughal emperor Ahmed Shah Bahadur [1–2]. By the late 19th century, however, many coins bore inscriptions referring to Queen Victoria of "Inglistan" (England). As late as 1948 Jodhpur was still producing coins in the names of George VI and Hanwant Singh [3–4].

Some of the states in north-west India, such as Awadh and Hyderabad, produced copper falus [5–6] or gold ashrafi [7–8], reflecting their commercial and political ties to Persia or Afghanistan. States in the Kutch region, such as Bhavnagar, Porbandar and Junagadh [11–12], had silver kori and half kori and copper dhinglo, dokdo [13–14], dhabu [15–16] and trambiyo. Also shown is a gold coronation kori from Kutch [9–10]. The inhabitants of Cochin used chuckrams, puttuns and fanams, while neighbouring Travancore also had anantarayas. The silver tamasha circulated in Kashmir, while copper cash and the gold pagoda paralleled the silver rupee and its subdivisions (right down to the tiny ⅟₃₂ rupee) in Mysore. The pagoda was the chief gold coin of the southern Indian states, and the issues of Mysore were very prolific [17–20].

INSCRIPTIONS

Most of the state coinage had legends in Persian (Farsi) or Nagari script, but it was often crude and blundered and therefore difficult to read. Fortunately, various symbols, approximating to mint-marks, were also included, and it is on these that collectors generally rely in order to assign their coins to the correct state. In general, coins often present an appearance of Arabic, with one or more horizontal lines dividing the text. English inscriptions were confined to the coins issued in Bikanir, Travancore and Jaora.

IMAGES

The exceptional use of Queen Victoria's crowned bust has already been mentioned, but she also appeared bare-headed on the rupee and mohur of Bhartpur in 1858. In the Muslim states, the use of effigies was usually frowned upon, but the Hindu states made occasional attempts at portraiture. Sayaji Rao III, Gaekwar of Baroda, was profiled on gold and silver coins [21–22], while the last mohurs and rupees of Bikanir bore a full-face bust of Ganga Singh.

An exception to the exclusion of portraits is to be found on the coins of Bahawalpur (now part of Pakistan) whose ruler, Sadiq Muhammad Khan, appeared bare-headed or wearing a fez on copper coins and silver rupees minted in 1940, although most of his coins featured his *toughra*, or sign-manual [23–4]. Travancore stuck gold sovereigns and half-sovereigns with the bust of Maharajah Rama Varma V. His

Royal Portrait

Machine-struck cash and chuckrams of Travancore not only bore the denomination in English but also had the monogram RV on the obverse, denoting Maharajah Rama Varma VI (1885–1924). However, his successor, Bala Rama Varma II (1924–49), exceptionally placed his own portrait on the chuckram.

successor, Bala Rama Varma II, appeared in profile on the copper chuckrams of 1938–45.

The Hindu kingdom of Tripura in Bengal had a long tradition of pictorial coins. These were mostly silver tankas or ramatankas with a horse and trident reverse, but other motifs included an allegorical scene alluding to the conquest of Chittagong [25–26], and the ritual bath in the River Lakhmia [27–28]. The nazarana mohur of Dhar (1943) had an armorial obverse and a Farsi inscription on the reverse [29–30]. A coat of arms, along European lines, also appears on the mohurs (1912–14) and silver half rupee (1923) of Assam, the rupees of Tripura and the mohurs of Rewah.

Both a portrait obverse and armorial reverse occur on coins of Datia, Indore and Gwalior. Scenery and landmarks are conspicuously absent, with the solitary exception of Hyderabad, which featured its Char Minar monument on the obverse of most coins from 1903 to 1948 [31–32], although a toughra was used in the series of 1911–30. The silver coins of Mewar (1931–2), struck in the name of "a friend of London" (Bhupal Singh), are unique in having a panoramic scene on the obverse [33–34].

Most of the coins were non-figural, although occasionally a pictorial element crept in, as in the paisas of Baroda, which showed a dagger or sword, or the paisas of Derajat, Lunavada and Elichpur, with their crude figures of lions. The coins of Indore featured a sacred cow and also used the motif of a radiate sun, while Tonk showed a horse and Mysore favoured the elephant.

The Mughal emperor Jahangir (1605–28) produced a handsome series depicting the signs of the zodiac [35–36]. The only coin known to have been issued by Rajkot appeared in 1945 and had the state arms (obverse) and the rising sun (reverse). A sun face obverse, sometimes with a kneeling cow reverse, appears on many of the coins of Indore [37–38].

1

2

3

4

5

6

7

8

9

10

11

12

13

14

15

16

COLONIAL AND MODERN INDIA

In 1498 Vasco da Gama rounded the Cape of Good Hope and reached India by sea. Within a few years the Portuguese had established trading posts on the west coast, but they were soon overtaken by the Dutch, Danish, French and British, all of whom formed settlements on the east and west coasts. All the foreign settlements produced distinctive coinage.

Left: Coins with the crowned profile of George VI circulated until 1950, when the series inscribed "Government of India" was introduced. Among the patterns of 1947–9 were square 2 anna pieces, one with a peacock in side view and one face on, displaying its tail.

PORTUGUESE INDIA

Although Bombay passed from the Portuguese to the British as part of the dowry of Catherine of Braganza in 1660, Portugal continued to have a major interest in the subcontinent. Its settlements gradually declined but it retained Goa, Damao and Diu until 1962, when they were seized by the Republic of India.

Crude copper tanga [1–2] were produced at each settlement, each with its own currency system. Thus the rupia of 2 pardao or xerafim [3–4] in Goa was worth 480 reis, while in Diu the rupia was worth 10 tanga or 40 atias or 150 bazarucos or 600 reis. In 1871 the currency was reformed on the basis of the rupia [5–6] of 16 tanga or 960 reis, and coins inscribed "India Portugueza", with the profile of Luiz I (obverse) [7–8] and the royal arms (reverse) were introduced. After Portugal became a republic coins mainly featured the arms and cross emblems [9–12]; the escudo of 100 centavos was adopted in 1958.

DANISH INDIA

The Danes established trading posts at Pondicherry and Tranquebar, on the south-east coast of India, in 1620, but sold their remaining interests to the British East India Company in 1845. Crude copper or silver dumps denominated in cash and fano (fanams) respectively, with the crowned royal monogram (obverse) and the date and value (reverse), were produced until 1845, but they are now very rare.

DUTCH INDIA

The United East India Company of the Netherlands had a number of settlements that issued their own coins in the 18th and early 19th centuries. These included Negapatam, ceded to the British in 1784; Tuticorin, ceded in 1795; and Cochin, ceded in 1814. The last of the Dutch trading posts, at Pulicat, was transferred to British rule in 1824. Illustrated here is a tiny silver rupee of Jagannathpur [13–14] and a lead bazaruk of the Dutch East India Company [15–16].

FRENCH INDIA

The French did not take an interest in India until 1664, when the Compagnie des Indes Orientales was formed. Trading posts were established between 1666 and 1721, from Surat on the west coast to Balasore on the Bay of Bengal. There were inland settlements at Arcot in south India and at Chandernagore and Murshidabad in the north-east. Following the defeat of the French by Clive at Plassey (1759), France lost all its settlements apart from Pondicherry, which, in 1954, voted to join the Republic of India. Copper and silver coins based on the rupee of 64 biches (paisa) were augmented by fanons (fanams) and caches (cash). Apart from an issue of 1836–7 most coins were undated and very crude. The basic type of the silver fanon (2 royalins) showed a European crown on the obverse and the fleur de lys of France [17–18] but in deference to local custom a Hindu crown was later substituted, often reduced in the smaller coins to little more than a jumble of dots [19–22]. The copper cash showed a single fleur de lys, or a mere fragment in the smaller denominations. Coins of British India were used from 1848.

BRITISH INDIA

The territories of the British East India Company, developed from 1660, were divided into the Presidencies of Bengal, Madras, Malabar and Bombay (now Mumbai). Each produced coins that conformed to either the Hindu or Muslim coinage systems [23–24], based respectively on the pagoda of 42 fanams or 3360 cash, and the gold mohur (such as this coin of the Bengal Presidency in the name of the Mughal Shah 'Alam II [25–26]) of 16 rupees or 256 annas. The vast majority of coins were inscribed in Farsi, but Madras used Nagari script, as shown on this silver half pagoda of 1808 [27–28]. The Bombay coinage featured the bale-mark emblem (obverse) and scales (reverse) from 1791 onward, and an armorial obverse was gradually adopted from 1804.

Standard coins for the whole of British India were introduced in 1835. The copper denominations [29–30] featured the arms of the East India Company while the silver coins portrayed the reigning British monarch; all coins had a wreathed value reverse. Shown here is a gold restrike of the copper half anna of 1892, with Victoria as Empress [31–32]. A new reverse, featuring a tiger, was adopted in 1946 when nickel replaced silver in coins from 2 annas upwards. As a wartime economy measure the pice (quarter anna) was redesigned in 1943, retaining the original diameter but reducing the metal content by means

Architects of Modern India
Following the death of Jawaharlal Nehru in 1964 rupee coins with his dates of birth and death were struck for general circulation until 1967. This set the precedent for coins marking the birth centenaries of Mahatma Gandhi (1969–70) and Nehru himself (1969).

of a large central hole [33–34]. These coins continued until 1947 and are of immense interest as they were struck at Lahore, Bombay and Pretoria (South Africa) as well as Calcutta. As well as three different types of crown, there are variations in lettering and the presence or absence of mint-marks.

REPUBLIC OF INDIA

In August 1947 the British handed over power to the Muslims of Pakistan and the mainly Hindu government of India. The Dominion of India became a republic in 1950. In the first decade of independence the old coinage system, based on the rupee of 16 annas or 64 pice, was retained. The obverses of 1950–7 were inscribed "Government of India" around the Ashokan column, while the reverses bore the denomination in English and Hindi surrounding a pictorial motif.

In 1957 the rupee of 100 naye (new) paise was adopted. The column of Ashoka continued but now with the country name in Hindi and English, while the reverse motifs prominently featured the numerals of value [35–36]. The use of various shapes, begun under the British, was considerably extended, each value having a distinctive shape. The designs were subtly modified in the 1970s and 1980s, but in 1988 a new series of pictorial reverses was released [37–38].

1
2
3
4
5
6
7
8
9
10
11
12
13
14
15
16
17
18
19
20

INDIAN OCEAN

A number of islands in the Indian Ocean, which were formerly part of the British or French colonial empires, issue their own coins. They range from Sri Lanka (formerly Ceylon), which has a coinage dating back to the 1st century BC, to the territories that have adopted distinctive coins only in quite recent times.

Left: Following the capture of the island of Ceylon from the Dutch in 1796, and its proclamation as a British crown colony six years later, copper coins were issued by the British in 1802. They bore an Indian elephant on one side and the value or the effigy of George III on the other.

SRI LANKA

The ancient coins of this island followed the pattern of the Chola dynasty of northern India, who subjugated the indigenous Veddahs and ruled until 1408. Ceylon then came under Chinese control until the arrival of the Portuguese in 1505. They, in turn, were supplanted by the Dutch in 1658. Local coinage was produced in each of these eras, mainly silver tangas such as this specimen from 1642 [1–2].

During the last year of the 18th century the British conquered the Dutch territories and made the island into a crown colony in 1802. The British retained the Indo-Dutch currency system, based on the rixdollar, on par with the rupee and divided into 48 stivers, each of 12 fanams. From 1839 to 1868 British third and quarter farthings [3–4] and silver threehalfpence also circulated in Ceylon, in addition to the local coinage. In 1872 the currency was decimalized, and the rupee of 100 cents was adopted. Bronze coins of this series bore the profile of the reigning monarch (obverse) and a palm tree (reverse) while the silver, or later nickel, coins had the value in numerals in an ornamental reverse [5–8].

Ceylon became a dominion in 1948 but continued to issue coins with the monarch's effigy until 1957. Thereafter the national emblem was substituted in a series introduced in 1963, with inscriptions in Sinhala and Tamil instead of English [9–11]. In 1972 the island became a republic under the name of Sri Lanka ("resplendent island"). A modified version of the coinage was adopted in 1975 [12]. A few commemoratives have been produced since 1957, when the 2500th anniversary of Buddhism was celebrated [13–16].

MALDIVE ISLANDS

This archipelago west of Sri Lanka was an independent sultanate from 1153 and had its own coins inscribed in Arabic from the 17th century. It became a British protectorate by agreement with the Governor of Ceylon in 1887. The rupee of 100 lariat (singular *larin*) became the rufiyaa of 100 laari in 1954, when the Maldives reverted to a sultanate after a brief period as a republic. Until 1968, when the second republic was proclaimed, coins bore the arms of the sultanate [17–20]. Since then coins have had pictorial motifs and numerals of value. Gold and silver coins in recent years have highlighted events or anniversaries of international importance.

MAURITIUS

Named after Prince Maurice of the Netherlands, this island was under Dutch control from 1598 to 1710, when it was acquired by the French,

Living Fossil

The coelacanth, a species of fish that existed 400 million years ago and pre-dated the dinosaurs, was believed to be long extinct when a live specimen was caught off the Comoros in 1938. Since then others have been found. This "living fossil" appears on a coin of the Comoros issued in 1984 to mark the World Fisheries Conference.

from whom it was captured by the British in 1810. At first the British retained the French currency of the livre of 20 sous; they then briefly issued coins in fractions of dollars [21–22] with a crowned anchor obverse, before adopting the rupee of 100 cents in 1877. Thereafter, coins portrayed the reigning monarch with the value on the reverse. From 1934, the silver coins had a pictorial reverse.

Mauritius became an independent state within the Commonwealth in 1968. Its coins continued to portray Elizabeth II until 1987, when the bust of Sir Seewoosagur Ramgoolam, the first prime minister, was substituted.

SEYCHELLES

Like Mauritius, this island group passed to Britain from France in 1810. It used the coinage of Mauritius until 1939, when distinctive coins, portraying the reigning sovereign, were introduced. These had the value on the reverse, but 5 and 10 rupee coins were added in 1974–9, with images of a beach scene and a turtle respectively. The Seychelles became an independent republic in 1976 and adopted a series of coins portraying the president, Sir James Mancham, with fauna and flora

on the reverse, but an armorial obverse was adopted the following year while retaining the same reverses [23–26]. Since 1983 there has been a prolific output of special issues marking all manner of events worldwide.

MADAGASCAR

A French protectorate from 1886 and a colony from 1896, Madagascar used French currency until 1943, when coins bearing the Free French emblem were introduced, followed in 1948–53 by a series showing the head of Marianne. The island became the Malagasy Republic in 1958 but did not issue coins thus inscribed until 1963, with poinsettia (obverse) and a zebu (reverse). It became a democratic republic in 1975 and reverted to the name of Madagascar in 1996, when the five-pointed star of the democratic republic reverted to the poinsettia emblem [27, 29]. Many coins are denominated in both French and local currencies, at 5 francs to the ariary [28, 30–32].

COMOROS

This archipelago came under French protection in 1886, and coins denominated in francs and centimes, but inscribed entirely in Arabic, were produced in 1890. Formerly a dependency of Madagascar, the Comoros attained self-government in 1961 and had coins with the effigy of Marianne and palm trees from 1964. It became a federal Islamic republic in 1975 and introduced coins inscribed in Arabic and French with the four stars and crescent emblem, with pictorial reverses [33–38]. Coins portraying Said Mohamed Cheikh celebrated independence.

Above: Gold crescent obverse, and silver pictorial reverse, issued as part of the Comoros "independence series".

INDOCHINA

The name Indochina was given collectively to the French colonies and protectorates in South-east Asia, on the eastern side of the peninsula shared with Thailand. The area was originally occupied by peoples from the Yellow River valley of northern China, who migrated as a result of ethnic cleansing during the Han dynasty. In the 2nd century BC, the Chinese conquered Indochina and controlled it until AD 938, leaving the indelible mark of Chinese culture. In more recent times the kingdoms and states of Annam, Tonkin, Cambodia, Cochin-China and Laos emerged. The French penetrated this area in the early 19th century and gradually gained control, creating the states of Cambodia, Laos and Vietnam.

Left: That the French regarded Indochina as the jewel in the crown of their colonial empire is reflected in the style of the coinage from 1879 to 1954, which is rich in the symbolism and allegory of the French Republic, with very little concession to local character.

FRENCH INDOCHINA

The extraordinarily diverse coinage of the region was gradually superseded from 1879, when the French introduced a uniform currency throughout the areas under their control. These coins had the inscription "République Française" on the obverse and "Indochine Française" on the reverse, the former usually accompanied by an allegorical subject and the latter with the value in European and Chinese characters. The coins were denominated in piastres of 100 sapeque, on par with the franc of 100 centimes.

Since it came under the control of the Vichy French government, Indochina was nominally an ally of the Japanese, who occupied it in World War II. French rule was restored in 1946 and new coins were then introduced. They were inscribed "Union Française" and "Federation Indochinoise", and bore the head of Marianne and ears of corn [1–4].

VIETNAM

This country occupying the eastern coast of the peninsula was formerly divided into Tonkin (north) and Annam (south). It gained complete independence from China in 1428 and developed into a mighty empire. Its prosperity was reflected in the wealth and diversity of its gold and silver coinage, which ranged from cast bent rings or "banana bars" and copper dongs to the beautiful tien and lang series of circular coins [5].

After the country came under French control, the emperors continued to rule. The last of them, Bao Dai (1926–55), was deposed in 1945 by the communist Viet Minh under the leadership of Ho Chi Minh. Ho established a provisional government in the north and struck dong, xu and hao coins with a five-pointed star [6–7] until 1954, when the Democratic Republic of Vietnam was established and aluminium coins with the communist emblem around a central hole were introduced [8–9].

Bao Dai fled from Hanoi to Saigon, where the French created the state of Vietnam in 1949. Aluminium coins of 1953 featured profiles or portraits of three women side by side [10–11]. In 1955, Bao Dai was deposed and (South) Vietnam became a republic. Coins inscribed "Viet-Nam Cong-Hoa" were issued, with rice plants or bamboo on the obverse and the value on the reverse [12–16].

CAMBODIA

The Khmer people have inhabited the region to the west of Vietnam for at least 2000 years. The Khmer Empire controlled much of South-east Asia at its zenith in the 12th century, but under attack from its neighbours it declined considerably. It sought French protection in 1863 and was incorporated in French Indochina in 1877.

Cambodia issued coinage based on the silver tical up to 1885, with tiny uniface pe depicting animals, birds or flowers. King Ang Doung imported British presses to mint coins such as the silver tical of 1847 with a view of Angkor Wat [17–18]. A series portraying Norodom I and dated 1860 (but not released until 1875) was produced in Belgium [19–20]. Independence was restored in 1949 under Norodom Sihanouk; coins inscribed "Royaume du Cambodge" appeared in 1953 [21–22]. The riel of 100 sen was adopted in 1959, but the previous motifs were retained.

In 1970, Sihanouk was deposed and the Khmer Republic was proclaimed by Lon Nol. No circulating coins appeared under this regime, although some gold and silver pieces were struck at the Royal Mint in 1974, shortly before the regime was toppled by Pol Pot. The People's Republic of Kampuchea abolished money. Apart from an aluminium 5 sen of 1979 [23–24], there were no coins until 1988 when some commemoratives began to appear. Pol Pot was ousted in 1989 and the State of Cambodia emerged the following year with coins thus inscribed. In 1993 Prince Sihanouk returned as head of state and the Kingdom of Cambodia was restored [25–26].

LAOS

Fa Ngum created the first kingdom known as Lan Xang ("land of a million elephants") in the 14th century and established his capital at Luang Prabang. The kingdom originally included parts of Thailand and Yunnan province in southern China, but it

United Country

After a long-running war between north and south, Vietnam was unified in 1976 as the Vietnam Socialist Republic (Cong Hoa Xa Hoi Chu Nghia Viet Nam) and coins thus inscribed have been used ever since. These have a star and cogwheel emblem on the obverse and a reverse bearing the value in currency based on the dong of 10 hao. Coins from 5 to 10,000 dong have been struck in brass, cupronickel or silver in recent years to mark the Olympic Games or to promote nature conservation.

gradually declined and by the early 19th century it had come under Thai control, whose coinage was widely used. The French established a protectorate in 1893. Autonomy was granted in 1949 but by 1953 the government was at war with the communist Pathet Lao. Laos gained independence in 1954, but civil war erupted in 1960 and continued until the creation of the Lao People's Republic in 1975.

Aluminium holed coins were introduced in 1952, based on the kip of 100 centimes [27–30]. Coins featuring the star and the hammer and sickle emblem were released in 1980 [31–32]. Large gold and silver coins were issued in 1971, and have reappeared since 1985.

Above: A silver bullion piece struck by the Chinese in 1943–4, denominated in kip, for trade in Laos.

15 16 17 18 19 20 21 22 23 24 25 26 27 28 29 30 31 32

CHINA

China is one of the world's largest countries, covering an area of almost 10 million sq km/3.7 million sq miles. It extends from Central Asia to the Pacific, and from the Gobi Desert to the Gulf of Tonkin. It is also the most populous nation on earth, with around 1.3 billion inhabitants. The Chinese were among the chief originators and developers of coinage. Their cash – distinctive copper coins with a square hole punched out of the centre – continued in use for nearly two millennia.

Left: The Dragon silver dollars, which were first struck at the Guangdong Mint in 1889, became the standard throughout the Chinese Empire. The weight of these coins was fixed at 7 mace and 2 candareens, the mace being a tenth of a tael.

ANCIENT CHINA

The bronze implements pioneered as currency by the Zhou dynasty were roughly contemporary with the very first coins of Asia Minor, but in China the former were actually predated by stone rings fashioned from limestone [1–2]. In addition to the well-documented "knife" and "spade" currencies, a variety of other implements circulated in the periods of the Zhou and Warring dynasties, including "bell money", "fish money" [3–4], imitation cowries and various other bronze artefacts used in barter [5–6].

The flattened, round copper discs known as cash [7], which more closely resemble today's circular coins, probably made their first appearance in the 4th century BC, although a handsome knife currency [8] reappeared at the beginning of the first millennium, thanks to the ruler Wang Mang. Cash often circulated alongside other items, such as the jewellery money of amulets and charms [9–10] exchanged under the Qing dynasty (1644–1911).

CHINESE EMPIRE

Although copper cash continued to circulate well into the 20th century, with many provincial variations, a standard unified coinage on western lines developed after the establishment of the central mint at Tianjin in 1905 [11–12]. Coins were struck rather than cast in the traditional manner. Subsidiary coins of values up to 20 cash were struck in brass, copper or bronze with a dragon motif, while silver coins were denominated from 10 cents to one dollar.

Tianjin manufactured the dies used at many of the provincial mints. In addition to the general issues for circulation throughout the empire, numerous provincial series were struck at regional mints in Anhui [13–14], Chihli [15–16], Fengtian, Fujian, Heilongjiang, Henan, Hubei, Hunan, Gansu, Guangxi, Guangdong, Guizhou, Jiangnan, Jiangxi, Jiangsu, Jilin, the Manchurian Provinces, Shaanxi, Shanxi, Shandong, Sichuan Xinjiang, Yunnan and Zhejiang. In some of these vast provinces there were several mints, each producing distinctive coins. In Xinjiang, for example, local coinage was produced at Aksu, Kashgar, Kucha, Urümqi and Wuxi in the latter period of the empire.

CHINESE REPUBLIC

The system of provincial and local mints continued after the republic was proclaimed in 1912. Indeed, it expanded in the 1920s and 1930s, as central government weakened and China disintegrated into regions controlled by warlords [17] followed by the long struggle between the Kuomintang ("national people's party") [18–22] and

Birds of Ill Omen

Silver dollars were issued in 1932, the reverse showing a junk with the rising sun in the background and three birds at the top. This seemed innocuous at the time, but the rising sun was the emblem of Japan and the birds were deemed to symbolize the Japanese air raids on Manchuria. The junk dollars were re-issued in 1933–4 with the sun and birds removed and in this form they were restruck during World War II in the USA, with an inscription added to celebrate victory over the Japanese.

the communists led by Mao Zedong. The situation was also exacerbated by wide variations in the value of currency in different parts of China, and latterly by inflation.

The bronze coins struck by the central government under the National Revenue Board had crossed flags on one side and the value in Chinese and English on the other, often incorporating a floral motif. Gold and silver coins portrayed Sun Yat-sen [23], Yuan Shi-gai [24] and other prominent figures. Interestingly, coins appeared in 1926 to commemorate the wedding of Pu Yi, the last emperor of China, who had abdicated in 1912. A new series portraying Sun Yat-sen was introduced in 1936 with a reverse reproducing an ancient bu coin.

Both the central government and the provinces produced numerous silver dollars portraying political and military leaders. Among the provincial issues, those coins issued under Japanese auspices in Manchukuo (Manchuria) in

the name of the Emperor Kang De (formerly Pu Yi) in 1932–45 are particularly noteworthy.

PEOPLE'S REPUBLIC

A soviet republic was proclaimed by Mao Zedong in 1931 and coins with a five-pointed star or the hammer and sickle superimposed on a map of China were issued in those areas under communist control. Extremely rare coins were also struck under communist auspices in various regions under local soviets [27–30], including some with very crude portraits of Lenin.

Although the People's Republic of China was proclaimed at Beijing in October 1949 it was not until 1955 that a regular coinage was introduced, based on the Renminbi yuan of 10 jiao or 100 fen, with a uniform obverse showing the state emblem and a wreathed value reverse. These motifs have been in use in the fen denominations for half a century without change. The jiao, first struck in copper-zinc in 1980, switched to aluminium in 1991 [25–26], when the 5 jiao, originally in the same alloy, switched to brass. In both values a new reverse incorporated a peony blossom. The yuan first appeared as a circulating coin in 1980, struck in cupro-nickel with mountains on the reverse, but changed to clad steel in 1991 with the peony reverse.

Silver and gold commemoratives have proliferated since 1980, mainly in yuan denominations, although they include the silver 5 jiao of 1983, which celebrated the seventh centenary of the sojourn of Marco Polo. Latterly, these commemorative and special issues have appeared in long series with specific themes, from the Olympic Games to the autonomous regions, founders of Chinese culture, poets and Chinese inventions. China has also produced tiny gold 3 and 5 yuan with a giant panda on one side and the Temple of Heaven in Beijing on the other. The Panda series has become immensely popular worldwide, even leading to issues in platinum since 1993 and large silver versions since 1997.

1

2

3

4

5

6

7

8

9

10

11

12

13

14

15

16

17

18

CHINESE TERRITORIES

On the fringes of China are several countries that were once part of its territory and are now independent, or conversely are now part of China, having had an independent existence with distinctive coinage. They include the former British and Portuguese colonies of Hong Kong and Macao.

Left: The ruined façade of St Paul's Cathedral, depicted on several coins, is one of the most impressive sights in Macao. The edifice is a reminder of the heyday of this former Portuguese colony, and was a bastion of Christianity in the Far East in the 17th and 18th centuries.

HONG KONG

China ceded the island of Hong Kong ("fragrant harbour") to Britain in 1841 at the end of the First Opium War, and a 99-year lease on adjacent territory on the mainland was granted in 1898. On the expiry of the lease Britain ceded the colony to the People's Republic in 1997. It has since been a special administrative zone, retaining its currency based on the dollar of 100 cents.

Locally struck coins were introduced in 1863, all but the tiny mil (one-tenth of a cent) bearing the crowned bust of Queen Victoria [1–2]. This established a precedent for all the coins down to 1997, with a reverse showing the name and value in English round the circumference and the corresponding Chinese characters in the centre. The sole exception was the 50 cents with the bust of Edward VII [3–4] on the obverse: its value in English appeared in the centre, with the name and date around the top and the Chinese equivalent around the foot.

The traditional formula continued with the coinage of Elizabeth II, three different effigies being used between 1955 and 1992. A silver 20 cents with the bust of Edward VII appeared in 1902–5, and this denomination was revived in 1975 as a nickel-brass coin with a scalloped edge [5–6]. Cupronickel $1 (1960), $2 (1975) and $5 (1976) had a reverse type showing the crowned lion emblem of the colony surrounded by the name and value in English and Chinese [7–8].

In preparation for the retrocession, a new series, with a bauhinia flower (obverse) and numeral (reverse) was introduced in 1993 and this included a bimetallic $10 piece [9–12]. A coin of this type with a pictorial reverse was released in 1997 for the opening of the Harbour Bridge. Gold $1000 coins began in 1975 with the Queen's visit, and since 1976 similar coins have greeted the Lunar New Year [13–14].

MACAO

The Portuguese acquired the peninsula of Macao with the islands of Taipa and Coloane as a trading post in 1557, although it did not acquire full colonial status until 1887. Portuguese coins were used until 1952, when a distinctive series based on the pataca of 100 avos was adopted. The obverse showed the crowned globe and shield emblem of Portugal, while the reverse bore the value in European and Chinese scripts [15–16]. A new series, with a shield (obverse) and Chinese characters (reverse) came into use in 1982 [17–18], and a pictorial issue appeared from 1992–3 [19–24] in anticipation of Macao returning to China in 1999 as a special administrative zone.

Commemorative silver and gold coins since 1974 have marked the opening of the Macao-Taipa Bridge and the Macao Grand Prix as well as the Lunar New Year [25–26]. An unusual feature of many modern coins has been the depiction of the ruins of St Paul's instead of the customary arms.

TAIWAN

The island of Taiwan, formerly known as Formosa, was occupied by Japan in 1895 but returned to China in 1945. Thither came the remnants of the Chinese nationalist forces when the communists drove them from the mainland. Since 1949, Taiwan has been the seat of the Republic of China (ROC), led by Chiang Kai-shek and his successors. Most coins since 1949 have featured Sun Yat-sen (obverse) and a map of the island (reverse) [27–28], with inscriptions entirely in Chinese and dates in years since the foundation of the republic in 1911. The 5 and 10 yuan, introduced in 1965, depict Sun's mausoleum at Nanking on the reverse. Many of the yuan coins since 1966 have portrayed Chiang Kai-shek.

Relatively few commemorative coins (from 10 yuan upwards) have appeared, honouring leaders of Chinese nationalism [29–30] or marking anniversaries of the republic. A silver 1000 yuan of 1996 marked the first popular elections, with side-by-side portraits of President Lee Teng-hui and Vice President Lien Chan on the obverse.

MONGOLIA

Once a mighty empire that conquered China and extended as far as Hungary, Mongolia came under the rule of the Manchus in 1691. In 1921, with Russian support, it asserted its independence and became a people's republic. Coins based on the tugrik of

Above: Flowers and candles depicted on sample coins from the Central Mint of Taiwan in the 1960s and 1970s.

Commercial Advertising

Gold and silver coins were issued by Macao in 1978 to mark the 25th anniversary of the Grand Prix. They depicted racing cars blazoned with advertising for Seiko, Luso Banking and even Rothman Pall Mall cigarettes, which appeared in the photograph supplied to the coin designer. The colonial authorities took exception to this so the coins were hurriedly withdrawn and replaced by designs without advertisements. The "advert" versions are now extremely rare.

100 mongo were issued from 1925, with the national emblem, followed by communist symbols in 1945 when Mongolia severed its last links with China. The collapse of communism led to the creation of the democratic state of Mongolia in 1990. Since 1994 coins have reverted to the emblem of the 1920s [31–32]. Mongolia has also produced a vast number of special coins, ranging from the Chinese New Year to the Japanese Royal Wedding of 1993. While coins in general circulation are inscribed in Mongol, in both the indigenous script and a modified form of Cyrillic, special issues are invariably inscribed in English.

HIMALAYAN STATES

Two of the countries that lie in the Himalayas, between China and India, have managed to preserve their independence, despite having been under the protection of their more powerful neighbours at various times. On the other hand, although it is now classified as an autonomous region of the People's Republic of China, Tibet has been under Chinese control since 1950, when its distinctive coinage was suppressed.

Left: In 1966 Bhutan celebrated the 40th anniversary of the accession of Maharajah Jigme Wangchuk with the issue of a set of seven coins. The four lower values were denominated in Indian currency, but the top values were 1, 2 and 5 sertums and were struck in gold or platinum.

TIBET

Nominally a tributary of China for many centuries, Tibet embraced Buddhism in the 8th century and thereafter became increasingly isolated from the outside world. A British military mission from India, led by Sir Francis Younghusband, invaded it in 1903. Influenced by the British, Tibet formally declared its independence in 1913, but this was suppressed by China in 1950. Following a revolt in 1965 it was made an autonomous region.

The coins of neighbouring Nepal were used from 1570, but in the 1720s Nepal began striking coins with a lower silver content for use in Tibet, based on the tangka of 15 skar or the srang of 10 sho or 100 skar. This was unsatisfactory and around 1763 the Tibetans began producing coins for themselves. From this early period dates the Suchakra Vijana tangka [1–2], but such coins were produced by hand in small quantities. A mint opened at Lhasa in 1791 under local auspices and struck Kong-Par tangkas, but was quickly suppressed by the Chinese, who opened their own mint in Lhasa in 1792 and struck silver sho in the name of Emperor Qianlong [3–4]. Sino-Tibetan coins continued intermittently until 1909–10, when the copper skar [5–6] was struck in the name of the Chinese emperor Xuantong (Pu Yi).

In the independent period, the Tibetan authorities struck a wide range of coins, from the copper skar to the gold srang [7–8] with a lion obverse and various motifs, notably the prayer-wheel, on the reverse. Even after the Chinese invasion of 1950 a few coins with the lion on a background of mountains continued as late as 1953.

BHUTAN

This landlocked Himalayan kingdom was conquered by Tibet in the 9th century and had a similar theocratic form of government. The southern part was annexed by Britain to India, but the northern part became a hereditary kingdom in 1907 and attained full independence in 1971.

For countless centuries, Bhutan had a wholly agricultural economy: self-sufficient in foodstuffs it relied on barter in all transactions, and barter is still widely practised. It had no coinage of its own and, when the need began to arise in the 18th century, it made use of the silver debs or half rupees of the Indian state of Cooch-Behar. About 1790 it began striking its own coins, originally in the same weight and fineness as the Cooch-Behar coins, but from 1820 onward debased by an admixture of lead or other metals, so that latterly debs were mostly copper or brass, with a silver wash to give them the appearance of precious metal. The design was very simple, with three lines of characters separated by horizontal lines, but including a symbol that helps to place them in chronological sequence, rather like the mint-marks

Nepalese Symbolism

The coins of Nepal are rich in the aniconic symbolism of Buddhism and Hinduism. While the obverse of the 50 paise coin since 1994 has featured the plumed crown of the Shah Dev dynasty, the reverse incorporates some of the items that compose the *ashtamangala* (the eight auspicious symbols). The date, in Hindi and Devanagari script, is 2051 in the Vikrama Samvat Era, 57 years ahead of the Common Era (that is, 1994).

on medieval English coins. They consisted mainly of the deb [9–10] and rupee [11–12] of debased silver.

This primitive coinage was replaced in 1928 by a series based on the Indian rupee of 64 pice. The obverse bore the bust of the ruler, Jigme Wangchuk, but the reverse was divided by horizontal and vertical lines to form nine compartments, with an inscription in the centre and ornate symbols in the others. They were undated but bore the symbol of the earth dragon in the Chinese zodiacal cycle. When re-issued they bore the iron tiger, dating them to 1950, though this symbol was retained when the half rupee was re-issued in a reduced weight to conform with the Indian coins current in 1967–8. In the interim a series based on the Indian rupee of 100 naye paise celebrated the ruler's 40th anniversary, followed in 1974 by a series portraying Jigme Singye Wangchuk, based on the sertum of 100 ngultrums or 10,000 chetrums [13–14]. Various Buddhist symbols appeared on the reverse.

Since 1974 Bhutan has produced numerous gold and silver coins for occasions ranging from royal anniversaries to international sporting events.

NEPAL

Distinctive coins, mainly square copper dams [15–16] were struck by several of the Himalayan mountain states from the late 15th century. Silver coins of good quality were produced at Patan [17–18] and Bhatgoan [19–20], while both circular and square mohars with their subdivisions were minted at Kathmandu [21–28].

In the late 18th century Prithvi Narayan Shah, ruler of Gurkha, welded these states into a single kingdom and struck silver mohars [29–30]. After his death Nepal suffered a long period of instability, reflected in the clay token inscribed in Newari, which was used as small change [31–32]. Order was restored in the 1840s when the Rana family established a hereditary premiership that took real power away from the king. This continued until 1950, when a popular uprising deposed the Rana prime minister and restored the power of the monarchy.

Prior to 1932 Nepal had a very complex currency system, based on the rupee of 2 mohar or 4 suka, 8 ani, 16 dak, 32 paisa or 128 dam [33–34]. Gold, silver and copper coins were struck on circular flans with geometric motifs contained in a square format (obverse) and a segmented device resembling flower petals (reverse). The currency was simplified in 1932 when the rupee of 100 paisa was adopted. Pictorial elements, such as crossed kukris, a hoe or a stylized lotus gradually crept in from that time. Symbols of the monarchy, such as the crown or sceptre, were depicted on the obverses [35–36]. Very few coins portrayed the ruler, King Tribhuvan, though he appeared on rupees of 1953–4.

A 2 rupee denomination was introduced in 1982 and thereafter became the preferred medium for commemoratives and special issues [37–38]. Previously, a few silver coins from 10 to 50 rupees had served this purpose. In more recent years both gold and silver coins of very high face values have appeared, including a gold bullion series denominated in asarfi.

KOREA

The "land of the morning calm" occupies a peninsula in north-eastern Asia, bordering China. The country allegedly had its own distinctive civilization over 4000 years ago, but recorded details date only from the 1st century BC, while the name Korea (Koryo) appeared in 935, when three kingdoms were merged into one. It came under Japanese influence in the late 19th century, became a protectorate in 1905 and was annexed in 1910. Liberated in 1945, it split along the 38th parallel: the north, under communist influence, became the People's Democratic Republic of Korea, and the remainder the Republic of Korea. Despite the collapse of communism everywhere else, North Korea remains a totalitarian state and Korea is still divided.

Left: The bronze 1 chon, the basic currency unit, was introduced in 1902. Japan's growing confidence is reflected by the imperial eagle, crowned and armed with sceptre and orb, and the fact that the inscriptions were mostly in Japanese.

KOREAN EMPIRE

Korea had a copper cash currency, on Chinese lines, for many centuries from AD 996 [1–2]. In the 17th century a new series, known as *shang ping* (stabilization money), was introduced [3–4]. A second series followed around 1742. The coins were cast at numerous mints all over the country, while each of the government ministries in the capital, Seoul, also produced them. They are identifiable by marks in the form of Chinese ideograms derived from a book entitled *Thousand Character Classic* (because the text consisted of exactly 1000 characters, none of which was repeated). These coins continued until 1888 when small silver and bronze coins, from 1 to 3 chon, were introduced [5–8].

Coins struck from modern presses were adopted in 1888, based on the warn of 1000 mun. The currency was reformed in 1892, when the silver yang of 100 fun was struck [11–12]; in 1893, the hwan of 5 yang or 500 fun was introduced [9–10], but this system was superseded a decade later by the won of 100 chon. Apart from the denomination, which was in English, all inscriptions were rendered in Chinese characters, and a phoenix or dragon was depicted on the obverse. During the brief reign of the last emperor, Kuang Mu, a few gold 10 and 20 won coins were struck. Following annexation by Japan in 1910, only Japanese coins circulated until liberation in 1945.

NORTH KOREA

The Cairo Conference of 1943 had decreed that Korea should be "free and independent" and presumably a unified sovereign state, but towards the end of World War II the Soviet Union declared war on Japan and invaded Manchuria and Korea from the north in 1945. At the same time, American forces landed in the south, and later that year the Potsdam Conference decided that Korea should be partitioned at the 38th parallel.

When the Soviet authorities barred the entry of UN personnel to supervise free elections in 1948, leading to reunification, the elections went ahead in the south and as a result the Republic of Korea was formally proclaimed on August 15. Unsupervised elections took place in the north ten days later and the Democratic People's Republic, with its capital at Pyongyang, was inaugurated.

In 1950 North Korean forces rapidly overran the south. US forces held on to Pusan and this became the bridgehead for the UN counterattack. The communists were on the point of defeat when China intervened, and the conflict see-sawed back and forth until 1953, when an armistice was arranged. The two Koreas have been in a state of warlike confrontation ever since, and all attempts by the UN to revive plans for reunification have foundered.

No coins were issued in North Korea until 1959, when three aluminium pieces, denominated 1, 5 and 10 chon, were released, with the communist emblem on the obverse and value on the reverse [13–14]. The chon was re-issued in 1970 and the 5 chon in 1974. These coins may be found with or without one or two stars flanking the numeral on the reverse [15–16]. A 50 chon appeared in 1987 with an emblem obverse, but the reverse depicted a Chulima rider; this coin also had a fixed date, with or without stars on the reverse. Higher values, from 1 to 10 won, in cupro-nickel, appeared from 1987, invariably commemorating Kim Il Sung, the "Comrade Great Leader". A vast number of gold and silver coins have been issued in more recent years [17–20].

A singular feature of the circulating coinage in the Democratic People's Republic from 1959 onward was the three-tier system, indicated by the presence or absence of five-pointed stars alongside the numeral of value on the reverse. Coins without stars were for general circulation among the people of the country; those with one star at the side of the numeral were issued to visitors from China and the former countries of the Soviet bloc; while those with two stars flanking the numeral were restricted to visitors from all other countries, who were compelled to exchange dollars, pounds and other "hard" currencies. As no new circulating coins have been produced since 1978 it is assumed that this system is still in force. The star system did not apply to the commemorative and special issues, which were anyway aimed very largely at the overseas market, as reflected in their thematic character.

SOUTH KOREA

The hwan of 100 chon was adopted in the south, but no coins appeared until 1959 when a series of three, from 10 to 100 hwan, had a numeral obverse and pictorial reverses showing, respectively, a rose of Sharon, a turtle warship and the bust of the first president, Syngman Rhee [21–22].

The currency was reformed in 1966 and the won (worth 10 hwan) was introduced. In this series the pictorial images occupied the obverse and the numerals the reverse [23–26], with a mixture of subjects, including the Pul Guk pagoda and the turtle warship, while the ship's inventor, Admiral Yi Sunsin, was portrayed on the silver 100 won. The permanent series has remained relatively stable since then, the only major change being the adoption of cupro-nickel in 1970 for the 100 won [27–28].

Since 1975, when the 30th anniversary of liberation was celebrated, South Korea has issued a number of silver and gold coins, though the range of subjects commemorated is much wider and less politically inspired [29–32].

Ironclad Battleship

The 50 hwan coins of 1959–61 and the bronze or brass 5 won coins of South Korea since 1966 have featured the so-called turtle boat invented by Admiral Yi Sunsin. With a fleet of these ironclad vessels he defeated the Japanese in Chinhai Bay in 1592, an action as decisive as the English defeat of the Spanish armada by Sir Francis Drake four years earlier.

JAPAN

The Empire of Japan consists of an archipelago off the north-east coast of Asia. According to legend it was founded in 660 BC by Jimmu Tenno, a descendant of the sun goddess Amaterasu. It is still believed that Japanese emperors are directly descended from him; they accede to the throne by divine right and are, effectively, living deities. For this reason, the image of the emperor remains sacred, and royal portraits never appear on coins. The sun symbol, which adorns the national flag, has appeared on some Japanese coins.

Left: The gold koban, introduced in 1601, resembled a large upright oval flat plate with a ribbed surface, on which various circular stamps were impressed . Sometimes an inscription was applied in black ink. Oban were similar pieces worth ten times as much.

ANCIENT JAPAN

The Japanese adapted Chinese coinage to their own purposes and introduced bronze cash in AD 708. From then until the middle of the 10th century coins of this type were issued with distinctive marks for each reign, but from then onward no regal issues were made at all, and the gap was filled by imitations of Chinese cash produced under the authority of the various *daimyos* (provincial nobility). During the Shogunate (1603–1867), there were many interesting and unusual coins. In 1624 the copper kwan-ei was introduced, and numerous variations appeared over the ensuing two centuries, augmented in the 19th century by the copper ei-raku and bun-kyu sen.

Unlike China, Japan made extensive use of gold and silver coinage from the 16th century onward, in the form of the large, flat oval oban and koban, oval silver chogin [1–2] or the small rectangular bu [3]. A notable oblong issue of 1765 was struck from confiscated silver ornaments.

MODERN JAPAN

When Emperor Meiji ascended the throne in 1867 he immediately dismissed Yoshinobu, the last of the shoguns, who had been the real rulers of Japan since the 17th century. Having restored imperial government he embarked on a comprehensive policy of westernization. In a single generation, this transformed Japan from a feudal backwater to an industrialized world power. One of Meiji's first reforms was the currency. Hitherto there had been no fixed ratio between gold, silver and copper, but he installed a Western-style mint at Osaka in 1869 and the following year coins based on the yen of 100 sen or 1000 rin were released. Illustrated here are the obverse and reverse of a copper pattern for the tiny 1 rin coin of 1870 [4–5].

The yen, derived from the Chinese word yuan (dollar), was originally a gold coin [6–7], but its size was reduced in 1874 and it was discontinued in 1880, as the public preferred the silver yen. Coins of this type [8–9] were minted regularly until 1914. Gold coins of 10 yen [10–11] and 20 yen [12–13] were introduced in 1871 and 1870 respectively. The former was struck until 1910, while the latter survived to 1920. The 20 yen was briefly revived in 1930–2, but coins of that period are very rare. When the 10 yen was revived in 1951 it was a small bronze coin. The tiny bronze rin was not minted after 1884, but the 5 rin or half sen continued until 1919.

Since their inception, modern Japanese coins have been dated by the regnal year of the emperor, and this has been inscribed entirely in Japanese since 1916, year 5 of the Taisho era.

Early types depicted a dragon or phoenix [16–17] as well as the chrysanthemum in a wreath [14–15] or as a central motif [18–19], but a greater degree of pictorialism crept in during World War II, with Fujiyama (1 sen), a peregrine falcon (5s) and a stylized flower (10s). The character for *dai* (great) was dropped from the country name following the defeat of Japan. New designs adopted late in 1945 were the peace dove (5s), rice (10s) [20–21], the phoenix and corn sheaf (50s) [22–23] and flowers (yen). Prior to 1948 the characters making up the country name were read from right to left, but this was reversed thereafter. A blend of symbolism and pictorialism developed in the postwar period; sometimes images that had previously been treated symbolically were rendered more realistically, as in the 50 yen of 1955–8, in which the chrysanthemum appeared as an actual flower, with leaves and stalk. Since 1955 the yen has been the smallest coin [24–25].

Postwar inflation led to higher denominations for everyday circulation. The first 100 yen piece appeared in 1957 as a silver coin but switched to cupro-nickel in 1967 [26–27]. When a 500 yen was required in 1982 it was struck in cupro-nickel from the outset. Similarly the metal used for the lower denominations was downgraded. The 10 yen, which had been a gold coin when it was last minted in 1910, was revived in 1951 as a bronze coin. The obverse featured the ancient temple of Hoo-do in an arabesque frame, and this continues to the present day. Similarly the gold 5 yen was struck until 1912 and next emerged in 1948 as a brass coin with the parliament buildings on the reverse.

COMMEMORATIVE AND SPECIAL ISSUES

Japan did not produce commemorative coins until 1964, when silver 100 and 1000 yen publicized the Tokyo Olympic Games [28–29]; both coins had symbolic motifs, although the obverse of the 1000 yen also featured

High Value

Japan was one of the first countries to introduce a base-metal high-value coin for general circulation. The 500 yen coin, launched in 1981, was worth about $2.50 or £1.30 at the then-current rate of exchange. The obverse depicts the paulownia flowers of the imperial *kiri-mon*.

Fujiyama wreathed in cherry blossom. Coins of 100 yen marked the Osaka Expo of 1970 [30–31] and the Sapporo Winter Games of 1972 [32–33].

Thereafter the pace of special issues quickened. Since 1985 coins of 500 yen have been the preferred medium for special issues, with occasional silver (5000 yen) or gold (10,000–100,000 yen). The 500 yen coins are struck in cupro-nickel and circulate generally. They cover all kinds of current events, from the opening of Narita Airport, the Selkan Tunnel and the Seito Bridge to the Asian Games and other sporting events. Royal events have also been celebrated, from the diamond jubilee of the Emperor Hirohito (1986) to the enthronement of Akihito (1990). No portraits were used, of course, the first occasion being marked by a view of the imperial palace and the second by a picture of the state coach. The centenaries of the cabinet system (1985), parliament (1990) and the judicial system (1990) are celebrated by coins.

Below: Of the current series, the brass 5 yen and cupro-nickel 50 yen have the distinction of being holed coins.

INDONESIA AND THE PHILIPPINES

Two great archipelagos extend the continent of Asia across the western Pacific. Indonesia, the world's largest island group, stretches along the Equator for more than 5000km/3000 miles, from the southernmost tip of Asia to northern Australia. The Philippines, much smaller and more compact, lie off the east coast of China. Both groups came in contact with Europeans in the 16th century, becoming colonies of Holland and Spain respectively; both were overrun by the Japanese in World War II.

Left: The silver coins of the Philippines, 1903–21, show Liberty with Mayon volcano in the background (obverse) and the emblem of the USA (reverse), symbolizing American control of the islands after the Spanish–American War of 1898.

NETHERLANDS EAST INDIES

Numerous kingdoms and sultanates spread across the East Indies and issued Islamic coins inscribed in Arabic and local languages. Shown here is a range of tiny gold coins of the 13th–17th centuries from Sallendra in Java [1]. These continued during the early period of Dutch rule, interrupted during the Napoleonic wars by the British occupation of Java and Madura (1811–16), when coins with the emblem of the British East India Company were briefly in use. The company also held Sumatra from 1685 until it was ceded to the Dutch in 1824; in that period copper kepings had the company emblem on one side and Arabic inscriptions on the other.

Coins equating the Dutch gulden with the Java rupee were supplied from Holland. They bore the crowned arms (obverse) and the VOC monogram of the Dutch East India Company or the name and date (reverse) [2–3], and supplemented a wide range of local pitis, kepings and rupees produced on various islands. During delays and shortages, makeshifts known as "bonks" were roughly cut from copper or tin rods. In 1856 the gulden of 100 cents was adopted and a new series

with arms (obverse) and Arabic inscriptions (reverse) was released [4–5]. A new type of bronze cent was introduced in 1936 with Dutch, Malayan and Javanese inscriptions round a central hole and rice panicles or flowers on obverse and reverse [6–7]. After Holland was overrun by Germany, some coins were struck in 1941–5 at the US mints in Philadelphia, Denver [8–9] or San Francisco, identifiable by their mint-marks after the date.

INDONESIA

The Netherlands Indies were occupied by the Japanese in 1942–5 and used the occupiers' currency. The Japanese fostered the nationalist movement, which had begun in the 1920s. The United States of Indonesia was proclaimed in August 1945 but a four-year campaign ensued before the Dutch finally bowed out. Coins inscribed "Indonesia" were introduced in 1951–2 [10–15]. Most featured the mythical *garuda* (the national bird) although the 50 sen [16–17] portrayed Dipanegara, who led the struggle for independence against the Dutch in the 18th century.

In the 1960s inflation drove coins out of circulation. Although the currency was reformed in 1965 (100 old rupiah to one new rupiah) no coins appeared until 1970–1, by which time the rupiah was the smallest denomination. This series had different pictorial motifs (fauna [18–19], flora and landmarks [22–25]). In later years, 5 rupiah coins appeared sporadically, promoting family planning [20–21] and serving as small change, but it was not until 1991 that a general issue of coins was resumed. In this series, from 25 to 1000 rupiah, the garuda obverse was combined with pictorial reverses [26–27]. Relatively few gold and silver commemoratives, mostly celebrating anniversaries of independence, have appeared since 1970. Separate issues of coins with the bust of Achmed Sukarno on the obverse, were produced for the Riau archipelago (1963–4) and West Irian, formerly Netherlands New Guinea (1964–71). Both sets had fixed dates of 1962.

TIMOR

This island in the Lesser Sunda group was partitioned between the Netherlands (west) and Portugal (east) in 1859. West Timor was incorporated with Indonesia from 1950, but East Timor remained under Portuguese rule and had coins in the Portuguese colonial style. In 1976 it was occupied by Indonesia, triggering off a long-running war that culminated in the attainment of independence in December 1999. The Democratic Republic of East Timor was later proclaimed, and distinctive coins with pictorial motifs, based on the escudo of 100 centavos, were introduced in 2004 [28–32].

Cowboys
The reverse of the 100 rupiah of Indonesia since 1991 shows the national sport of cow-racing.

PHILIPPINES

An extensive copper and silver coinage was produced in the Philippines in the Spanish colonial period, based on the peso of 8 reales, with subdivisions of quarto and octavo real. The obverse showed a lion resting on twin hemispheres, while the crowned arms of Spain occupied the reverse. A wide range of foreign coins, with appropriate countermarks, circulated in the 19th century before the currency was reformed in 1861, and the peso of 100 centimos was adopted, with the head of the monarch (obverse) and crowned arms (reverse) [33–34].

Under American rule from 1898 the currency changed to the peso of 100 centavos, and this continued until 1967, when the names changed to piso and sentimo. The seated or standing figure of Liberty appeared on the obverse, while the reverse featured the American eagle and shield until 1935 [35–36], when the Commonwealth of the Philippines was proclaimed with a measure of autonomy. Although the shield on the reverse changed, the coins continued to bear the name of the United States of America.

Occupied by the Japanese in 1941 and liberated in 1944–5, the Philippines became an independent republic in July 1946, but coins reflecting this change did not appear until 1947 and most denominations did not appear with the republican arms until 1958. An entirely new series portraying national heroes was released in 1967 [37–38] and since then has undergone changes in metal, size and shape, with pictorial reverses replacing the original arms or seal devices in 1983. The current coins, introduced in 1995, have the value on the obverse and arms on the reverse.

In 1903 the Commission of Public Health established a leper colony on the remote island of Culion. Special coins, from half centavo to 1 peso, were struck by Frank & Company with the caduceus emblem on the reverse. In 1927 a new series portrayed José Rizal with the national arms on the reverse.

1
2
3
4
5
6
7
8
9
10
11
12
13
14
15
16
17
18
19

MALAYSIA AND SINGAPORE

The countries in this group were all formerly under British rule and have maintained close ties through membership of the Commonwealth since they attained independence in the 1960s. They formed part of the great Javanese empire of Majapahit and converted to Islam in the 14th century. From the 15th century onward the coins of the numerous petty states generally conformed to Islamic standards. Johor struck octagonal gold kupangs with Islamic inscriptions [1–2], but for small change Chinese-style cash, such as the tin jokoh of Perak [3], or the silver tanga, such as this example from Melaka of 1631 [4–5], were preferred. The Portuguese and Dutch penetrated the region in the 16th and 17th centuries, followed by the British East India Company, which acquired the strategically important island of Penang off the coast of Kedah in 1786.

Left: The tenth anniversary of the Republic of Singapore was celebrated by the silver $10 of 1975, with a pictorial reverse emphasizing its importance as one of the world's largest commercial ports.

STRAITS SETTLEMENTS

This British crown colony was formed in 1825 by combining the trading posts at Penang – shown here are copper pattern cents of 1788–1810 [6–9] and a quarter-dollar of 1788 [10–11] – and Melaka with Singapore, the settlement founded by Stamford Raffles in 1819. Coins bearing the name of the East India Company but denominated in the local currency, based on the dollar of 100 cents, appeared in 1845 with the profile of Victoria (obverse) and wreathed value (reverse) [12–13]. The name was changed in 1862 to "India Straits", then to "Straits Settlements" in coins from 1872 to 1935 [14–15].

BRITISH NORTH BORNEO

This territory was administered by a chartered company until it was overrun by the Japanese in 1942 and declared a crown colony in 1946. It changed its name to Sabah on joining the Federation of Malaysia in 1964. Coins bearing the company arms were struck by the Heaton mint from 1882 until 1941 [16–17].

SARAWAK

The land of the white rajahs came into being in 1840, when the Sultan of Brunei granted territory on the island of Borneo to James Brooke, a British adventurer who had quelled a rebellion on the sultan's behalf, and whose initials appear on this copper keping [18–19]. In 1888 the state of Sarawak was placed under British protection. It was occupied by the Japanese in 1942 and ceded to the British Crown in 1946 by Sir Charles Vyner Brooke, who is portrayed on the silver 20 cents of 1910 [20–21]. It joined Malaysia in 1963. Sarawak issued its own coins from 1841 to 1941, with the profile of the rajah (obverse) and a wreathed or encircled value (reverse).

MALAYA

The Currency Board of Malaya was established shortly before World War II and uniform coinage for use in the Straits Settlements and the Malay States was introduced in 1939, with the crowned profile of George VI (obverse) and the value (reverse) [22–23].

Although it was interrupted by the war, this coinage was resumed in 1945 and continued until 1956, though no coins were dated after 1950. A new series, with the crowned bust of Elizabeth II, circulated from 1954 to 1961 and was inscribed "Malaya and British Borneo" on the reverse [24–25].

MALAYSIA

The Malayan Federation was formed in February 1948 by Melaka and Penang with the nine Malay states. It became an independent member of the Commonwealth in 1957 and used coins of Malaya and British Borneo.

In September 1963 the Malayan Federation joined with North Borneo (Sabah), Sarawak and Singapore to form the Federation of Malaysia. Coins inscribed "Malaysia", in currency based on the ringgit of 100 sen, were introduced in 1967, when the Currency Board was dissolved. The standard obverse featured the parliament building in Kuala Lumpur and the crescent and star emblem, while the reverse bore the value [26–29]. A new series, with a floral obverse and indigenous artefacts on the reverse, was introduced in 1989 [30–31]. Commemorative coins have appeared since 1969.

SINGAPORE

This island at the tip of the Malay Peninsula became a separate crown colony in 1946. It joined Malaysia in 1963 but seceded in August 1965 to become an independent republic.
Singapore continued to use the coins of Malaya until 1967, when a distinctive series based on the dollar of 100 cents was adopted. This followed the same pattern as the coinage of Malaysia, with the value on the reverse, but from the outset had different pictorial motifs on each obverse: birds and fishes on the middle values, with a fountain and high-rise apartment block (1 cent) [32] and Singapore's trademark mythical beast, the Merlion ($1). Armorial types with flora and fauna on the reverse have been used since 1985 [33–34]. Commemoratives have

South-east Asia's Own Olympics

Coins with seven interlocking rings have marked the four-yearly South-east Asia and Pacific Games, involving Malaysia, Singapore, Indonesia and the Philippines.

appeared since 1973, and there have been annual issues for the Chinese Lunar New Year since 1991.

BRUNEI

This sultanate arose in the 16th century and eventually ruled most of Borneo and even parts of the Philippines but declined in the early 19th century. It was eventually confined to a small area near the mouth of the Brunei River. Its fortunes recovered after World War II thanks to the discovery of oil in the region; it is now one of the world's wealthiest countries.

Cash or pitis of lead or tin appeared briefly about 1700, but it was not until 1868 that tin coins were re-introduced, with the state umbrella (obverse) and text in Jawi script (reverse). Western-style bronze coins, struck by Heaton of Birmingham, appeared in 1887, before Brunei adopted the currency of the Straits Settlements and later of Malaya. On the dissolution of the Currency Board distinctive coins were resumed, portraying Sultan Hassanal Bolkiah (obverse) [35] with ornamental motifs (reverse) [36–38]. New portraits were adopted in 1977 and 1993.

Gold and silver commemoratives have appeared since 1977, with various portraits of Sultan Hassanal on the obverse, mainly celebrating royal events or national anniversaries.

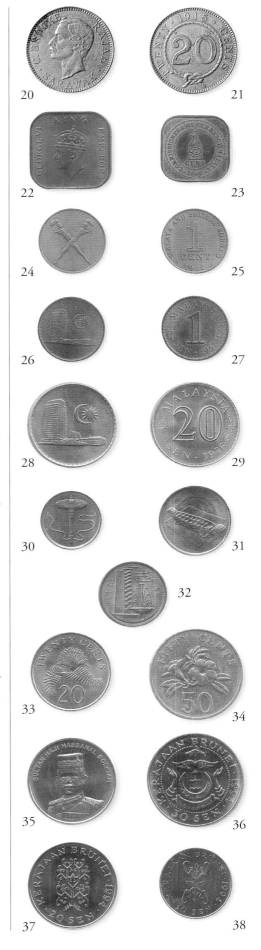

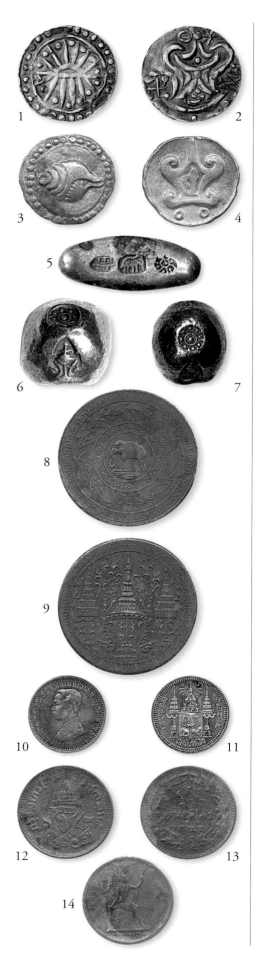

THAILAND

The ancient kingdom, known to its inhabitants as Muang Thai ("land of the free"), was the only country in South-east Asia never to fall under the control of a European power. Malay, Mon and Khmer kingdoms prospered in the region before the arrival of the Thai people, who began their migration from southern China and Laos during the 6th century. The emergence of a Thai-dominated nation began with the rise of the Sukhothai kingdom in the mid-13th century, under which distinctive bullet-shaped coins first emerged. In 1782 Rama I moved the capital to Bangkok and founded the dynasty that endures to this day. The Dutch, French and latterly the British played a part in the westernization of the country.

Left: The 10 baht coin of 1987, celebrating the anniversary of the Asian Institute of Technology, shows King Rama IX himself lecturing to students. It is one of many recent coins to show the hands-on approach of the royal family in everyday life.

SIAM

Silver and tin units were circulated in antiquity by the Indochinese kingdom of Funan [1–2], and later by the Mon people of Dvaravati [3–4]. In the north-east, the Kingdom of Langchang used bar-shaped coins of varying lengths, known as "leech money" [5] or "tiger tongue money", throughout the 16th and 17th centuries. More widely, gold and silver bullet-shaped coins developed from the original "bent rings" and endured as currency until the end of the 19th century [6–7]. The pieces had a standard weight based on the baht (15.4g/½oz), which was used as a unit of weight until the 1930s.

Bullet money was gradually superseded by western-style coinage from 1859 [8–9], the year in which Queen Victoria sent Rama IV a coining press as a gift. From then until 1937, coins were minted in a range of denominations, based on the baht on par with the tical and tamlung and worth 4 salung, 8 fuang, 16 sik, 32 pai, 64 att [12–13] or 1280 solot, while 20 baht equalled a chang.

From the outset these coins combined symbolism with images of Buddhist shrines and temples. In 1887 a series with the bust of Rama V (Chulalongkorn) was adopted [10–11], while the reverse of the lower values depicted a heavenly nymph, seated with a shield and spear, looking suspiciously like Britannia on British coins [14]. Buddhist symbolism continued on the higher values. The currency was reformed in 1908 and reduced to the baht of 4 salung or 100 satang, but similar types continued. Coins of this period were struck in many different metals, including tin, bronze, brass and cupro-nickel as well as silver and gold.

THAILAND

The new name was officially adopted in place of Siam by royal decree of June 1939. To this period belongs the bronze holed satang [15–16] followed by tiny tin or aluminium coins [17]. In September 1945 the country reverted to the older name but since May 1949 has been known as Thailand. Coinage continued to be inscribed solely in Thai characters until 1945, when western numerals were briefly used to denote value and date (in the Thai calendar). Most coins, however, have continued to be inscribed solely in the indigenous script. Definitive coins bear the effigy of the reigning sovereign. Rama IX (Bhumifhol Adulyadej) ascended the throne in 1946 as a teenager and many different portraits of him have been used. Sometimes the differences are very subtle, such as the effigies with one or three medals on the king's chest, or the portraits of the 1980s with or without a space between the collar and the lower hairline. The present series, from the tiny aluminium satang [17] to the bimetallic 10 baht, was introduced in 1987. It has the king's portrait on one side and symbolism, royal insignia or temples on the reverse [18–22].

COMMEMORATIVE AND SPECIAL ISSUES

An extraordinary feature of modern Thai coinage is the wide range of commemorative and special issues, the vast majority of which are produced in base metal for general circulation and add considerable interest to the everyday currency. They have been produced in denominations of 1, 2, 5, 10 and 20 baht in cupro-nickel. Although many have the portrait of Rama IX on the obverse this is by no means standard. In many cases, conjoined busts of the king and Queen Sirikit have been used, facing left or right [27–28]. Other coins have devoted the obverse to the

Princess Mother [30] and the various princes and princesses of the blood royal. In effect, Thai coins are the nearest thing today to the portrait gallery of the Roman emperors. The coins that portray the junior members of the royal family are invariably intended to celebrate events in their lives, from the investiture of Prince Vajiralongkorn as crown prince (1972) [29] to royal birthdays and weddings. These are as assiduously chronicled in coins as the anniversaries of the king's reign. In some cases the formal portrait gives way to a more pictorial treatment. Thus the Food and Agriculture Organization coin of 1977 showed the king instructing a farmer, while coins of 1991, celebrating the award of a Magsaysay (Philippines) scholarship to Princess Sirindhorn showed her working with children (obverse) and the decorative scroll of the award (reverse).

When it comes to the centenaries of national institutions, an appropriate pictorial motif appears on the reverse, but conjoined busts or facing portraits side by side of Rama IX and one of his ancestors are commonly featured on the obverse. Triple portraits have been used in coins marking the centenary of the Thai Red Cross (1993) and the 72nd anniversary of Chulalongkorn University (1989). The reverses of these coins tend to be symbolic in character [23–26] – again the parallel with the allegories of the Roman Empire is close. A more pictorial approach has been used in coins publicizing wildlife conservation [31].

Graduation Coins

When Princess Sirindhorn and her sister Chulabhorn graduated from university, their success was celebrated by sets of three coins in 1977 and 1979, with their portraits on the obverse, and appropriate symbolism on the reverse.

Above: In the 19th century, multilingual trade coins, struck locally in cast tin, circulated in the port of Singgora (Songkhla). This example has Thai and Arabic characters on the obverse, and a Chinese legend on the reverse.

15 16 17 18 19 20 21 22 23 24 25 26 27 28 29 30 31

AUSTRALASIA AND OCEANIA

This vast area in the Pacific Ocean includes Australia, the world's smallest continent, together with New Zealand and a number of archipelagos scattered over the eastern and southern Pacific. The area was first traversed by Europeans in 1521 but was not properly surveyed until the 18th century, largely as a result of the three voyages of the British explorer and navigator Captain James Cook. All the territories have been subject to European colonization, primarily of British and French origin.

AUSTRALIA

Although Chinese, Spanish and Portuguese navigators sighted the great southern land it was not until 1770 that its east coast was properly surveyed by James Cook, who named it New South Wales because of an imagined similarity to that part of Britain. The first permanent settlement took place in 1788 when the penal colony at Port Jackson was founded. The six Australian states of New South Wales, Van Diemen's Land or Tasmania, Western Australia, South Australia, Victoria and Queensland were settled as colonies during the period 1823–59. They joined together in 1901 to form the Commonwealth of Australia. The country is a member of the Commonwealth, with Elizabeth II as head of state.

Left: A polygonal 50 cent coin was issued in 1970 to celebrate the bicentenary of Captain Cook's first voyage to the Pacific, during which he charted the east coast of Australia.

PRE-DECIMAL COINAGE

With a few exceptions, the Australian colonies used the coins of the mother country, and this continued for several years after the Commonwealth of Australia was formed. The silver threepence, sixpence, shilling and florin (2 shillings) were introduced in 1910 and bore the right-facing crowned bust of Edward VII, who died that year, with the Commonwealth arms on the reverse. The left-facing bust of George V was substituted the following year, when the bronze halfpenny and penny were added to the series [1–4]. These coins had a prosaic reverse with the value in words across the middle.

A new series appeared in 1938 with the bare-headed profile of George VI and pictorial images on the reverse. A kangaroo appeared on the bronze coins [5–6], while the silver featured ears of wheat (threepence) [7] or a merino ram (shilling), but the sixpence retained a modified version of the arms and the florin [8] had a more elaborate crowned version of the arms. These reverse motifs were retained for the series of 1953–64, with the profile of Elizabeth II on the obverse [9]. A crown (5 shillings) with a Tudor crown on the reverse was restricted to 1937–8. The florin was the medium for coins celebrating the jubilee of federation (1951) and the Queen's visit (1954) [10].

GOLD COINS

The only regular coinage produced in the 19th century consisted of gold sovereigns and half sovereigns [11–14]. Following the discovery of gold in South Australia, pound coins with a crown (obverse) and value with the weight and fineness around the circumference (reverse) were minted at the Government Assay Office in Adelaide in 1852 [15–16]. Three years later a branch of the Royal Mint opened at Sydney and began coining sovereigns and half sovereigns with the profile of Queen Victoria (obverse) and a crown over "Australia" within a wreath (reverse) – the first coins to bear the name of the continent.

Australian coins continued until 1870 [17–18] but thereafter Sydney struck gold coins conforming to the prevailing British designs [19–20], distinguishable by the S mint-mark alongside the date. Branch mints were later opened at Melbourne (1872) [21–22] and Perth (1899). Production of gold sovereigns ceased in 1931.

DECIMAL COINAGE
Australia switched to the dollar of 100 cents in 1966. The bust of Elizabeth II by Arnold Machin appeared on the obverse [23], while reverses up to 20 cents featured examples of Australia's unique wildlife [24]. The circular silver 50 cents bore an elaborate version of the arms; when it next appeared, in 1969, the coin was struck in cupronickel with a polygonal shape. The series was re-issued in 1985 bearing the Maklouf profile [25] and in 1999 with the Rank-Broadley obverse [26]. The 1 and 2 cent coins were discontinued in 1991 and aluminium-bronze coins denominated $1 (1984) [27] and $2 (1988) [28] replaced banknotes.

Bimetallic $5 coins also appeared in 1988 but this denomination has since been largely employed as a commemorative. Australia has produced a vast range of commemoratives and special issues [29–31] in recent years, many in thematic series, in silver, gold and platinum and including, recently, coins with coloured surfaces.

KEELING COCOS ISLANDS
Ordinary Australian coins circulate in the overseas dependencies of Christmas Island and Norfolk Island. In the

Holey Dollar and Dump
The first distinctive coinage in Australia, authorized in 1813 by Governor Lachlan Macquarie, consisted of Spanish silver dollars with their centres cut out and tariffed at 15 pence, while the outer rings were circulated at 4s 9d. The work of cutting the coins and stamping them to denote their new value was entrusted to William Henshall, a convicted forger. In 1988, Australia issued a pair of legal tender silver coins, consisting of a 25g/1oz holey dollar and a 25 cent dump, as part of the celebrations marking the bicentenary of the first colony.

Keeling Cocos Islands, however, a distinctive series was issued in 1977, based on the rupee of 100 cents. It bears the bust of John Clunies-Ross (obverse), the self-proclaimed king of the islands in the 19th century, and a palm tree (reverse). Previously, various plastic and ivory tokens for use by workers in the coconut plantations were produced in 1910–13 and 1968 [32].

1

2

3

4

5

6

7

8

9

10

11

12

NEW ZEALAND

The Dominion of New Zealand is a member of the Commonwealth and has Elizabeth II as its head of state. It consists of two large islands and has an area rather larger than that of the United Kingdom but with only a twentieth of the population. Its economy is based on agriculture, with wool, meat and dairy products accounting for the bulk of its exports.

Left: In 1977, New Zealand celebrated the Queen's Silver Jubilee with a silver dollar showing the house at Waitangi where the treaty of cession was signed in 1840, echoing the Silver Jubilee crown of 1935, whose reverse had depicted the signing ceremony.

The Maori who migrated from Hawaii between the 10th and 14th centuries called the islands Aotearoa, "the land of the long white cloud". Abel Jan Tasman was the first European to sight the land and named it after the Dutch province of Zealand. Its coast was surveyed in detail in 1769 by James Cook, who annexed it to Britain. This rash act was ignored by the home government and for more than half a century New Zealand was visited only by whalers and sealers. By 1814, missionaries were establishing posts around the Bay of Islands and adventurers came in search of gold. In 1840, Captain William Hobson signed the Treaty of Waitangi with Maori chiefs and New Zealand was annexed as a dependency of New South Wales. A silver crown issued in 1935 for the silver jubilee of George V pictured the meeting of Hobson and the Maori chief, Waka Nene.

New Zealand was detached from New South Wales in 1852 and granted self-government. In the 1860s the population rose sharply following the discovery of gold, but continuing wrangles over land resulted in the Maori Wars of 1861–71. In the 1890s, New Zealand declined to join the Australian colonies in federation and became a separate dominion.

EARLY COINAGE
Remarkably, New Zealand used British coinage well into the 20th century. Periodic shortages of coins were met by

the traditional expedient of tradesmen's tokens, which began in 1857 and amounted to about 150 different types by 1881 when they were discontinued, although they continued to circulate until 1897. Later, Australian coins circulated alongside British ones.

New Zealand introduced distinctive silver coins in 1933, with the crowned bust of George V [1] on the obverse and various pictorial motifs on the reverse: Maori clubs (threepence) [3], the extinct *huia* bird (sixpence) [4], a Maori warrior (shilling) [2], a kiwi (florin) [5] and arms (half crown). Bronze coins did not appear until 1940, when the halfpenny featured a *tiki* or Maori idol [7] and the penny a *tui* bird [8]. These reverse types continued in later issues, with the profiles of George VI (1937–51) [6] and Elizabeth II (1953–64). Beside the centennial florin of 1940, silver crowns were issued on three occasions, for the silver jubilee (1935), the royal visit (1949) and the coronation (1953) [9]. To mark the centennial (1940) a half crown was issued [12], and half crowns were also issued in 1962 [10–11].

DECIMAL COINAGE
New Zealand adopted the dollar of 100 cents in 1967, with coins in bronze (1 and 2 cents) or cupro-nickel (5 cents to $1). The Machin bust of the Queen appeared on the obverse, while the reverse motifs were a stylized fern leaf (1 cent) [13], kowhai blossom (2 cents)

Non-Event

In 1949 a crown featuring a silver fern leaf and the Southern Cross was struck at the Royal Mint and shipped to New Zealand to celebrate the visit of George VI. The trip was cancelled on account of the king's illness, but the coins were issued anyway. When Queen Elizabeth and the Duke of Edinburgh visited New Zealand five years later no coins were issued to mark the occasion.

[14], tuatara (5 cents) [16], Maori *koruru* or carved head (10 cents) [15], kiwi (20 cents) [17], Captain Cook's brig *Endeavour* with Mount Egmont (Taranaki) (50 cents) [18] and the national arms crowned and flanked by fern leaves [19]. The 50 cent coin was re-issued in 1969 with an edge inscription to celebrate Cook's bicentenary.

Apart from the 1 and 2 cents (discontinued in 1988), the basic series has continued to this day, with the more mature effigies of the Queen by Maklouf (1986) [20] and Rank-Broadley (since 1999). In 1990 the large cupro-nickel dollar was replaced by a smaller aluminium-bronze coin featuring a kiwi [24]; at the same time a circulating $2 in the same alloy depicted a great egret [21] while the 20 cents now showed a tiki flanked by Maori curvilinear panels [23].

COMMEMORATIVE COINS

To mark the 150th anniversary of annexation in 1990 the circulating coins were temporarily replaced by issues showing a stylized bird (5 cents), a Maori sailing canoe (10 cents),

Cook's ship (20 cents) and tree-planting (50 cents); the dollar showed the signing of the Treaty of Waitangi.

Large dollars in cupro-nickel or silver were produced extensively from 1969 to commemorate historic anniversaries and events, including royal visits in 1970, 1983 and 1986, while royal birthdays, jubilees and wedding anniversaries [22] have also been assiduously celebrated. New Zealand hosted the Commonwealth Games in 1974 and 1989, issuing a single coin the first time and a set of four the second time. In more recent years coins have marked the Rugby World Cup and the Olympic Games. A series of 1992, ostensibly honouring Columbus, included coins in tribute to Kupe, the mythological leader of the Maori migration to New Zealand, as well as Tasman and Cook. A $5 coin of 1990 paid tribute to the Anzac forces of World War I, while a $20 of 1995 saluted the bravery of Charles Upham, the New Zealand double winner of the Victoria Cross.

New Zealand does not possess its own mint and has therefore relied mainly on the British Royal Mint for its coins, but this has given rise to some curious errors. In 1967 a consignment of bronze 2 cents was struck with the obverse of the Bahamas 5 cents instead. In 1985 a supply of cupro-nickel 50 cent coins was found to have the Canadian dollar reverse showing a Voyageur canoe. While examples of the Bahamas error are quite common, only nine of the Canadian hybrid coins have so far been recorded.

Above: A dollar depicting Mount Cook, known to the Maori as Aorangi, was issued to celebrate the 1970 royal visit.

NEW ZEALAND DEPENDENCIES

Several countries in the South Pacific are dependencies of New Zealand. Coins of the latter originally circulated in these territories – and still do, in the case of Niue – but in more recent years, indigenous coinages have developed, and these are inscribed with the names of the islands and relevant pictorial reverses.

Left: The British oarsmen and gold medallists Sir Matthew Pinsent and Sir Steve Redgrave are portrayed on the reverse of the $50 coin issued by Niue to mark the 1992 Olympic Games. Steve Redgrave holds the record as Britain's greatest Olympian, winning gold medals at five consecutive Olympic Games from 1984 to 2000.

COOK ISLANDS

This archipelago of 15 islands some 3000km/2000 miles north-east of New Zealand is named in honour of James Cook, although the Spaniard Alvaro de Mendaña was probably the first European to sight it, in 1595, while the Portuguese Fernandes de Quieros landed there in 1606. Cook visited the islands in 1773, 1774 and 1777 and named them the Hervey Islands, after one of the lords of the Admiralty.

The Cook Islands had their own monarchical system, but in 1888 Queen Makea Takau sought British protection. They were annexed by New Zealand in 1901 but were granted internal autonomy in 1965, though New Zealand continues to be responsible for defence and external affairs. The islands used New Zealand coins exclusively until 1972, when a series

Above: Dollar issued by New Zealand in 1970 to mark the bicentenary of the discovery of the Cook Islands.

bearing the Machin bust of Elizabeth II [1, 3, 5] was introduced. These coins followed the weights, alloys and specifications of their New Zealand counterparts, with pictorial reverses featuring a taro leaf (1 cent), pineapple (2 cents), hibiscus (5 cents) [2], orange (10 cents) [4], fairy tern (20 cents) [7], bonito fish (50 cents) [6] and Tangaroa, the Polynesian god of creation ($1) [8]. The reverse of the 20 cents changed in 1972 to depict a Pacific triton shell. The series was re-issued in 1978 with an edge inscription marking the 250th anniversary of the birth of Captain Cook, and the same device was repeated in 1981 to celebrate the wedding of Prince Charles and Lady Diana Spencer. In 1987 the Maklouf profile was substituted, the size of the dollar reduced and a scalloped shape adopted on the dollar, while a $2 coin depicting an island table and a $5 showing a conch shell [9] were introduced.

Numerous commemorative or special issues have appeared since 1986 [10–11], notably the series of 16 (1996) featuring world wildlife and the multicoloured coins depicting the cartoon character Garfield (1999).

NIUE

Discovered by Cook in 1774 and originally named Savage Island, Niue was originally administered as part of the

Cook Islands but has been a separate dependency of New Zealand since 1922. New Zealand coins are still in general circulation and Niue must be unique among the nations of the world in not having introduced a base-metal circulating coinage of its own. This defect, however, has been more than remedied since 1987 by the release of a considerable number of commemorative or special coins in denominations from $1 to $250, in cupro-nickel, silver or gold. The overwhelming majority are from $5 upwards and in fact it was not until 1996 that Niue got around to issuing a $1 coin, with a reverse depicting HMS *Bounty*, scene of one of the most famous mutinies in the history of the Royal Navy.

While some coins have the Maklouf profile of Elizabeth II on the obverse, the majority bear the crowned arms of New Zealand instead [12]. The first coins were of $5 denomination and portrayed the tennis stars Boris Becker [13] and Steffi Graf. This set the tone for subsequent issues; tennis is a sport that has been rather neglected on the coins of other countries, but from Niue have come coins honouring Martina

First Rounded Triangle
To the Cook Islands goes the credit for producing the world's first triangular coin with rounded edges, the $2 of 1987–94: both circulating and proof versions were minted in each year.

Navratilova and Chris Evert as well as Steffi Graf (1988), the final between Germany and Sweden in the Davis Cup (1989) and a further issue devoted to Steffi Graf (including silver $50 and $100 as well as $250 gold coins) in the same year. After that, Niue looked elsewhere and, discovering that soccer was a lucrative theme, issued coins portraying such football stars as Franz Beckenbauer and even the entire Italian squad (1990). Themes of other series range from endangered wildlife to war heroes such as Douglas MacArthur and Admiral William Halsey, and Cook's voyages of discovery vie with the Soviet Union's Luna 9 moon landing.

TOKELAU ISLANDS
About 3000km/2000 miles north of New Zealand lie the Union or Tokelau Islands – Atafu, Nukunono and Fakaofo – whose inhabitants are Polynesian by race and Samoan in language and culture. These remote atolls were acquired by Britain in 1889 and bandied about for many years, at times administered as part of the Gilbert and Ellice Islands Protectorate and then, from 1926 to 1948, attached to Western Samoa. Since then they have been a New Zealand dependency.

In 1978 a cupro-nickel dollar was issued, merely inscribed "Tokelau" with the date round the top, over the Machin bust of Elizabeth II (with neither her name nor titles) [14]. What appeared to be Morse code running round the rim were patterns of three dots representing the three atolls. The reverse depicted a breadfruit with the value in Samoan ("Tahi Tala") [15]. An edge inscription proclaimed "Tokelau's First Coin". This established the pattern for subsequent coins, from $1 [16–17] to $100, and though the Maklouf profile was adopted in 1989 the Queen's name remains conspicuously absent. The reverses depict aspects of island life, although a series of 1991 featured salient events in the Pacific War, from the attack on Pearl Harbor to the raising of the Stars and Stripes on Iwo Jima.

10

11

12

13

14

15

16

17

PNG, NAURU AND VANUATU

Apart from Nauru (formerly Ocean Island), these countries lie to the north of Australia. They include Vanuatu, formerly the New Hebrides, which was administered by France and Britain as a condominium, and the eastern part of New Guinea (the world's largest island after Greenland), which was formerly partitioned between Germany and Britain. The western portion of New Guinea was once part of the Dutch East Indies and is now Irian Barat, part of Indonesia.

Left: The toea*, or Emperor of Germany bird of paradise, is not only featured on coins of Papua New Guinea but has lent its name to the unit of currency.*

GERMAN NEW GUINEA

The southern portion of east New Guinea was annexed by Queensland in 1883. A year later Germany annexed the northern part, which became Kaiser Wilhelmsland. British and German coinage circulated in the respective territories, but in 1894–5 a distinctive series for use in Kaiser Wilhelmsland was produced by the New Guinea Company, whose German name appeared on the obverse of the bronze 1 and 2 pfennig coins, with the value on the reverse. The higher values, comprising the bronze 10 pfennig, silver half, 1, 2 and 5 marks and the gold 10 and 20 marks, had an obverse showing the *toea* (the national bird), with a wreathed value on the reverse [1–5]. Shortly after the outbreak of war in August 1914 German New Guinea was invaded and occupied by Australian forces. In 1920 Australia was granted a mandate by the League of Nations and ordinary Australian coins were adopted.

BRITISH NEW GUINEA

The administration of the southern portion, known as British New Guinea or Papua, passed from Queensland to the British Crown in 1888, but was transferred to the Commonwealth of Australia in 1901. It became a self-governing territory in 1906. British or Australian coins were used until 1929, when cupro-nickel halfpennies and pennies were introduced as small change, followed by the cupro-nickel

threepence and sixpence, and the silver shilling, in 1935. A singular feature of the coinage was that all five denominations had a central hole [6–7]. The obverse bore a Tudor crown flanked by two maces on the two lowest values and the shilling, while the others featured the crown and royal monogram flanked by the date. The reverses had the name of the territory, value and date, with cruciform or geometric patterns in the middle.

A bronze penny was adopted in 1936 with the monogram of Edward VIII, and was one of the few distinctive colonial coins of his short reign [8–9]. New pennies with the "GRI" monogram appeared in 1938 and 1944, with sporadic issues of higher values up to 1945 [10–11].

PAPUA NEW GUINEA

The Japanese invaded New Guinea in 1942 and a ferocious campaign ensued before Commonwealth forces regained control. A mandate from the United Nations was granted in 1946 and in 1949 Papua and New Guinea were united. In 1973 the territory was granted self-government, and full independence as a member of the Commonwealth was achieved in 1975.

Coinage was introduced that year, based on the kina of 100 toeas, the eponymous bird of paradise appearing on the standard obverse, with other examples of fauna on the reverse [12–13]. Simultaneously a gold 100 kina portrayed the prime minister, Michael Somare. Coins from 1 to 20 toeas have been issued in the same designs ever since [14–19].

A few heptagonal 50 toeas appeared in the 1980s, solely as commemoratives, but the crown-sized 5 and 10 kina are the preferred medium, together with gold 100 kina. The relatively few special issues have included coins for the visit of Pope John Paul II (1984) and the Commonwealth Games (1991). An enormous 25 kina in enamelled silver appeared in 1994 to mark the centenary of the first coinage.

NAURU
One of the world's smallest and most isolated countries, the Republic of Nauru has an area of just 21sq km/8sq miles and a population of 13,000. It has the curious distinction of being the only country in the world without a capital. Composed largely of phosphate deposits, now exhausted, Nauru could eventually disappear as the island succumbs to rising ocean levels resulting from global warming. Some of the phosphate revenue was invested in Australian real estate, notably Nauru House, one of the highest buildings in Melbourne, but having enjoyed the highest per capita income of any Third World country, Nauru is now on the brink of bankruptcy. In the 1990s the islanders attempted to create a tax haven, but this ended in 2004. Recently the island's main revenue has come from Australia, which uses it as a detention centre for asylum seekers.

Discovered in 1798 by a whaler, John Fearn, who named it Pleasant Island, Nauru continued as a tribal kingdom with mixed Melanesian and Polynesian inhabitants until 1888, when it was annexed by Germany as a dependency of New Guinea. The exploitation of the phosphate deposits began in 1905. Nauru was occupied and administered by Australia from 1914 and invaded by Japan in 1942. In 1947 the United Nations placed it under joint British, Australian and New Zealand government until it became an

Heptagonal Coins
In 1980 Papua New Guinea introduced a 50 toea denomination and adopted the seven-sided format pioneered by Britain. It has so far been confined to coins commemorating the South Pacific Festival of Arts (1980) and the Ninth South Pacific Games (1991).

independent republic in 1968 under the presidency of Hammer de Roburt. Australian coins are in everyday use but silver $10 and gold $50 pieces have been issued by the Bank of Nauru since 1993 to commemorate the Olympic Games, the World Cup, the Queen Mother [20] and other subjects of global interest.

VANUATU
Named the New Hebrides by Captain Cook in 1774, these islands east of Papua New Guinea were declared a neutral zone in 1878, administered jointly by British and French naval officers. A condominium was proclaimed in 1906, but the only distinctive coins were those provided by the French after 1966 (see "French Pacific Islands").

In 1980 the country became an independent republic within the Commonwealth and adopted the name of Vanuatu. Coins thus inscribed, with the national emblem (obverse) [21, 23] and flora or seashells (reverse) [22, 24], were struck in denominations from 1 to 100 vatu. Several FAO coins have appeared [25–26], along with coins from 10 to 100 vatu celebrating the end of the Victorian era (1995), the Olympic Games, Captain Cook and the 25th anniversary of the Voyager 1 spacecraft – an eclectic mixture.

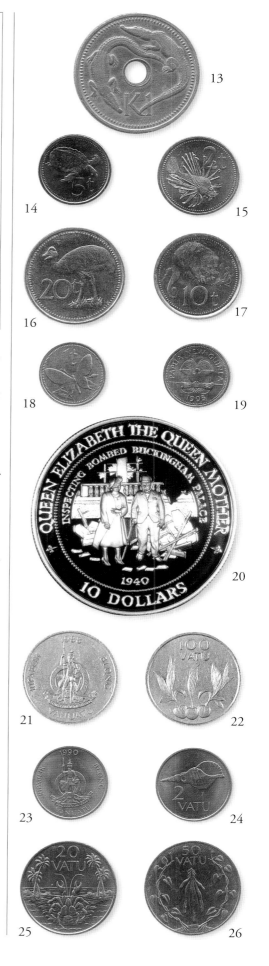

FIJI, SOLOMONS, KIRIBATI AND TUVALU

These countries are archipelagos scattered over the south-western Pacific. Though all three were sighted by European navigators in the 16th and 17th centuries they were surveyed by Captain Cook in the 18th century and thereafter fell within the British sphere of influence.

Tuvalu, formerly the Ellice or Lagoon Islands, was claimed for the British Crown in 1892 by the captain of HMS Royalist, *depicted on the $20 of 1993.*

FIJI

In 1643, Abel Jan Tasman was the first European to sight Fiji, and the islands were visited by James Cook in 1774. William Bligh and the loyal members of the crew of HMS *Bounty*, set adrift in an open boat by the mutineers, sailed through the Fiji group on their epic voyage to Timor (1789), but it was not until 1840 that the islands were comprehensively surveyed.

Traders and adventurers arrived in 1801 in search of sandalwood, and by 1850 there was a sizable and cosmopolitan population in Suva, the capital. By that time the islands were united under King Cakobau, but in 1874 incessant tribal warfare induced him to seek British protection in order to restore law and order. In the colonial period the British developed the sugar industry, bringing in indentured coolies from India. When Fiji attained independence in 1970 the Indian majority were held back by the indigenous Fijians, a dangerous situation that resulted in two military coups in 1987, the declaration of a republic and Fiji's expulsion from the Commonwealth. It was re-admitted in 1997.

British (from 1881) and Australian currency (from 1910) was in circulation until 1934, when distinctive coins were introduced. The holed halfpenny and penny were originally struck in cupro-nickel, then brass (1942) and bronze (1949), with a crown and the name of the monarch on the obverse and the country name, value and date on the reverse [1–2]. Thus Fiji was one of the few colonies to issue coins in 1936 in the name of Edward VIII. The silver sixpence, shilling and florin appeared in 1934, with a crowned bust of George V on the obverse and reverse motifs of a turtle, outrigger canoe [3–4] and colonial arms respectively. A 12-sided nickel-brass threepence was added in 1947, featuring a thatched hut between palm trees on the reverse. These coins, with the crowned effigy of the monarch, continued until Fiji adopted the dollar in 1969. A new series bore the Machin bust of the Queen and artefacts representing indigenous culture: kava bowl (1 cent) [6–7], palm-leaf fan (2 cents) [5], ceremonial drum (5 cents), throwing club (10 cents), *tabua* (whale's tooth) on a braided cord (20 cents), sailing canoe (50c) [8–9] and arms ($1) [10], the specifications following the Australian standard. The Maklouf effigy of the Queen has been used since 1986.

Numerous commemorative coins have appeared since independence in 1970. In addition to conventional circular coins Fiji has experimented with pentagons, polygons [11–13] and even segments which, when fitted to similar coins from Western Samoa and the Cook Islands, form a complete circle.

Pacific Conflict

The Solomon Islands were the scene of some of the fiercest fighting between Japanese and US forces in 1942–3, especially on Guadalcanal. From 1991 onward, several coins were issued to mark the 50th anniversaries of the battles of the Coral Sea and Guadalcanal, beginning with a dollar commemorating the Japanese attack on Pearl Harbor.

SOLOMON ISLANDS

Discovered in 1567 by the Spanish, these islands were partitioned between Germany and Britain and were declared protectorates in 1885 and 1893 respectively. The German islands were occupied by Australia in 1914 and in 1976 the protectorate was abolished. Since becoming an independent member of the Commonwealth the islands have issued coins portraying Elizabeth II with indigenous artefacts on the reverse, as well as numerous commemoratives [14–19].

KIRIBATI

Pronounced "Kiribas", the islands' name is the Polynesian rendering of "Gilbert", as they were previously thus named after Captain Thomas Gilbert, who first visited them in 1778. With the Ellice Islands, the Gilberts were administered from Fiji as a British protectorate, becoming a crown colony in 1915. The Phoenix group was added in 1937 and the Central and Southern Line Islands in 1972. These sparsely populated islands are spread over more than 2.5 million sq km/1 million sq miles of ocean, but their total land area

is relatively small. The Gilbert Islands became a separate colony in 1976 and a republic within the Commonwealth in 1979, adopting the present name. Until then Australian currency was in use, but Kiribati has since issued its own coins, with arms (obverse) and indigenous fauna (reverse) on the low values and a sailing canoe and thatched hut on the dollar coins [20–21].

TUVALU

Formerly the Ellice Islands, this group has an area of 25sq km/10sq miles, and constitutes one of the world's smallest independent republics. In 1974 the inhabitants voted to separate from the Gilbert Islands and in 1976 became a "constitutional dependency" of the British Crown, under the name of Tuvalu. Complete independence for the population of 9000 was achieved in October 1978. Distinctive coins were adopted in 1976, bearing the Machin effigy of Elizabeth II with marine fauna on the reverse [22–23]. Since 1994 the Maklouf profile has been substituted. A few silver ($5, $10 or $20) and gold ($50 or $100) coins have appeared since 1976, marking anniversaries of independence or royal events, from the wedding of Prince Charles and Diana Spencer (1981) to the Duke of Edinburgh Award and birthdays of the Queen Mother.

Fitting the Pieces Together

Kiribati has produced relatively few special issues, although they include segmented Millennial coins resembling pieces of a jigsaw puzzle (1997), inscribed with the Latin for "times are changing".

1

2

3

4

5

6

7

8

9

10

FRENCH PACIFIC ISLANDS

Second only to Britain, France was the major colonial power in the South Pacific, and it still maintains a strong presence in that region. The Bank of Indochina established branches at Nouméa, New Caledonia, in 1888 and at Papeete, Tahiti, in 1905 and was responsible for paper money. French coins were in use until 1949, when separate issues for the French territories were introduced. The Bank of Indochina was succeeded in 1965 by the Institut d'Emission d'Outre-Mer (Overseas Issuing Institute), whose initials appear on the obverse of the nickel coins issued since 1975 [6, 14]. Separate issues are made for French Polynesia and New Caledonia, the CFP ("Change franc Pacifique" or "Pacific franc exchange") franc being tariffed at 1000 to 8.38 euros.

Left: An image of Moorea, one of the most spectacularly beautiful islands anywhere in the world, is featured on the 50 franc coins of French Polynesia.

FRENCH POLYNESIA

Porinetia Farani, as it is known in the local language, is a French overseas collectivity, comprising several island groups scattered over 2.5 million sq km/1 million sq miles of the South Pacific, with a total land area of 4,200 sq km/1,600sq miles and a population of 270,000. The largest island is Tahiti, which is also the location of the capital, Papeete. Captain Cook visited Tahiti in 1769, naming the archipelago the Society Islands, and Captain Bligh of the *Bounty* spent some time there in 1788–9 gathering breadfruit plants, which were to be established in the West Indies as food for the plantation slaves. Pomare II converted to Christianity in 1797 and British missionaries were in a favoured position until 1843, when France established a protectorate that became a colony in 1880 when Pomare V abdicated. The Society Islands joined the Marquesas and the Tuamotu archipelago in 1903 to form the colony known collectively as the French Settlements in Oceania.

French coins were used until 1949 when French Oceania attained self-government within the French Union. Aluminium coins from 50 centimes to 5 francs had the allegorical figure of Marianne on the obverse and a palm-girt scene on the reverse [1].

In 1957 the territory was renamed French Polynesia and chose to remain within the French Community. Coins in the same designs as those of 1949, but inscribed "Polynésie Française" on the reverse, were adopted in 1965 [2]. Higher denominations (10, 20 and 50 francs), struck in nickel, were added in 1967, with the head of Marianne (obverse) [5–7] and reverse motifs of a carved pole [3], frangipani blossom [4] and the jagged peaks of Moorea respectively. A 100 franc coin with the Moorea reverse, struck in nickel-bronze [8], was added to the series in 1976.

French coins also circulate widely, reflecting the continuing military presence associated with the testing of nuclear devices at Mururoa Atoll. Since January 1996, however, nuclear testing has been discontinued and the military garrison greatly reduced. Today the main sources of revenue come from tourism and the cultivation of *noni* fruit for the pharmaceutical industry.

NEW CALEDONIA

This archipelago 1800km/1100 miles east of Australia was discovered in 1774 by Captain Cook, who bestowed on it the name then used by poets to denote Scotland. As in Tahiti, British missionaries brought Christianity and a measure of Western civilization, but it was the French who established a protectorate there in 1853. They used it as a penal settlement, deporting many thousands of Communards in the aftermath of the abortive revolution of 1870–1. Normal colonial development began only in 1894.

New Caledonia used French coins exclusively until 1949 but, following its establishment as an overseas territory within the French Community in 1946, aluminium coins for small change were introduced. These had the same obverse as the coins of French Oceania [9] but the reverse featured the *kagu*, the national bird [10–11]. Nickel coins appeared in 1967 with the head of Marianne on the obverse [14] and on the reverse a Melanesian sailing pirogue, or flat-hulled canoe (10 francs) [12], zebu cattle (20 francs) [13] and a hut surrounded by Norfolk Island pines (50 francs) [15]. Nickel-bronze 100 francs with the pines reverse were added to the series in 1976.

Associated with New Caledonia are the three tiny volcanic islands of Uvea (Wallis), Alofi and Futuna, known as the Wallis and Futuna Islands, lying between Fiji and Samoa. The group was discovered by the Cornishman Samuel Wallis in the 18th century, but Christianized by French missionaries who arrived in 1837, and French protectorates were established over the islands in 1887–8. Each island has its own king to this day. In 1959 the inhabitants voted to become a separate overseas territory, thus severing political dependency on New Caledonia. A French overseas collectivity since 2003, the territory continues to use the coinage of New Caledonia.

NEW HEBRIDES
Named the New Hebrides by Captain Cook in 1774, because of a fancied resemblance to the islands off the west coast of Scotland, these islands east of Papua New Guinea had previously been visited by the Portuguese Pedro de Queiros (1606) and the Frenchman Louis de Bougainville (1768). Rival missionaries and sandalwood traders

Reference to Earlier Currency
The squiggles flanking the carved mask on the reverse of the 10 and 20 franc coins of the New Hebrides are pieces of *tridacna* or clam shell, used as money before the advent of coinage.

established themselves in the islands throughout the 19th century and urged their respective countries to annex them. Even British settlers favoured French protection when their own government seemed indifferent. An ad hoc dual system developed, but was unsatisfactory in regard to the settlement of civil disputes. The situation was aggravated by periodic uprisings by the indigenous inhabitants. In 1878 France and Britain negotiated a deal whereby the islands were declared a neutral zone, administered jointly by British and French naval officers, but this was impractical and led eventually to joint rule. A condominium was proclaimed in 1906, with two separate police forces and a judicial system headed by two judges (one British and one French) and a president, who did not have to be either nationality, appointed by the king of Spain.

British, French and Australian currency was used but the only distinctive coins were those provided by the French authorities from 1966 onward, with the head of Marianne on the obverse and indigenous carvings on the reverse [16–20]. In 1980 the New Hebrides achieved complete independence, becoming the Republic of Vanuatu, a member of the British Commonwealth (see page 149).

1

2

3

4

5

6

7

8

9

POLYNESIAN KINGDOMS

Polynesia (from the Greek for "many islands") is the generic name for the vast number of islands scattered across the central Pacific from Hawaii in the north, whence the hardy seafaring Polynesians set out to colonize the other island groups in the 10th and subsequent centuries. The tribal communities eventually developed into kingdoms with their own coinage.

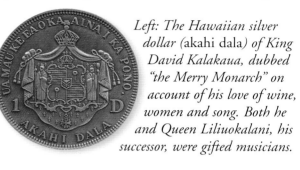

Left: The Hawaiian silver dollar (akahi dala) *of King David Kalakaua, dubbed "the Merry Monarch" on account of his love of wine, women and song. Both he and Queen Liliuokalani, his successor, were gifted musicians.*

HAWAII

This archipelago was visited by Captain James Cook in 1778. At that time the eight main islands were under the rule of petty kings and tribal chiefs, but by 1795 Kamehameha I had welded them into a single nation. American missionaries and traders gradually transformed Hawaii, creating the sugar and pineapple industries and bringing in indentured labourers from Japan and the Azores. American businessmen engineered the downfall of the monarchy in 1893, and for a brief period in 1894 Hawaii was a republic before it was admitted to the USA in 1898, becoming a territory in 1900 and a state in 1959.

Copper cents with a facing bust of Kamehameha III on the obverse and the value in the Hawaiian language on the reverse appeared in 1847. A regular coinage was introduced in 1881–3, with the profile of David Kalakaua on the obverse [1–2]. The reverses featured a crowned value (5 cents), wreathed values (10 cents and ⅛ dollar) and the crowned arms (quarter, half and dollar). Coins with the bust of Queen Liliuokalani dated 1891 or 1895 (the latter bearing a striking resemblance to the Syracusan decadrachms of the 5th century BC, complete with dolphins surrounding the portrait) were commissioned by Reginald Huth, a wealthy British collector, and are regarded as

patterns. Restrikes or imitations of Hawaiian coins have been produced in recent years as tourist souvenirs.

TONGA

Named the Friendly Islands by Captain Cook in 1773, Tonga is an archipelago in the South Pacific, south of Samoa and east of Fiji. Intertribal warfare was brought to an end by Taufa'ahau, who adopted the name of King George Tupou I when he converted to Christianity in 1845. Aided and abetted by the British missionary Shirley Baker, who became prime minister, he united the islands into a single kingdom by 1862. Tonga became a self-governing British protectorate in 1900 and a fully independent kingdom within the Commonwealth in 1970.

The coinage of Britain, and latterly of New Zealand, circulated in Tonga, and the first indigenous coins were the gold pieces of 1962 called the koula (from the Tongan word for "gold") with its half and quarter. A standing figure of Queen Salote appeared on the koula and half koula and a profile on the quarter koula, with the royal arms on the reverse. Circulating coinage, based on the pa'anga of 100 seniti, was adopted in 1967, with Salote's effigy on the obverse [3] and various reverse motifs of a giant tortoise (1 and 2 seniti), wreathed value (5 and 10 seniti) and the coat of arms (20 and 50 seniti and 1 pa'anga) [4]. These coins were posthumous, as Salote had died in 1965. A series of seven coins, including the platinum hau (100 pa'anga) and its subdivisions, also appeared in 1967 to celebrate the coronation of her son and successor Taufa'ahau Tupou IV, with his portrait (obverse) and arms (reverse), followed by a permanent series with his profile replacing his mother's [5–7]. A series introduced in 1975 bore a facing bust of the king in military uniform, with motifs promoting the Food and Agriculture Organization programme [10–11]. Since then Tonga has produced numerous coins in all shapes and sizes [8–9] for a wide range of topics, often issued in thematic sets. These have ranged from veteran and vintage cars to celebrate the automobile centenary [12–13] to sporting events such as the Olympic and Commonwealth Games and the America's Cup yacht races, as well as tributes to members of the British royal family [14].

Christmas Coins

From 1982 to 1988 Tonga released heptagonal coins to celebrate Christmas, with appropriate reverse motifs ranging from Dürer's *Praying Hands* to the Three Wise Men. Struck in cupro-nickel for general circulation, they were also minted in silver, gold or platinum in very limited editions.

Despite its comparative remoteness, Tonga has made a big splash in the coin world with a number of startling innovations. As well as the first gold coins from Oceania, Tonga experimented with high-denomination coins (the hau worth 100 pa'anga) struck in palladium, a rare metal of the platinum group. In the 1980s, when the bullion value of silver rose sharply, a number of special issues were struck in silver-plated cupro-nickel. Some coins of 1967–8 were countermarked to commemorate the king's 50th birthday or the anniversary of Salote's death, in much the same way that stamps are overprinted for this purpose.

WESTERN SAMOA

The islands of Samoa were discovered by the Dutch Jacob Roggeveen in 1772 but were later the subject of a three-cornered tussle between Germany, Britain and the USA. Although the group had an indigenous monarchy, it was partitioned between Germany and the USA in March 1900, and the eastern portion remains under US rule. In 1914 German Samoa fell to forces from New Zealand, which was granted a mandate by the League of Nations. Western Samoa remained under this mandate until it attained independence in 1962.

Distinctive coins were introduced in 1967, based on the tala (dollar) of 100 sene (cents) [15–16]. The obverse bore the profile of Malietoa Tanumafili II, a direct descendent of the kings of Samoa, who holds his position for life, although it is intended that his successors should be elected for five-year terms. The reverses focus on various fruits [19–20], with the state arms on the tala. Since 1969 Western Samoa has issued a large number of special coins, commemorating the Queen's silver jubilee [17–18] and featuring sporting events such as the Commonwealth and Olympic Games [21–22] and the Americas Cup yacht races, while local heroes such as Robert Louis Stevenson (known as Tusitala – "the teller of tales") [23–24] and German governor Dr Wilhelm Solff are not forgotten.

GLOSSARY

Accolated *see* **conjoined**.

Aes grave (Latin, "heavy bronze") Heavy coinage of the Roman Republic from 269 BC.

Aes rude (Latin, "rough bronze") Irregular lumps of bronze used as money before the adoption of regular coinage, *c.* 400 BC.

Aes signatum (Latin, "signed bronze") Regular bars or ingots cast to a standard weight, stamped to guarantee their weight, 289–269 BC.

Alliance coinage Coins struck by two or more states in conjunction.

Alloy Mixture of metals, such as bronze (copper and tin).

Aluminium Lightweight silver-coloured metal used for coins of low denominations.

Aluminium-bronze Durable, gold-coloured alloy of aluminium and copper.

Angel Gold coin named for its image of Archangel Michael, first used in France in 1340 and introduced to England in 1465, with a value of 6 shillings and 8 pence.

Annulet Small circle used as an ornament or spacing device in inscriptions.

Antoniniani Roman imperial coins named after the emperor Caracalla (Marcus Aurelius Antoninus) in whose reign they were first minted.

Assay Test to determine the fineness of precious metal.

Base metal Non-precious metal or an alloy containing neither gold nor silver.

Beading Border of raised dots round the rim of a coin.

Billon Alloy of copper with less than 50 per cent silver.

Bimetallic Made of two different metals or alloys; such coins usually have a centre in one metal and outer ring in another.

Bit (1) Segment of a coin that has been cut up in order to circulate at half or one quarter the value of the entire coin. (2) Nickname of the 1 real piece that circulated in North America in the 17th and 18th centuries, worth one eighth of a dollar, or 12½ cents.

Blank Disc of metal cut or punched out of a strip or sheet, on which a coin is struck. Also known as a flan or planchet.

Blundered inscription (1) Jumbled lettering in inscriptions on barbarous coins, reflecting the illiteracy of the makers copying Greek or Roman coins. (2) Unreadable inscription as a result of a mis-strike.

Bon pour (French, "good for") Inscription on 1920s French tokens used during a shortage of legal tender coins.

Bracteate (from Latin *bractea*, a thin piece of metal) Coin struck on such a thin blank that the image impressed on one side shows through on the other.

Brass Alloy of copper and zinc.

Brockage Mis-struck coin with only one design, normal on one side and incuse on the other, caused when a struck coin clings to the die and strikes the next blank to pass through the press.

Bronze Alloy of copper and tin.

Bullet money Globular pieces of silver with impressed marks, used as currency in Thailand from the 14th century until 1904.

Bullion Precious metal whose value is reckoned solely by its weight and fineness.

Bullion coin Coin struck in precious metal, now usually with an inscription giving its weight and fineness, whose value fluctuates according to the market price of the metal.

Carat (US karat) Term used to denote the fineness of gold, being ½₄ of the whole. Thus 22 carat gold is .916 fine.

Cartwheel Nickname of the British penny and 2 pence copper coins of 1797, weighing respectively 1oz/28.35g and 2oz/56.7g, with raised rims resembling cartwheels.

Cased set Set of coins in mint condition, packaged by the mint.

Cash (from Portuguese *caixa* and Tamil *kacu*, a small coin) Cast circular coins in copper or bronze with a square central hole, used as subsidiary coinage in China.

Cast coins Coins made by pouring molten metal into moulds, rather than by striking discs of metal with dies.

Clad Descriptive of a coin with a core of one metal covered with a layer or coating of another.

Clipping Removing slivers of silver or gold from the edge of coins, an illegal but widespread practice until the 1660s, when milled coins began to be struck with grained edges.

Cob Irregularly shaped silver piece sliced from a bar of silver and crudely stamped for use in Spanish America in the 16th to 18th centuries.

Coin weight Piece of metal of exactly the weight of a known coin, used to check weight and fineness of matching coins.

Collar Ring within which the obverse and reverse dies operate to restrict the spread of the blank between them; it is often engraved with an inscription or pattern that is impressed on the edge of the coin.

Commemorative Coin struck to celebrate a historic anniversary or personality or publicize an event.

Conjoined portrait Obverse portrait with two heads or busts in profile, facing the same direction and overlapping. Also known as accolated or jugate.

Convention money Coins struck by neighbouring states and mutually acceptable; specifically the issues of Austria and Bavaria, which spread to other German states in the early 19th century.

Copper (1) Metal widely used for subsidiary coinage for more than 2500 years, usually alloyed with tin to make bronze, but also alloyed with nickel or silver. (2) Nickname for small denomination coins.

Counterfeit Imitation of a coin for circulation, intended to deceive the public and defraud the state.

Countermark Punch mark applied to a coin to change its value or authorize its circulation in a different state.

Crown gold Gold of 22 carat (.916) fineness, so called because it was first used in England in 1526 for the gold crown; it remains the British standard.

Cupro-nickel (US copper-nickel) Alloy of copper and nickel.

Currency Money of all kinds, including coins, paper notes, tokens and other articles, passing current in general circulation.

Current Descriptive of coins and paper money in circulation.

Cut money Coins cut into smaller pieces to provide proportionately smaller values for general circulation.

Debasement Reduction of a coin's precious metal content.

Decimal currency Currency system in which the basic unit is divided into 10, 100 or 1000 subsidiary units.

Demonetization Withdrawal of coins from circulation, declaring them to be worthless.

Denomination Value given to a coin or note of paper money.

Device Term derived from heraldry for the pattern or emblem on a coin.

Die Hardened piece of metal bearing the mirror or wrong-reading image of a device, used to strike one side of a blank.

Die break Raised line or bump in a relief image caused by a crack in the die.

Dump Coin struck on a very thick blank.

Eagle US gold coin with an American eagle obverse and a face value of $10, circulating until 1933.

Ecclesiastical coins Coins struck under the authority of an archbishop or other prelate, prevalent in the Middle Ages and surviving in coins of the Papacy.

Edge The side of a coin, perpendicular to the obverse and reverse surfaces, which may be plain, inscribed or grained.

Edge inscription Lettering on the edge of coins designed to prevent clipping.

Effigy Portrait or bust on the obverse of a coin.

Electrum Naturally occurring alloy of gold and silver prevalent in the ancient coins of the Mediterranean region; it was also known as white gold.

Engraving Technique of cutting designs and inscriptions in dies used for striking coins.

Epigraphy Study of inscriptions engraved in stone or metal, usually to determine the date and provenance of an artefact so inscribed.

Error Mistake in the design or production of a coin.

Exergue Bottom segment of the face of a coin, usually divided from the rest of the field by a horizontal line and often containing the date or value.

Face Obverse or reverse surface of a coin.

Face value Value of the denomination applied to a coin, distinct from its intrinsic value.

Facing Descriptive of a portrait facing to the front instead of in profile.

Fantasy Piece purporting to be a coin but either emanating from a non-existent country or never authorized by the country whose name is inscribed on it.

Field Flat part of a coin between the legend and effigy or other raised parts of the design.

Flan *see* **blank**.

Forgery Unauthorized copy or imitation, produced primarily to deceive collectors.

Gold Precious metal used for coins since the 7th century BC.

Grade Description of the condition of a collectable coin for the purposes of valuation and trade.

Graining Pattern of close vertical ridges around the edge of milled coins, originally devised to eliminate the fraudulent practice of clipping. Also known as reeding or milling.

Gun money Emergency Irish coinage of 1689–91 struck from gunmetal by the deposed James II in order to pay and supply his troops during the Williamite or Jacobean War.

Hammered Descriptive of coins struck by hand, using a hammer to impress the dies.

Hoard Group of coins buried or hidden in the past.

Holed coin (1) Coin minted with a central hole. (2) Coin pierced after striking, to wear as jewellery or a talisman.

Hub Right-reading metal punch used to strike working dies.

Incuse Descriptive of an impression that cuts into the surface of a coin.

Ingot Piece of precious metal, cast in a mould and stamped with its weight and fineness.

Intrinsic value Net value based on the metal content of a coin, as opposed to its nominal or face value.

Iron Metal used in primitive currency such as the spits of ancient Greece, and for emergency coinage in both World Wars.

Jugate (from Latin *jugum*, yoke) Alternative term for **conjoined**.

Key date The rarest date in a long-running series.

Klippe Coin struck on a square or rectangular blank hand-cut from sheet metal, originally in a time of emergency.

Laureate Descriptive of a design incorporating a laurel wreath, either adorning the brows of a ruler or enclosing the value.

Legal tender Coin declared by law to be current money.

Legend Inscription on a coin.

Long cross coinage English pennies first issued by Henry III, on which the arms of the cross on the reverse reached to the rim.

Lustre Sheen or bloom on the surface of an uncirculated coin.

Maundy money Set of small silver pennies distributed by the British sovereign to the poor on Maundy Thursday (preceding Good Friday), a medieval custom still enacted. Ordinary coins were originally used but special 1, 2, 3 and 4 pence coins were first minted in 1822.

Milling Mechanical process for the production of coins, in use from the 16th century. Also known as graining.

Mint Establishment in which coins are produced. Also used as a grading term.

Mint set Coins still enclosed in the package or case issued by the mint.

Mint-mark Mark on a coin identifying the mint at which it was struck.

Mis-strike Coin on which the impression of the die has been struck off-centre.

Moneyer Mint official in pre-industrial era responsible for striking coinage of legal weight and quality.

Mule Coin whose obverse and reverse designs are wrongly matched. Can be comprised of different denominations or even separate foreign currencies.

Nickel Base metal used extensively in coinage as a substitute for silver, frequently alloyed with copper to make cupro-nickel.

Non-circulating legal tender Coins that, though technically valid for use, do not circulate in practice (such as silver and gold

commemoratives). Abbreviated to NCLT.

Numismatics (from Latin *numisma*, coin) The study and collection of paper money, coins and medals.

Obverse "Heads" side of a coin.

Overdating Method of changing a date without the expense of engraving an entirely new die. One or more digits are altered by superimposing other numerals using a punch.

Overstrike Coin produced when a previously struck coin is substituted for a blank, on which traces of the original design remain.

Pattern Design piece prepared by a mint for approval by the issuing authority, not actually put into production. Patterns may differ from issued coins in metal or minor details, but many bear designs quite different from those eventually adopted.

Pellet Raised circular ornament, sometimes used as a spacing device in the inscription.

Pieces of eight Nickname for Spanish silver 8 real coins.

Piedfort (US piefort) Coin struck on a blank of two or three times the normal weight and thickness.

Planchet *see* **blank**.

Platinum Precious metal first used for coins in Russia in 1819 and occasionally in recent years for proof coins.

Plate money Large, cumbersome copper plates used as money in Sweden, 1643–1768.

Privy mark Secret mark incorporated in a coin design as a security device or to identify the particular die used.

Profile Side portrait often used on the obverse of coins.

Proof Originally a trial strike but in recent years a coin struck to a very high standard, often in precious metals.

Punch Piece of hardened metal bearing a design or lettering used to impress a die or a coin.

Reeding *see* **graining**.

Relief Raised parts of the design.

Restrike Coin produced from the original dies, but long after the period in which they were current.

Reverse "Tails" side of a coin, usually featuring arms, the value or a pictorial design.

Rim Raised border around the outside of a coin's face.

Scissel Clippings of metal left

after a blank has been cut; sometimes a clipping accidentally adheres to the blank during striking, producing a crescent-shaped flaw.

Scyphate (from Greek *scypha*, skiff or small boat) Cup-shaped, used to describe Byzantine concave coins.

Series All the issues of a coin of one denomination, design and type, including modifications and variations.

Siege money Emergency currency issued under siege.

Silver Precious metal widely used for coinage from the 6th century BC onward.

Steel Metal refined and tempered from iron and used in a stainless or chromed version for coinage since 1939. Copper-clad steel is now extensively used in place of bronze.

Tin Metal used for small coins in Malaysia, Thailand and the East Indies, and in British halfpence and farthings (1672–92). It is more usually alloyed with copper to form bronze.

Token Coin-like piece of metal, plastic or card issued by merchants, local authorities or other organizations, often during periods when government coinage is in short supply, but also produced extensively as a substitute for money.

Trade coin Coin produced for use outside the country of origin as part of international trade, such as British and American trade dollars.

Truncation Stylized cut at the base of the neck of a portrait, sometimes the site of a mint-mark, the engraver's initials or a die number.

Type A major variety of a series of coins.

Type set Set comprising one coin of each type in a series.

Uniface Coin with a device on one side only.

White gold Ancient term for **electrum**, a natural alloy of gold and silver. This differs from the modern term for the "hard" metal produced by alloying gold with platinum, nickel or palladium.

Year set Set of coins produced annually by a mint, usually containing a specimen of each coin issued during the year.

Zinc Metal alloyed with copper to produce brass; zinc-coated steel was also widely used in Europe during both World Wars.

INDEX

PICTURE ACKNOWLEDGEMENTS

The publishers would like to thank A H Baldwin and Sons Ltd, London for their kind assistance in supplying a substantial number of images from their photographic archive for use in this book.

All images in the book were supplied by James Mackay and A H Baldwin and Sons Ltd, London except for the following:

12 (coins 1–6): supplied by Heritage Galleries and Auctioneers (HeritageAuctions.com), Dallas, TX, USA; 27 (coins 18–19): supplied by New World Treasures, Iron Mountain, MI, USA; 48 (coin inset, top): supplied by Said International Ltd, Valletta, Malta; 149 (coins in panel): supplied by Guenter Roeck, www.theresia.name/en; 149 (coin 20) supplied by Chard (1964) Ltd, www.24carat.co.uk.

Paul Baker supplied the following images of coins: 20 (coins 11, 14 and 15); 27 (coins top-left, in panel; coins 21–22); 32 (coins 12–13); 34 (coins 3–4; 6–11); 35 (coins 12–15); 45 (coins 24–26); 53 (coins 12–13; 16–17; 20–23); 56 (coins 3–6); 57 (coins 15–20); 58 (coins 6–7; 10–11); 59 (coins 21–32); 63 (coins 12–15); 64 (coins 12–13); 65 (16–19; 24–25); 66 (coins 8–9; 12–17); 67 (coins 22–27 and 29–30); 71 (coins 34–37); 72 (coins 9–14; 17–18); 87 (coins 32–33); 90 (2–7; 9; 14–17); 91 (coins 25–26; 36–7); 96 (coins 7–18); 97 (coins 26–27; 30–33); 98 (coins inset, bottom-right; 16–17); 99 (coins 27–28); 100 (coins 1–2; 15–16); 101 (28–29); 108 (coins 15–16); 109 (coins 22–27; 32–33); 111 (coin bottom-right, inset); 112 (coin top, inset); 113 (coins 33–34); 118 (coins 13–16); 119 (coins bottom-left, in panel; coins 33–34); 123 (coins 27–38); 124 (coins 1–4; 8–9) 125 (coins 23–26; 31–32); 130 (coins 13–14); 132 (coins inset, top-left; 13–14); 133 (coins 15–16; 29–32); 135 (coins 20–23; 28–33); 136 (coins 10–13); 137 (coins 35–36); 144 (coins 1–2; 10–11); 146 (coins 1–6); 147 (coins 10–11; 14–17); 242 (coins 6–11); 149 (coins 21–22); 244 (coins 1–4; 8–9; 11); 151 (coins 12–19; 22–23); 152 (coin inset, top-right; 2; 6); 153 (coin in panel; coins 14–19); 154 (coins 1–4; 6–9); 155 (coins 17–20; 23–24).